Finding the Way to Home:

A Child-Centered Approach to Transitioning Children from Foster to Adoptive Families

Redmond Reams, PhD

ChildVox Press

For

Kelly and Sarah

and

Missy, Mike, Jr. and all the other children in the child welfare system

Acknowledgements

I want to thank all my beta readers: Amy Amador, Freda Bax, Cindy Boersma, Kay Delay, Kendra Morris-Jacobson, Laura Orgel, Michael Weiner, Samantha Wilson. They offered me their time and wisdom. Despite their best efforts, all remaining faults are my sole responsibility.

Table of contents

7   Introduction

12   Chapter 1 - Overview of Model

27   Chapter 2 - Participants' Characteristics and the Transition Process

77   Chapter 3 - The First Visit

97   Chapter 4 - Subsequent Early Visits

107   Chapter 5 - Shifting to Visits without Foster Parents

121   Chapter 6 - Day-long Visits

129   Chapter 7 - Overnight Visits

147   Chapter 8 - Highlighting the Transition in the Foster Relationship

161   Chapter 9 - Moving from Foster Home to Adoptive Home

181   Chapter 10 - Post-Move Contact between Child and Former Foster

       Parents

195   Chapter 11 - Sibling Groups

243   Chapter 12 - Birth Parents Still Involved

249   Chapter 13 - Foster Home is a Short-Term Placement

253   Chapter 14 - Foster parents are Against Using the Model

263   Chapter 15 - Child has Experienced a Prior Disrupted Adoption

273   Chapter 16 - Conflict among Adoptive Parents

275   Chapter 17 - Conflict between Adoptive and Foster Parents

279   Chapter 18 - Long-Distance Adoption

283   Chapter 19 - Older Child Resists the Adoptive Transition

285   Chapter 20 - Recommendations for Child Welfare Agencies

Introduction

Many books have been written about the child welfare system and foster children (*e.g.,* Mitchell, 2016; Roberts, 2001) and there are also many books about adoption and adopted children (*e.g.,* Davis, 2105; Gray, 2012; Miller Wrobel, Helder, & Marr, 2020). This book focuses on the intersection of those two realms: the transition of a foster child *into* an adoptive home; more specifically, those children who are adopted by people they *don't* know before, that are strangers to them, whether kin or unrelated. Although there has been work done in the United Kingdom around models for this transition (e.g., Beek, Neil & Schofield, 2021; Browning, 2015; Lanyado, 2003), this does not exist in the United States.

In 2022 in the United States, there were 53,665 children adopted out of the child welfare system and, of those children, 20,948 were adopted to parents other than their foster parents (U.S. Department of Health and Human Services, 2024). From these numbers, it is clear that the majority of these children are adopted *by foster parents they are already living with.* There is an invisible but significant transition that occurs for these children and the foster parents (Waterman, 2003). For the children that are not adopted by their foster parents, that are adopted by strangers, this book proposes a child-paced, relationally-focused model for how to shape the adoptive transition. When the people children trust to keep them safe and loved are changed, that is stressful for children (e.g. Dozier & Bick, 2007; Lanyado, 2008) and can be traumatic. It is also stressful for the foster and adoptive families, including the other children in those homes. Research says that well-managed transitions lead to better adoptive outcomes (Neil, Young & Hartley, 2018; Selwyn, Meakings, & Wijedasa, 2015).

The origin of this book occurred in 1971 when I was 14 years old. My older brother was serving in Viet Nam as a combat medic and the mother of my 3-year-old niece and 2-year-old nephew was considered to be neglecting them. The child welfare agency placed them to live with my parents and I. They had never met my dad, their grandfather, before he arrived and drove them over 800 miles to our home. I remember how quiet they were when they arrived and for weeks afterwards. They seemed to lack a certain spark. They played, laughed, and cried but it all seemed muted. I enjoyed playing with them. I was the youngest of three brothers and the only one left at home and it was nice to be the big brother for once. They stayed with us for a year and during that time they had no contact with their mother; I'm imagining, at least partly, due to distance. After that year, the court determined that the children could resume living with their mother, and my dad and I drove them back to their mother. When we pulled up to her house, my dad had the kids get out, told me to stay in the car, and walked them up to the front door. Their mother answered the door, my niece and nephew went inside, my dad came back to the car, and we drove away. It took less than five minutes. I remember the feeling of abruptness—how could they be in my life one minute and gone the next? I couldn't wrap my head around how sudden that shift was for those young children. I never saw them again. My brother, struggling mightily with his PTSD, consented to their adoption by their mother's new husband. I have worked with many foster and adopted children since then as a therapist and as a consultant to child welfare agencies for adoptive transitions, but I still often think about my niece and nephew.

How you might use this book

This book presents the full model with all its bells and whistles. You may use it as a practical user guide, but there are many other ways to use it

- as a buffet of optional strategies for you to select from and integrate into your own way of transitioning foster children into adoptive homes;

- as an invitation for deeper thought into situations that aren't covered here, e.g., adoption by foster parents of children already in their care, international adoptions, transitions between foster homes, and removals from birth families;

- as an integrated model of strategies that can be used together over the course of an adoptive transition;

- as an ideal that may be aspired to, but which also may be modified to reflect the practical parameters in a particular context (perhaps because of the particular set of adults, characteristics of the child, agency guidelines, sociocultural considerations, funding limitations, the workload of a child welfare caseworker, etc.);

- some children are transitioned into a permanent guardianship arrangement that may not be with the foster parents they are living with (although it often is) and this model may be used in those transitions as well;

- as a window for adults (caseworkers, foster parents, adoptive parents, other court and child welfare personnel) to see into the emotional realities of the child throughout the process of adoptive transitions, as well as the emotional impacts on foster and adoptive parents; or

- even as fodder for child welfare professionals and policymakers to disagree with, which will hopefully spur them to clarify their own thinking about adoptive transitions.

Structure of the book

The first two chapters focus on describing the model, its rationale, how the participants influence the process through what they bring personally to the transition process, and the initial planning needed before visits begin. The next eight chapters provide a step-by-step description through the first visit between child and adoptive parents, later visits with the foster parent still present, visits without the foster parents around, overnight visits, moving day, and post-move contact between the child and the former foster parents. Chapter eleven deals with the complexities when transitioning multiple children in a sibling group into an adoptive home. The following eight chapters focus on special situations such as adoption when the adoptive and foster homes are far apart or when a teenager is resistant to the adoption and other scenarios. The final chapter lays out recommendations for child welfare agencies to support this model and adoptive transitions in general.

The adoption stories of several foster children are woven throughout this text in order to provide texture to the model, and to illustrate how individual circumstances play a role. These are fictional vignettes. Each story is a composite, bringing together common themes that I have observed, and which provide the foundation of this model.

Taken together, the stories of Diego (age 5 years), Isabella (age 14 years), and Hakim (age 18 months), as well as the story of siblings Brett, Krissy and Maggie (ages 7, 4 and 2 respectively) will hopefully help you grasp what it looks like to apply this model in the real world. While they are not based on actual events, they are crafted to represent situations that *might as well* have happened within my career. In that way, they are real stories, if not literal ones.

Caveats

This model comes out of my experience as an external consultant guiding adoptive transitions and also as a child psychotherapist who provided input during my clients' transition processes. I developed this model and have attempted to document my experience and thinking for the benefit of caseworkers, foster parents, adoptive parents, and therapists involved in adoptive transitions who want to facilitate them more planfully and with greater sensitivity to the child.

The underlying concepts of this model are generally supported by research, but the whole model has not yet been tested. Instead, the model is based upon my own clinical experience, and upon the theories of Mary Ainsworth, John Bowlby, Magda Gerber, Daniel Hughes, Mary Main, Donald Winnicott, and others. This model should not be regarded as the only way to facilitate transitions. This model will hopefully spark the development of more models and research efforts towards identifying the best ways to manage adoptive transitions. Each child—and their context— is unique, so the model should only be used as a guide, with the child's individual situation remaining the focus. In some aspects of the model, developmental influences are made explicit, but the child's developmental level should be a consideration throughout all aspects of an adoptive transition. I have tried to weave in cultural considerations, but I am not aware of any culturally specific approaches to adoptive transitions. Of course, all cultures have rituals and beliefs about life transitions, which could and should be integrated to create culturally meaningful adaptations of this model of adoptive transitions, or a new model altogether. I hope that this book provides a useful building block for further thinking and research that addresses the adoptive transition through a variety of cultural and identity lenses.

I use the plural form of the terms for adoptive parents and foster parents, but adoption and fostering by one parent is a viable alternative (Wise, 2007). I avoid gender-specific pronouns, recognizing that children and adults in the adoptive process are of all gender identities. I do not attempt to directly address transitions between foster homes, although there are elements of this model that can be applied to such circumstances. This model explores an extremely wide range of potential variables; obviously not all of them will occur during any single adoptive transition, but most adoptive transitions include some of them. Some jurisdictions have begun to use the terms "resource parents" or "resource family parents" to refer to individuals that have historically been referred to as "foster parents" or use the term "first parents" rather than "birth parents". I stay with the older terms to avoid confusion since the majority of jurisdictions and the general public still use them. This model primarily focuses on the transition of a single child; it also addresses sibling group transition as a specific scenario.

This model is imperfect, incomplete, and not comprehensive to all circumstances and jurisdictions. I welcome feedback from any interested party at redmondreamsphd@gmail.com.

Chapter 1

Overview of Model

Imagine for a minute that a woman from the State Department comes one day and visits you where you live. She congratulates you and tells you that you have been chosen to be part of a secret government spy program. Her description of the program is confusing and you don't really understand the implications for yourself except that somehow you and this woman will supposedly be on a team together. You are stunned and do not ask any questions but assume that you will have a chance to clarify what this means before you agree to anything.

The next day she comes back and, to your surprise, informs you that it is time to leave and that she has police backup; you don't have a choice. You have 30 minutes to pack whatever you want to take with you even though you don't know where you are going. She won't answer your questions but maintains a friendly demeanor.

She drives you to the airport and the two of you get on a military plane that flies for hours and hours before landing in a big city in China. You're not sure which one. While on the flight, she tells you that you will spend the foreseeable future in China to be part of this confusing secret government program, and never go back to the place you used to live. You want to call your family and friends; she says that is not possible for security reasons. After you land, she introduces you to your local contact, a person who only speaks Chinese, and who you will evidently live with. She then surprises you with a hug and says she has to hurry to catch her flight back to your home country.

Imagine the feelings you might be having a week later, in two months, in a year; feelings about your prior life and the relationships contained in it; feelings about this mysterious woman who disappeared, perhaps permanently; and about your local contact who you have to learn how to live with; feelings about your future in China, your unclear role in a new culture, and the possible dangers of living there. Wouldn't you experience some anxiety, sleep difficulties, longing for your old life, anger outbursts, confusion, and difficulty believing that all of this is really happening? It might have been hard for you to understand the government program and your role in it, but wouldn't it have been better to have an opportunity to say goodbye to family and friends, learn a few phrases in Chinese, get to know this woman more, and prepare yourself for the big changes?

Young children transitioning from one placement to another in the child welfare system are like the adult in the scenario above, except they likely have already been traumatized and/or neglected in their birth family and from having undergone prior stressful transitions. The thesis of this model is that more planful transitions will benefit these children and the adults involved, which is especially important when adoptive placements are involved.

When a young child is transitioned from a foster home to an adoptive home, many emotional and practical agendas influence the process. There are as many agendas as there are players: foster parent(s), adoptive parent(s), child welfare caseworker, and other involved professionals (judge, child's therapist, child's attorney, Court Appointed Special Advocate (CASA) or Guardian Ad Litem (GAL), community health nurse, early interventionist), in addition to the child or children. Adult agendas can act as barriers to an effective transition into a new placement for the child.

In addition to these agendas, adults may incorrectly assume that parts of the process that are no big deal to them are also fine for a young child (van der Kolk, 2007). Young children perceive many other key elements of a transition process—including time, relative safety, distance from attachment figures—differently than adults do. In addition, past abrupt separations from attachment figures may have sensitized the child to the possibility that transitions will be, at least, anxiety-provoking and potentially traumatic. This model is focused on creating an adoptive transition that provides the child with a narrative that they can positively integrate into their identity **for the rest of their life.**

As shown in Figure 1, the process of the transition starts out with a select group of adults meeting and planning without the child during a pretransition phase. After the planning is tentatively complete, the child meets the adoptive parents in the foster parents' presence. Once the child feels safe enough with the adoptive parents, the child has short visits (less than 3 hours) with adoptive parents, without the foster parents around.

These progress to all-day visits (6-8 hours) with adoptive parents. The next big step for the child and adoptive parents is overnight visits which, if successful, leads to moving day. After the move, the child has contact with the former foster parents while living with the adoptive parents.

As you'll learn, the model prioritizes the interests of the child in several ways.

- We assume that the child is the most vulnerable participant, and that the adults have committed to giving precedence to the child's needs.

- We pause and pay attention to and reflect upon what we see emotionally and behaviorally in the child, and notice when the child is ready to take the next step in the process. This idea is captured in Sally Provence's variation of an Alice in Wonderland quote, "Don't just do something. Stand there and pay attention. Your child is trying to tell you something."

Figure 1

Flow Chart of Adoptive Transition Model

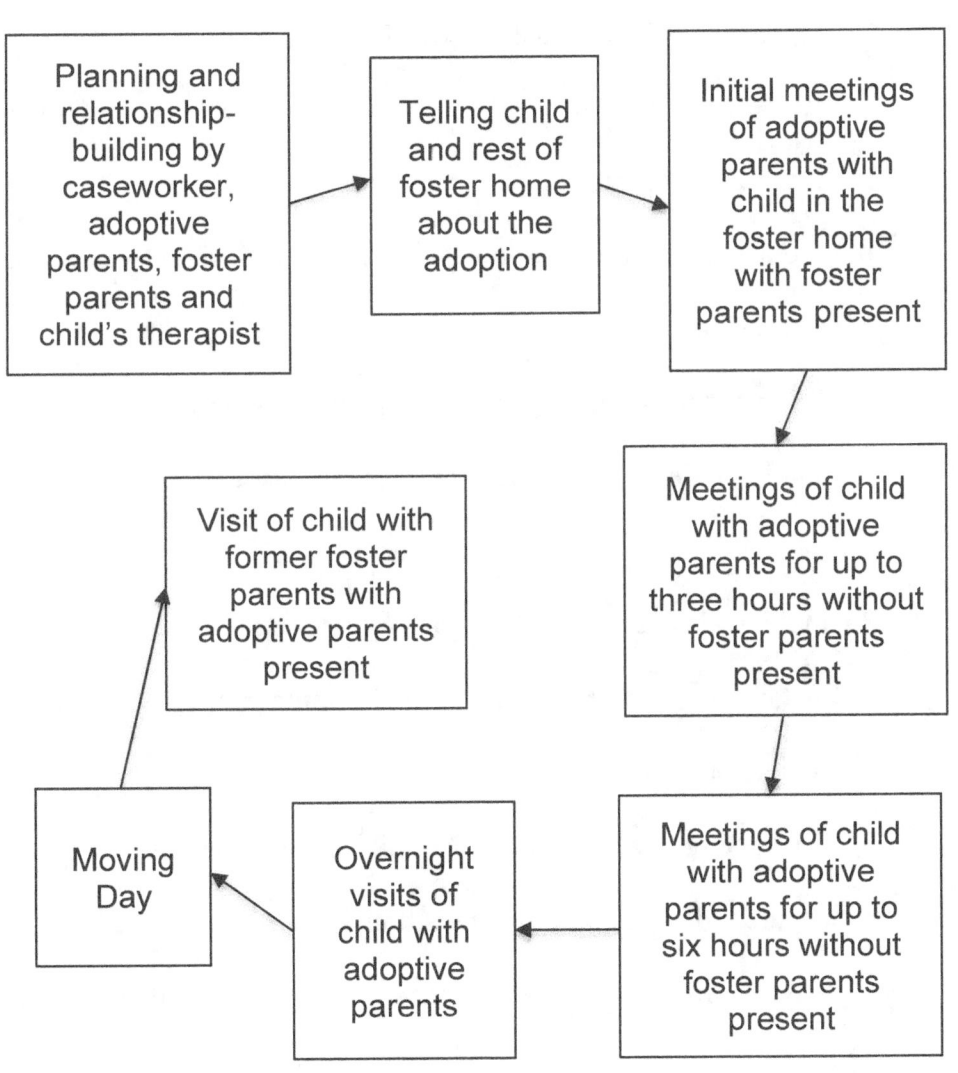

- We identify opportunities to demonstrate, to the child, their importance to the adults. This is achieved through the choices adults make to ensure that the child's interests are the factor that set the pace of the whole process. Children sense this and absorb it, not because they've been told so, but because their environment actually wraps sensitively around them.

- We avoid triggering a child's past losses and traumas as much as possible.

- We strive to be thoughtful and respectful regarding the cultures and identities of the child, the birth parents, the foster parents, the adoptive parents and/or the caseworker–and how those individuals may have been a target for bias and oppression historically and/or currently by the child welfare system or society at large.

- We prevent new traumas for the child, by anticipating their sense of safety/danger about the transition.

- We give the child a move guided by adults who are attuned to their needs and prioritize them, presenting a contrast to their prior experiences of moves.

- We highlight the importance of relationships through building the child's trust with their adoptive parents and by honoring the changes that occur in the important existing relationships the child already has with their foster parents.

Part of the complexity of this model is that it endeavors to focus on simultaneously the minds of the child, the adoptive parents, and the foster parents (Rustin, 2008). Thus, the model is also attentive to the adult participants' emotional and relational realities in several ways.

- It invites participants to reflect and notice concerns they have internally that might prevent them from being sufficiently present with and thoughtful about the child and themselves. We assume that all humans have sensitivities, both conscious and unconscious, and that these are not shame or blame-worthy.

- It facilitates communication between participants about the inevitable hurdles they will face in relationship with each other.

- It minimizes the risk of extra hurdles between the adult participants.

- It ensures that all adults (caseworkers, foster parents, adoptive parents, etc). feel that they are valuable and respected sources of input.

- It raises the likelihood that adoptive and foster parents will want to be "repeat customers" of the child welfare system.

Main goals

The two main goals of the model are to 1) build degrees of safety incrementally by facilitating the beginnings of attachment between child and adoptive parents and 2) support the transition of the foster parents' role in the child's life from caregivers (providers of love, protection, and nurturing) to extended family (a substantive but secondary degree of care and interest).

Building the attachment between the child and the adoptive parents

The basis for secure attachment is a caregiver who actively considers the child's needs, present and future, in all their forms. They are responsive to the child's current mental life: their wants, hopes, plans, fears, embarrassments, grievances, loves, hates, ideas, and many other feelings the child experiences with or without awareness (e.g., Fonagy & Campbell, 2016). In other words, they can respond to what is going on *inside* of the child, not just to their external behavior. This leads to more sensitive parenting. Children implicitly feel this sensitivity. They feel the involvement of the parent's mind and the effort the parent puts into trying to understand what is the best response for their sake at a given moment. The child may never notice the individual parenting decisions, but they experience the overall environment in which things just seem to go relatively smoothly for the child—and in response to their needs. This sensitivity is what this model is trying to help the child feel in the adoptive transition. Thus as the child moves through the steps of the transition, the pacing and adult actions would all feel attuned to the child.

Of course, all parents occasionally drop the ball with their children—children react to this with a range of possible negative emotions. Ideally, parents notice this reaction, validate it, and shift back on track. Children can experience these mistakes as blips that can be quickly repaired, not something traumatic. They come to anticipate their parents' miscues as a part of daily life, and will trust these imperfect parents to respond to their own reaction as children by working towards repair. They will then come to experience brief negative reactions as tolerable and easily fixed—an important part of emotional regulation.

Many children entering foster care do not have secure attachments with their birth parents but are sometimes able to form them with their foster parents depending on their foster parents' own attachment status (Dozier et al., 2001,) and if they have stability in their placements (Jacobsen et al, 2016). Thus, when the adoptive parent attempts to form a relationship with them, the foster child's likelihood to trust or mistrust these new adults is based on their experiences with previous caregivers. It is especially important that the adoptive parents approach the beginning days of this new relationship with a focus on tuning into the child's state of mind and being responsive (Steele et al., 2009). Adoptive parents need the support of foster parents and caseworkers to have the information and moment-to-moment guidance as they begin interacting with the child (described in Chapter 3). A durable foundation of secure attachment can form if the child feels that the adoptive parents are sensitive to and prioritizing their feelings during the transition. Building the relationship between the child and the adoptive parents is an obvious goal of an adoptive transition but not the only one.

Support the transition of the foster parents' role in the child's life from caregivers to extended family

Foster children deal with more loss than most people do in their whole life—from their initial removal from their family of origin to changes in foster placement (Bekman & Bellas, 2022; Mitchell, 2016). In my study of over 200 adoptive transitions, children averaged 2.4 placements (Reams, 2021). In this model, children do not fully lose contact with their foster parents. Instead, the foster parents shift their role from day-to-day caregivers to extended family members with intermittent contact. Even though the relationship is continuing and so a total loss of another relationship is avoided, the adoptive transition still represents a loss for both the child and the foster parents of the relationship they have had (Davis, 2015).

This model acknowledges that loss by talking about it to the extent made possible by the circumstances. The loss is processed both before and after the transition because contact continues. The child learns that loss and change do not equate permanent and total disappearance, as when they left previous foster homes. These post-transition visits (Reams, 2023) are a crucial part of the model that prevent the child from dealing with abandonment at a time when they are trying to build new attachments. They also learn that they are important enough to continue existing in the minds of caregivers after they have left the foster home—enough of a priority to those parents that they will still want to have contact with the child (Browning, 2015; Lanyado, 2008).

Focusing on the child's point of view in this model

In many life situations, decision making is informed by adults' perception of what is best for a child. A goal of this model is that the child's feelings (especially regarding safety as outlined in Table 1) are prioritized over "what adults think is best" (Browning, 2015). Adult decisions that do not take into account how a child will experience those decisions may traumatize the child. Adoption is such a well-intentioned decision. The adults may know that the adoptive parents are loving, safe people but to the child they are complete strangers.

The child's view of safety with new people (in this case, adoptive parents) is layered. Children with secure attachments to consistent caregivers move through the levels of safety in Table 1 easily and relatively quickly. Children in the child welfare system work through them at their own pace in the adoptive transition and beyond. There is not necessarily a linear progression through the steps; the child may perceive an adult doing something that puts them at higher risk. This perception of higher risk can flow from a child feeling like the foster parents are less protective in some way or the adoptive parents are more threatening.

The child's perception is often not reality and the adults had no intent to make the child feel more at risk. Nevertheless, the child's sense of safety has shifted and it needs to be noticed and taken into account, even if

Table 1

Levels of safety for a child with a new person

1. New person will not hurt or kill me when a safe person is nearby and alert.
2. New person will not hurt or kill me when a safe person is nearby but distracted.
3. New person will not hurt or kill me when a safe person is in another room.
4. New person will not hurt or kill me when no safe person is present but other people are around (i.e., in public without foster parents) and will keep me safe from other people.
5. New person will not hurt or kill me when I am awake in private with them.
6. New person will not abandon, hurt, or kill me while I am asleep.
7. New person will not abandon, hurt, or kill me when I make them irritated or mad.
8. New person will not abandon me in potentially dangerous situations (as defined by the child) and instead will protect me. They even seem to want to nurture me.
9. New person will consistently appear to proactively keep me safe from injury and other people, and will offer me nurturance consistently enough that I let it in.
10. New person will protect me consistently and will give me nurturance for long-enough that I accept it regularly and come to expect it and rely on it to some extent.

Some may feel that the inclusion of fear of mortal threat is overly extreme. Yet the attachment system evolved in mammals to avoid being killed by predators, including by members of one's own species or family

(Ebensperger, 1998). The child is not necessarily consciously fearing for their life; instead, the child has registered a potential threat and the nervous system reacts as if it is life-or-death given the child's history of attachment relationships.

The child will need consistent and responsive support throughout the adoptive transition from a safe person, i.e. a foster parent. We make the following recommendations:

- After every contact between adoptive parents and child, foster parents provide the child with an opportunity to discuss how it went. Doing so is **not** a requirement for the child, though. Children often debrief at a later time of their choosing.

- Ideally, every child in an adoptive transition has a preexisting individual therapist they have a trusting relationship with (Lanyado, 2003, 2008).

- Inform important adults in the child's life (e.g., teacher, school counselor, coach, neighbor, best friend's parent, youth pastor, child care provider, mentor) that the child is going through an adoptive transition—and inform the child that those figures know. This enables emotional support and planning goodbyes. These resources are also useful to talk about feelings in addition to the foster parents because some of the child's feelings will be about the foster parents themselves.

Developmental factors

In thinking about the child's point of view, we need to remember that they will often not use words to express feelings and other reactions directly. They may not be aware of their own distress or able to identify it as a specific feeling rather than a general distress. When they are aware of a specific feeling, they may not have words for that feeling or have enough sense of safety to be able to express their feeling with the words that they do have. Even if they have all the preceding, do they have any expectation that they will be listened to, understood, and responded to positively? Indirect manifestations of distress at different developmental levels may include:

- *Infants and toddlers*—developmental regression in recently acquired skills, increased clinging, withdrawal, new sleep or feeding difficulties, dissociating/"spacing out".

- *Preschoolers*—developmental regression, clinging, increased tantrums, aggression toward peers and/or adults.

- *School-age children*—controlling and/or rejecting behavior toward peers and adults, increased anger outbursts and aggression, withdrawal, and school refusal.

- *Teenagers*—controlling and rejecting behavior toward adults, rebellion, increased drug use, increased withdrawal and decreased communicativeness, running away.

Feelings of distress usually indicate that the child needs to spend more time in the current step of the adoptive transition. It may even mean that the child needs to take a step backwards in the process to help settle and feel safe. Deciding between these two alternatives is based on how great the distress is, the timing of the distress, and how recently the child moved onto their current step. When in doubt, move back a step. This is often resisted by adults because it can feel like a failure or creates practical difficulties.

Moving back a step is a loving gesture that recognizes the child is not yet ready but will be with some more time and care. We will go into this evaluation of when to move forward versus taking a step back in much more detail when we look at the process of visits.

Developmental considerations also arise when adoptive and foster parents respond to the questions of children in adoptive transitions. Answer the child's questions with sensitivity to that child's ability to understand and make sense of what is being said. Listen and determine what information the child is specifically asking for; be wary of assuming the child is asking for more information than they concretely ask for. Answer the child's questions in a way that is as simple as possible and developmentally appropriate. For instance, if the child asks, "Does mommy still love me?", instead of inquiring what is in the child's mind behind that question, just answer, "Yes, she does" and wait to see if the child asks a follow-up question. Be careful not to give too much information in your answers, as when responding to an older individual. Praise them for asking questions, and encourage more.

If a question brings up intense feelings for the foster or adoptive parent, it's perfectly fine to say "Good question. I need to think about that before I answer." The foster parent or adoptive parent would then process the question, their feelings, and potential answers with someone they trust. They would also meet their commitment of returning to the child and offering a responsive answer.

A child's question may be a vehicle for indirectly bringing up a feeling. Listen for tone of voice or nonverbal behaviors as signals; the child may or may not even be aware of their feelings, or able to describe them. Answer the child's question but also address the potential feeling the child might be having (e.g., "Some kids meeting someone new feel a little nervous."). Notice that the statement to the child was phrased as "some kids" rather than assuming the child's specific experience. This approach gives the child an opportunity to talk about the topic without putting them on the spot or telling them how they feel.

Chapter 2

Participants' Characteristics and the Transition Process

Each of the participants in an adoptive transition is a specific individual who will bring a unique set of experiences to the process. How the transition goes will be influenced by the participants' characteristics and their ability to operate as a team. In this chapter, we consider some of the meaningful attributes of the child and each adult.

Child characteristics

Degree of contact child still has with birth parents

Many children who are ready for an adoptive transition have stopped visits with their birth parents, whose parental rights have been legally terminated. Ideally, the child has had a goodbye visit with the birth parents to help them feel resolved with the ending of that relationship.

With or without a goodbye visit, many children still dream of a reunion with their birth parents. If the child has a therapist, this is an important topic to address. Whether there is a therapist or not, the foster parents would discuss this with the child—and not just as a one-off conversation, but rather as a dialogue that extends over time, ideally with the child expressing feelings and asking questions. Even if the child has begun to accept the reality of never being reunited with the birth parents, they may still idealize one or both of the birth parents. This should not be challenged, as it needs to fade gradually over time as the child gains more experience with positive relationships with parents and more capacity to reflect on those relationships with all their caregivers, especially with the help of their Lifebook (defined in chapter 8). Instead of challenging it, another option might be a response like "I know you wish that were true, I wish that was true also."

If the child is still having contact with the birth parents but there is not going to be any post-adoption contact, arranging a good-bye visit is important. The goals of this goodbye process are:

1. Child and birth parents have an opportunity to express their love for each other.

2. Child and birth parents have an opportunity to express sadness that they will not be living together and that they will miss each other.

3. The birth parents acknowledge to the child that the judge has decided that it would be best for the child to not live with the birth parents for the rest of their childhood and that the birth parent will abide by that decision even if they do not agree with it.

4. The birth parents express a desire for the child to be happy with the family they will be living with.

5. The birth parents have an opportunity (but are not required) to apologize for any past actions as they see fit.

6. The child can give the birth parent something they have made for them in anticipation of this meeting (perhaps a handmade card).

7. The birth parents give the child a letter that expresses their love, their missing them, their acceptance of not living together and their wish for their future happiness, which is placed in the child's Lifebook. This letter needs to be reviewed and preapproved by the caseworker and the child's therapist. The birth parent would be

given the opportunity to revise the letter based on feedback so as to achieve an acceptable version.

8. The birth parents and child are photographed for the child's Lifebook. The birth parent can also have a copy of the photograph.

9. The birth parents have had the opportunity to talk through any anger at the judge, caseworker, or any other figure in the child's life and can manage their anger so that these feelings are not expressed during this time. This meeting is for the benefit of the child and not a time for the parent to express negative feelings even if they feel them strongly.

Some birth parents will be resistant to cooperating with visits that mark the transition in their relationships with their child. They may experience an adversarial relationship with the child welfare system and feel that they have been treated unfairly. Yet a lot of the resistance may also flow from pain and hurt and grief over losing this life-defining connection with their child. The experience often has an enormous impact on their own sense of identity, self-esteem, and meaning in life. Regardless of their role in the child's experience of harm, their pain is still real.

It is important to assess whether or not the birth parent can be appropriate enough with the child. A central question is whether they have been able to talk through their pain about their child's removal, time in foster care and adoption and about what a session with the child might look and feel like. Who can do this with the birth parent? Often the child's caseworker may have had too many negative interactions with the birth parents to be a resource for this role. An ideal person is an emotionally supportive person identified by the parent and could include a loving relative, religious leader or therapist. If not a person with a stable connection with the parent is not available, then a professional that has had a positive (or even neutral) connection with the birth parents could be considered: therapeutic visitation therapist, caseworker for adoptive parents, past parenting group leader, child's therapist. The birth parent needs to review the goals of the meeting listed above and agree to each in advance of the goodbye meeting. Role-playing what they would say at the goodbye meeting with the child is useful, as well as how they might react to various behaviors of the child. The birth parent writing a draft letter to the child for the goodbye meeting can also be a good way for the birth parent to prepare. The in-person meeting would only happen if the birth parent can prioritize the needs of the child, but the birth parent would be given the chance to write the child a letter either way.

The child also needs to be prepared for the goodbye meeting with their birth parent, of course. This would be done by their therapist, in conjunction with the foster parents. If the child does not have a therapist, then the foster parents are the next choice. The child should be helped to think about what they want to express to their birth parent. Consider prompting them to create a handmade gift (perhaps a goodbye card). Lots of feelings will come up for the child—sadness, loss but also anger. All of these need to be accepted and given room for expression. They are all normal and to be expected.

If post-adoption contact between the child and birth parents is anticipated, begin negotiations between birth parents and adoptive parents as soon as possible for how that contact will occur. Negotiating the open adoption process and agreement is beyond the scope of this manual (see Goldberg, 2019). Design and start implementing the process by which birth parents and the child acknowledge to each other the impact of the open adoption on their relationship, including the birth parents' support for moving forward with the adoption.

Whether the child has post-adoption contact or not with birth parents, the child's emotional relationship with them will continue throughout their life. Whether in the form of memories, or if the child was too young to have remembrances of their birth parents, Lifebook material or even just the idea of what they might have been like, a child's birth parents are an essential part of the child's identity.

Child has trauma history

At an oversimplified level, children that have been traumatized seek to avoid reminders of the trauma (perhaps by shutting down or spacing out or isolating) that will spike anxiety for them and yet they also continuously scan the environment for signs of danger so they will not be caught off-guard and can try to prepare and protect themselves from incoming danger. Both of these trauma-related tasks are quite demanding of the child and can leave them overloaded and easily emotionally overwhelmed and thus acting-out.

In scanning the environment, the child will spot what they take to be a sign of impending danger but which the adults know is safe. This is a trauma trigger. Triggers may include one or more of the adoptive parents physically resembling a trauma perpetrator. In addition, certain physical movements or situations (e.g., bath time) may also act as a trauma trigger. For instance, a child who had been disciplined by being dipped into scalding water was intensely fearful of bathtime. Children often do not remember the specific events that are the source of the trigger. As van der Kolk (2015) has noted, trauma often returns as a reaction rather than as a memory.

The transition process would be designed with sensitivity to the potential to remind the child of past trauma and also respect the child's coping strategies for living in what feels like a dangerous world. Adults may know the world is safer than the child thinks but no amount of words will convince the child of that. It takes years and years of safety to shift that sense of dangerousness even somewhat. Consider what the child's reactions in the past have taught the foster parents about the child's trauma triggers.

Notice and take seriously aspects of the child's reactions in the present that may indicate exposure to a trauma trigger or the child's anticipation of such an exposure. If the child who has been traumatized has a therapist, they will be an important source of input. (Note: almost all children entering an adoptive transition have experienced at least one relational trauma when they were removed from their birth home, but experiencing a potential trauma is not a guarantee that a person will become traumatized). There is more specific discussion of trauma and adapting visits outside the foster home in Chapter 5. Trauma will likely impact the child's capacity to feel safe with new people and will likely emerge as triggers that they experience with the adoptive parents. All the recommended procedures in this manual may need to be modified to take into account a child's particular trauma reactions and their nervous system responses. Modifications may be made with creativity and thinking both about the underlying purpose of the original transition procedure but also the point of view of the child, especially when they are terrified. In considering how the child's trauma history may affect the relationship with the adoptive parents, focus on the most recent or egregious known incidents, while also remembering those traumas that may be less documented or spotlighted; such as:

- occurred as a result of witnessing traumatic events that occurred directly to others in a home or in the community;
- were a result of neglect rather than physical or sexual abuse;
- occurred in current or past foster homes; and
- were inflicted by other children or animals.

There may be information in the child's Lifebook to account for the trauma history. Whether it is in the Lifebook or not, the adoptive parents need as **full** a trauma history in writing as possible so they can hold that history until it makes developmental sense for the child to learn it. All youth need to know their full trauma history by the time they turn 18 (and often before) so they can make sense of the intrusive thoughts, feelings, images, bodily reactions they are experiencing. This helps them to recognize that they are not going crazy when they have posttraumatic symptoms. Youth live with their history for all their lives and need time to start making sense of it.

Child has history of losses

During this transition, the child is losing their existing relationships with foster parents, others in the foster home, and their community. This may reverberate with previous forms of loss they have experienced (Bekman & Bellas, 2022; Lee & Whiting, 2007). These include:

- placement changes, including their original removal;
- losses the child may have experienced before they left their birth home;
- houselessness;
- deaths of significant others, including pets;
- abandonment or perceived abandonment by parental and sibling figures; and
- loss of possessions through moves.

All of these losses affect a child's sense of identity (Bekamn & Bellas, 2022; Heineman, 2007). Verbal and/or behavioral expressions of the child's grief may come at any point in the transition process. They may be easily recognized as grief, as when the child says to their foster parent with tears, "Momma, I don't want to move away." These grief expressions may also be disguised (e.g., the child hits another child who is cradling a baby doll). A particular step or steps in the adoptive transition may need to slow at a particular point to address the child's grief in a developmentally appropriate way (e.g., Trozzi, 1999).

Child has ongoing relationships

A strength the child will have are the ongoing relationships with people they have some degree of trust in. These trusted individuals may be able to validate the safety of the adoptive parents for the child and can be valuable assets in the transition. The child simply observing positive interactions between two groups of adults (those with established relationships with the child and the adoptive parents) can go a long way to building a sense of trust in the adoptive parents in the child's mind. These individuals with ongoing relationships may include:

- foster parents;

- grandparents, siblings, and other birth relatives;

- caseworkers;

- teachers, mentors, youth pastors and coaches;

- neighbors;

- psychotherapists and school counselors; and

- guardian ad litems, court-appointed special advocates, and attorneys.

The child may also lose contact with some of these individuals as part of the transition. Thus, it is important to be sensitive to the child's experience in losing their relationships with many of the important individuals in their lives, not just the relationships they have with their foster parents.

Child has mental health needs

In this section, selected mental health issues a child may have will be discussed for how they may impact adoptive transitions.

Children with very disrupted relationship histories often require slower adoptive transitions. These children may have a diagnosis of

Reactive Attachment Disorder, although not necessarily. Adoptive parents may need extra training in attachment-building interactive behaviors, such as Dyadic Developmental Psychotherapy (Hughes, Golding & Hudson, 2019). It can be tempting to move quickly through the adoptive transition since these children often show little distress. Specifically, they:

- may not show any anxiety in first meetings with adoptive parents;
- may not show any distress at the changes in their relationship with foster parents;
- may not show any markers of developing attachment with adoptive parents;
- may seem quickly and easily (even excessively) connected with adoptive parents;
- may sabotage adoptive transition as it proceeds further; or
- may show little interest or avoid contact with foster parents after moving day.

Children who are clingy and have developmentally-excessive separation anxiety may become anxious and emotionally dysregulated when they are starting to visit with adoptive parents away from foster parents. Before the transition proceeds, the child may need:

- if old enough, instructions for managing their body's arousal states (e.g., mindfulness, deep breathing);

- soothing and reassurance from foster parents;

- anti-anxiety medications;

- a more-incremental process of visiting with the adoptive parents at a distance from the foster parents (e.g., playing with adoptive parents on the porch or in the front yard while the foster parents look on through a window);

- Taking an object used for reassurance in the foster home with them on the visit (e.g., a stuffed animal or "blankie"); or

- having a method of the child feeling connected with the foster parents while away from them, perhaps through an object the child carries with them (a photo or possession of the foster parent) or through scheduled phone calls or texts.

Children who are neurodivergent form attachments even though it may be less obvious based on surface behaviors. They may become overloaded by social or environmental stimuli, and may need:

- a more gradual introduction to adoptive parents, including techniques developed for children with struggles reading social cues and understanding social interaction, like social stories (Gray, 2015);

- particular sensitivity to the potential for visits outside the foster home to be overwhelming for the child from a sensory perspective (e.g., Stock Kranowitz, 2022), foster parents are a good resource for ideas for planning more manageable visiting activities;

- various forms of visual communication (e.g., communication picture board) to support their understanding of the sequence involved in a particular visit or in the adoptive transition process; or

- particular emphasis on continuity and predictability within the transition. It may be useful to solicit input from their educator, skills trainer, or even the child, if they are older;

- creation of a space within the bedroom of the adoptive home that has comforting sensory qualities created with fabric, lighting, headphones, etc. that the child knows is a soothing space for when they become overwhelmed.

Foster parent characteristics

The foster parent's attitudes toward the adoption may have been influenced by many factors: practical ones (e.g., how many children they have in their home at that time and how challenging they are), emotional ones (e.g., how painful the last adoptive transition was or was not), relational ones (e.g., how well the two foster parents are getting along in their partnership at that time), body-based ones (e.g., are they struggling with insomnia), child-based ones (e.g., how emotionally available the child is for a deep attachment). All of the possible factors within these categories can not be explored here. Some will be examined below. What is important to remember is that every foster parent has an internal emotional life woven of many influences; some of these may be known about and some may be out of awareness, some may be shared with others and some may be kept private. Foster parents benefit from reflecting on their history and state of mind and how it may influence their participation in the transition. By doing so, the quality of the transition also benefits.

Many foster parents have helped at least one child transition out of their home previously. Their experiences and learnings, both positive and negative, are part of what they bring to this transition. The emotional impact of the transition is strongest during their first such transition.

Foster parents will have a past that includes losses and their degree of resolution. These losses may include:

- deaths of parents or siblings;

- miscarriages, stillbirths, or death of a child;

- estrangement with family members;

- prior departures of foster children to birth or adoptive homes that went poorly and/or resulted in severing of contact; or

- divorce or separation.

Foster parents have hopefully been provided some degree of support from friends, spouse, and/or therapists while processing their feelings related to those losses. If there hasn't been resolution, then the impending change in the relationship with this child may be experienced as a loss by the foster parents that resonates with feelings from the preceding losses, confronting foster parents with intense feelings of grief (Hebert et al., 2013; Lynes & Sitcoe, 2019).

The foster parents may not demonstrate their emotions about the move for a variety of reasons (their own coping mechanism, neurodiversity in how they experience or express feelings, desire to protect the child from adult emotions, consciously not feel anything about this child moving out because they avoid feelings of loss without even being aware of it). This is a dilemma for the child, who may perceive the lack of foster parents' expressed feelings as meaning that the child is not emotionally meaningful to the foster parents (Lanyado, 2008). There will be more about foster parents' experience of loss in Chapter 8.

Foster parent struggles to manage their feelings of grief/loss

It is to be hoped that all foster parents have a secure attachment to the foster children in their care and thus will have some degree of loss when the children move. Yet some foster parents struggle to manage their grief and loss which can increase the difficulty of the adoptive transition. This is especially possible if the foster parents previously had asked to be considered as possible adoptive parents. When they identify themselves as an adoptive option for a child already in their home, then they often, whether they are aware of it or not, deepen their connection to the child despite knowing the outcome is not guaranteed (Waterman, 2003).

The foster parents may experience a range of feelings (e.g., disappointment, anger, grief) at having not been preferred over the adoptive parents to adopt this child by the child welfare decision makers. When this occurs, foster parents may need more time and support to help them emerge as full and willing participants in the adoptive transition, but it may be more emotionally complicated for them to say goodbye to a child that they never wanted to let go of, and to support adoptive parents who were their prior competitors. It is very important to provide opportunities for them to process these emotions within the planning team, and/or privately.

Foster parent does not have a significant attachment to the child

Sometimes a child is being adopted from a foster home where the foster parent has not developed a secure attachment to the child. There are a variety of reasons that this may occur:

- the short time a child has been with a foster parent (this will be dealt with in a special section later on);

- a poor fit between the temperaments of the foster parent and child;

- the child has a history of not being emotionally connected to their past caregivers for whatever reasons and so is unresponsive or rejecting of overtures from the foster parents;

- the child has very challenging behaviors, especially if those behaviors pose a safety risk to the foster family, their home, or other children in the family; or

- the foster parent deals with their prior relationship history by not forming secure attachments to foster children in their home.

Whatever the reason the foster parents have not developed a strong connection to the child, they may feel less motivation to participate or "go the extra mile" for the child during the transition. They are not against the transition process (see Chapter 14 for this situation), but when the child looks to them for the second-to-second affirmations of the safety of their new circumstances, they may not notice this need. The resulting less than optimal support they might give lacks the reassurance the child needs. Foster parents can't fake their way through this but they can make an effort to be as engaged and thoughtful as possible when they are interacting with the child about the adoption, especially when with the adoptive parents. Sometimes, if the foster parents and adoptive parents form a bond, foster parents can generate some motivation for the adoptive process through resonating with the adoptive parents' excitement about the child.

If the foster parent does not have a secure attachment with the child, then the child is less likely to have a secure attachment with the foster parent

(Dozier et al, 2001). This may also complicate the adoptive transition in a variety of ways. This may make it harder for the child to depend on the foster parent to be a reliable source of reassurance while they get to know the adoptive parents. The child may have a version of an insecure or disorganized attachment with the foster parent, which may complicate letting go of the foster parent as the primary caregiver. It will be important to try to understand the changing relationships from the child's perhaps distorted view of how relationships work and adapt the model laid out here, keeping in mind the basic principles previously described.

Foster parents are a member of a group that has been discriminated against by the child welfare system

Individuals from many groups (e.g., BIPOC, people with disabilities, families in poverty, LGBTQIA+) are and have been discriminated against by the child welfare system. Individuals from these groups are sometimes rejected as foster parents for no other reason. Even if accepted, they often experience microaggressions and explicit bias from other child welfare staff. As humans who always carry assumptions and biases about others based on some characteristic, we need to be reflective and thoughtful about our actions and our reactions to feedback. When these assumptions and biases are part of historical patterns that have caused great pain, the emotional stakes are raised and there is greater potential for hurt and misinterpretation. Those exercising power, whether formally as a caseworker or informally as a foster parent, need to be especially careful not to use that power based on assumptions about others. All the adults involved in the transition process need to strive to be thoughtful about their biases and open to feedback. Even members of previously discriminated against groups can be biased towards individuals from their own group or other groups also.

These histories of discrimination can influence the adoptive transition process. Foster or adoptive parents may already have felt microaggressions or overt discrimination by representatives of the child welfare system by the time they get to this step. Caseworkers from these marginalized groups may also bring their own histories of being discriminated against as well.

As planning is occurring, these past oppressive experiences may lead to expectations that others will not be collaborative or voices will not be heard or someone will dominate the process. These slights will often actually occur, hopefully not intentionally, but still hurtfully because of implicit beliefs. There is more and more written about how to have hard, productive conversation when there have been offenses (e.g., Kim & Del Prado, 2019). Because these hurts can derail an entire adoptive transition, an attempt will be made to outline a series of steps that the two individuals might take with each other, with the benefit of a third person or not.

1. The person who has been hurt needs to express that they feel hurt and what the other person did or said or didn't do or say that felt hurtful to them. In communicating this hurt, they ideally would try to use a hurt but non-accusatory tone and avoid expressing the assumption that the other person intended to hurt them or is a "bad" person or is the same as other people that have done harm intentionally from their group (e.g., just another entitled white man) even if those assumptions are floating around inside trying to gain traction.

2. The other person needs to start with acknowledging that they have caused hurt, that the hurt feelings are significant and apologize in a remorseful tone without trying to explain themselves at all. People do not like to have the self-image of being someone who hurts others and so look to dodge this, even though hurting others is common. It is very hard to not say, in essence, "Yes I hurt you but it doesn't really count because I didn't mean it or it was a joke or I was trying my best or …"

3. The person who was hurt can then evaluate whether they can accept the apology then and there or, whether they are too hurt to do that, and so they thank the other person for the apology but say that they need more time to process what happened. Whether they accept the apology or not, it is important for them to know that they are not saying their feelings have stopped being hurt and that they are fine. In either case, it is useful at this point for the hurt person to ask the person who hurt them something like, "How do you

understand what just happened?" The advantage of asking is to get more context regarding how much the hurtful person understands the hurt they caused and perhaps has some insight about why they did it. This can flesh out the apology and enhance the repair between the two individuals. The person who caused the hurt may need some time to think about this question.

4. In response to the question of "How do you understand what just happened?", it is useful for the person who caused the hurt to not answer immediately and instead think some about it. This delay communicates that the question is being taken seriously. Without the delay, it is easy to succumb to the temptation to rationalize actions as actually okay and the apology will have been undermined. Another temptation can be to put some of the responsibility for the hurt onto the person who has the hurt feelings. Regardless of whether that has any merit, the other person is still hurting and will not be able to take that in from the very person that hurt them. Instead, it is important for the person who has caused the hurt

to think about whether they have a bias, whether they are aware of it or not, that may have gotten expressed (e.g., that two gay men could not effectively raise a daughter). Another possibility is that they made an assumption about the other person that was inaccurate (e.g., that the person in a wheelchair could not give a foster infant a bath). Without realizing the impact, they may have done something in the interactions that was hurtful (e.g., talked over someone else). They may have referred to historical traumas insensitively (e.g., talked about the residential school that the foster teen attended in glowing terms and generalized that those placements are often very helpful to certain teens in talking with parents of an indigenous background). This is not an exhaustive list. If the person who caused the hurt can identify such an error, then they can take ownership for that. In addition to acknowledging the error, they would remain open that there may be other factors too that contributed to them causing the hurt. If they can not identify such an error, then it is important for them to acknowledge that and commit to thinking more about what was going on with them. It's good for them to apologize again and acknowledge that there is still hurt they have caused. Whether they can own an error or not, they can also ask for feedback from the person they have hurt if the hurt person is willing to give any at that point in time. If they are not willing, then that can be graciously accepted.

5. The person who has been hurt would carefully reflect on whether they can give constructive feedback or instead might seek to hurt the other person back or are uninterested in giving feedback to the person who so recently hurt them or want that other person to do more work reflecting about what their role was. The act of asking for feedback was a vulnerable act (because it opens them up to attack) on the part of the person who caused the hurt. This vulnerability can be productively acknowledged even if feedback is not going to be given. If feedback is going to be given to the person who caused the hurt, then it specific and direct feedback is

most useful but also recognized and communicated as one person's perception and not a fact (e.g., "From my point of view, I think you assumed incorrectly I could not do that because I am a member of this group. I would have preferred it if you had asked me directly if that was something I was able to do.").

6. If the person that was hurt decides to give feedback, then the person who caused the hurt should receive it with gratitude. It is a gift to have someone else's perception of us even though it is almost always uncomfortable. We may not agree with the perception, just as we almost always do not fully agree with how someone else evaluates a movie. We only have our own sense of ourselves and how we come across; someone else's perception gives us much to think about and reflect on and is worthy of gratitude.

This description of a back and forth interaction is optimal. Even assuming it can not be achieved in its entirety, there is value in aspiring to achieve it and to give each other grace for the sake of creating a good transition for the child.

Adoptive parents' characteristics

All of the characteristics discussed below go into helping to form the adoptive parent's state of mind regarding the adoption. The adoptive parent's dream of having a child has often had to wait a long time; finding a suitable partner, perhaps going through infertility treatments, taking classes required by the child welfare agency, completing a home study, getting selected by the child welfare decision makers as the right family for a child. All of this waiting means that by the time they get to an adoptive transition, adoptive parents are very often ripe, to bursting, to have this adoptive child in their family. This can lead to a desire to move the process along as quickly as can be.

Adoptive parents can also have a view of foster children as in need of rescuing, especially by them. This can lead to a fantasy and expectation that the child will be grateful for how much the adoptive parent is giving and is going to give to the child. Instead, the child might be hesitant to engage or easily break down into tears or have tantrums. Adoptive parents may then feel that the child is too difficult for them or that they are doing it wrong or the child is not grateful enough (see Heineman (2001) for an example with a therapist and a child).

A fear-based perspective can also dominate an adoptive parent's perspective. They may feel that they had so many setbacks previously that something is fated to go wrong again, e.g., the birth parent will reemerge as a placement option or the child will thoroughly reject them or the foster parent will conclude that the adoptive parents are no good as parents and stop the transition.

In each of these scenarios, adoptive parents need a calm person to remind them about the long-term game plan of having the best transition and that they will be good parents and that the foster child has their own viewpoint based on their experience in the world, for better and worse. It is normal for adoptive parents to get agitated as they head into a transition process. The calm person might be their caseworker or the child's caseworker or the foster parent or a friend or parents of theirs or perhaps a therapist. Adoptive parents need a support system for the emotional roller coaster that an adoptive transition can be.

Adoptive parents are a member of the child's birth family (kinship placement)

When a child is going to be adopted by a birth family member, there are some important differences than when the child is going to be adopted by a non-related stranger. Most importantly, there is a chance that the child and their relative have some level of a preexisting relationship. The extent of the preexisting relationship can vary greatly - from no contact at all to one or two visits some years back which the child may have an uncertain memory of to annual contact at large family gatherings to more regular contact every few months at family dinners.

In implementing this model, it is important to view the kinship relationship from the point of view of the child. The adult relative may feel they know the child somewhat based on visits and updates from the birth parents including photos and videos. For the child, the sense of how well they know the adult relative is much more based on how much and the nature of in-person contact, i.e., did the child and adult relative actually interact or were they just in the same house for a period of time and, if they did interact, what were the child's feelings associated with the interaction? Also, the child's developmental stage when the contact occurred is important - if the child saw the adult relative often and played with them when they were between two and four years old but has not seen them since and is now ten years old, then the child may not have much conscious memory of that relative.

The nature of the preexisting relationship from the child's point of view will affect the child's sense of safety with the adult relative. The child may believe that they will not be hurt imminently by the adult relative from the beginning, however, that does not mean the child feels safe with the adult relative when they are alone with them without the foster parent present. Most times the child will not have been alone with the adult relative much, instead they will have been with the birth parent and the adult relative. This is similar to the initial visits in this model. Sometimes adult relatives believe that because they feel they know the child relatively well, the adoptive process can happen relatively quickly. When using this model, it is important to follow the child's signals about when they are ready to progress to the next stage of the model. The preexisting relationship may help early steps go more quickly in some cases. In addition, the child knowing the adoptive parent ahead of the transition does not change the other main aspect of the transition process: the child and foster parent dealing with the loss involved in no longer living together.

Adoptive parents have previously adopted children

A prior successful adoption often significantly lowers the anxiety adoptive parents might otherwise feel going into this adoption. Two important questions to consider about the first adoption. What is the view of the adoptive parents with respect to the attachment between them and that adopted child? What were the adoptive parents' feelings about how the prior transition was structured and how it went? The adoptive parents bring insights that can be useful in identifying transition steps or activities to include or exclude. Use prior adoptive experience as a source of wisdom — while recognizing that the current child who is moving is different from the first child these parents adopted and may have different needs during the transition.

If there were disruptions or dissolutions of past adoptions, ask the adoptive parents to describe how they have processed that ending and their understanding of what led to it. It is useful to highlight that the adoption cessation may have been experienced as a traumatic experience for the adoptive parents and that they will likely be triggered at points in the current adoptive transition or afterwards. Help the adoptive parents identify supports for helping them with those triggers (e.g., their own therapists). Even if the prior adoption did eventually end, it is still important to ask about the adoptive parents' views about that prior adoptive transition.

Adoptive parents reside significantly far away from foster parents

(This is addressed in Chapter 18.)

At least one adoptive parent has the capacity to take substantial parental leave

If the adoptive parents have the capacity, it is strongly recommended that at least one parent take substantial parental leave (at least three months, preferably six or more). Doing so enhances their ability to support post-transition visits of the child with former foster parents and, most importantly, it supports the development of the relationship between the adoptive parents and the child. It is incredibly difficult for a child to enter a new adoptive home and then spend time in child care situations that require them to learn how to trust even more new caregivers. In some adoptive families, this may be unavoidable. In those cases, the best alternative is childcare provided by a psychologically healthy relative, with a small owner-run child care as the next best option (NICHD Early Child Care Research Network, 2005).

Adoptive parents feel neither parent can take substantial parental leave

Parental leave is important even if the child will be attending school or preschool. Leave can be used for after-school hours and times when school is not in session (e.g., spring break or summer). There are several reasons why adoptive parents may conclude that taking parental leave is not possible.

- If adoptive parents don't see the importance, educate them in a nonjudgmental way about attachment, bonding, prioritizing the child's needs in this early part of the relationship, etc.

- Parental leave can often create a financial hardship (especially in the case of single adoptive parents,) consider asking them to be creative about generating a fund to live off of while on a leave (e.g., asking adoptive parents' own family and networks for support, soliciting donations via crowdsourcing, using a credit card, taking out a second mortgage or credit line on their home, using some retirement funds early, or taking a second job for a limited period of time). The tone used in this request is important as there may be issues of social class and privilege operating. It is recommended that the tone be one of looking at possibilities with no shame attached and being mindful of how the adoptive parents may experience the discussion.

- If the adoptive parents' employer is resistant, then remind them that they are required to comply with the Family and Medical Leave Act (FMLA) if they have 50 or more employees, which requires up to 12 weeks of parental leave for adoptive parents.
  - Note: FMLA parental leave needs to be used up in the 12 months following the adoption. Learn more about FMLA at the Dept. of Labor website https://www.dol.gov/agencies/whd/fmla.

Adoptive parents may not have considered the possibility of alternating or combining parental leave windows. For example, each parent could take 12 consecutive weeks of leave, or both parents could divide the week by each working 2.5 days/week. Either arrangement results in 24 total weeks of leave.

Adoptive parents' psychological profile

Adoptive parents bring personalities formed by their prior relationships, temperament, and life experiences including successes, trauma, and loss. The most relevant personality strengths they may bring to the adoption include reflectiveness, emotional regulation, and empathy. Adoptive parents may have significant emotional needs, as with all people. There is no shame in this. It is incumbent on adoptive parents to implement strategies for coping with and managing these needs. This includes:

- remaining attentive to their needs and to the possibility that an adoptive transition may reveal new ones;
- self-identifying issues that affect them and communicating this to their supportive others (spouse, parents, siblings, friends, therapist, caseworker);
- allowing others to raise the possibility that an issue is active;
- reflecting with self-compassion about the concerns being activated (how, when, by what or whom, etc.);
- practicing empathy for others who have concerns that might also have been activated;
- talking with supportive people about their feelings;
- creating a plan for managing and self-regulating intense feelings when they come up (e.g., breathing, grounding exercises,

removing oneself briefly from the situation, refocusing on goals, etc.); and

- if another participant in the transition has been hurt by one's actions, intentionally or not, creating a plan for repairing those hurts with the other participant and working with the issue going forward—and communicating that plan to the foster parents, caseworker and any other relevant individuals and accepting feedback on the plan before then implementing it.

Adoptive parents have previously experienced difficulty adding children to their family

Difficulty previously adding children may have occurred as a result of infertility, miscarriage/stillbirth, and/or not being chosen as the adoptive family for a child. All of these are losses that will be triggered to some extent by the adoptive transition. Many individuals or couples may have previously been in therapy or support groups to work on these loss issues. If that therapist or group is available, it may be useful to resume with them during the process of the adoptive transition and beyond to work on issues that may come up again.

It is often complicated for adoptive parents to manage both the preexisting grief and the new excitement of adoption. This mixture of feelings can manifest differently for each of the adoptive parents, which can create strain in their relationship. Open communication about each adoptive parent's experience is very helpful. Each parent will need to accept that they will handle these complicated feelings differently from their partner in order to lower tension between them. Recognizing that this experience is common, adoptive parents might share some details of their experience with the foster parents and caseworker, who can sympathize and provide support.

Adoptive parents are members of a group who have been discriminated against by the child welfare system

As mentioned previously, individuals from many groups (e.g., BIPOC, people with disabilities, LGBTQIA+, people in poverty) have historically been discriminated against by the child welfare system when they function as foster parents. This is also true when they apply to become adoptive parents.

Individuals from oppressed groups experience discrimination directly in society, and can come to expect its recurrence. Caseworkers and foster parents are representatives of the child welfare system and are seen as such by prospective adoptive parents, even if they do not identify with or consciously agree with the system's history of discrimination. Caseworkers and foster parents can also come from oppressed groups, but they have greater familiarity with the child welfare system than the adoptive parents. Implicit assumptions, unconscious defenses, power dynamics, and conscious anxieties will come into play when adoptive parents, foster parents and caseworkers interact and may surface during the adoptive transitions. This is especially loaded when adoptive parents come from oppressed groups.

As was mentioned before, communicating about our assumptions regarding others is both essential and challenging. Misunderstandings are often not maliciously intended, yet still may cause hurt and still need to be attended to. Recognizing the validity of the others' feelings is a great starting point, even if the source of the feelings is not understood or the feelings are disagreed with. The goal of this communication is to preserve the working relationship among the participants and thereby safeguard the welfare of the adoptive child and the adoptive transition.

Caseworker variables

Caseworker's preexisting stance toward adoptive transitions

As a group, caseworkers present significant variability in how they approach adoptive transitions. A caseworker may have their own existing model they have used for transitioning children into adoptive homes or they may have a model that they have been trained to use by others or they may use different strategies for each transition responding to the circumstances. Whatever model they use, how satisfied are they with that approach? Further, what is their openness to trying a new model? Consider whether the caseworker is choosing to use their current model out of their own belief in it or are they going along with it because a higher up in the chain of command has required them to. Even if the caseworker is ordered to use this approach, the model presented here includes flexibility for modifications based on the caseworker's sense of what the child and the involved adults need.

Relational focus versus task focus

When caseworkers are chronically overloaded, they may perform their role in a more task-oriented way in an effort to perform their role with efficiency and achieve the most good for the most people. The focus on relationships prioritized in this model is not optimally compatible with efficiency in completing practical tasks, but it is crucial for accomplishing relational goals. This model presents a relational approach to adoptive transitions in a way that is maximally efficient within reason and achievable for the goals of creating new relationships with adoptive parents and transforming relationships with foster parents. Hopefully, this makes it more attractive to task-focused caseworkers.

Consider the level of support the caseworker has from their supervisor, peers, and agency. Child welfare work is incredibly under-resourced and high-stress, with incredible stakes on the line: the welfare of vulnerable children. This model calls for a lot from caseworkers:

- reflectiveness regarding the ongoing process of the adoptive transition and their role in it;

- sensitivity to interpersonal cues;

- empathy and compassion to both the child and the involved adults;

- openness to shifting plans based on reactions from the child; and

- juggling multiple agendas, both practical and interpersonal, in the adoptive transition while responding to all the other issues on their caseload.

All these characteristics are more easily handled when caseworkers have reflective supervision, a sense of teamwork with colleagues, community support, governmental resources for the agency's mission, and so much more. In short, when caseworkers have support from their professional networks, they have the capacity to be more thoughtful and empathic.

There may be a degree of overwhelm and burnout with the job of caseworker. Burnout is said to occur when important work loses its meaning, which can make it hard for caseworkers to emotionally invest in an involved model like this one. Even if a caseworker is not "burnt out," an overwhelming workload can make it harder for a caseworker to fulfill the role for caseworkers as presented in this model. This model, however, has a clear mission to benefit children in a deep relational way, which can also be an antidote for burnout when used effectively.

Characteristics of other involved parties (e.g., CASA, child's attorney, birth parents, psychotherapist).

Birth parents

Birth parents may exhibit a wide range of stances toward their child's adoption, including:

- acceptance of a changed, but continuing, role for themselves in the child's life;

- frustration at what they perceive as the latest example of their being wrongfully hurt by the state;

- denial of the reality of adoption, and a persistent belief they will be reunited with the child somehow;

- disengagement from child and their parenting role, and little emotional reaction to adoption;

- substantial grief about losing the child, including pervasive sadness and/or anger; or

- appreciation that adoption is better for their child in the long run.

The birth parent may also genuinely be in different stances on different days depending on their emotional regulation, feelings in the moment toward the child welfare worker/system, and space to process their feelings.

The birth parent may try to actively sabotage the child moving on to the adoptive family, including with the following actions:

- devaluing adoption and adoptive parents while in contact with the child;

- making extreme demands about parameters of openness in adoption during negotiations with adoptive parents;

- refusing to participate in a goodbye process with the child; or

- attempting to delay the adoption through legal actions.

These and similar attempts need to be understood in the context of the birth parent's state of mind and potential grief process and what they might consciously and unconsciously be attempting to accomplish (e.g., holding onto the child, protecting their self-esteem, avoiding shame, processing grief). Keep these underlying goals in mind while interacting with the birth parent, rather than responding to their surface behaviors.

If the birth parent is supportive of the child's adoption, then they can be asked to:

- provide copies of photos or videos or narrative about the child's history for the Lifebook;

- attend moving day (if other parties consent);

- send a tangible, permanent message supporting the adoption that could be saved such as a letter or text or email or video;

- offer a more temporary message, such as a phone call to the child, supporting the adoption.

There is much more about scenarios that include active contact with birth parents in Chapter 12.

Other family of origin (e.g., grandparent, aunt, uncle, siblings)

Extended family members may have had variable amounts of contact with the child over the years, which in some cases may have yielded a deep relationship. These individuals may have extensive knowledge about the child's history and traumas, which hopefully is documented in the Lifebook. Further, the child may have relationships with them that need to be honored as part of the adoptive transition.

Extended family members are also a carrier of the child's cultural heritage. When it is appropriate for them to have ongoing involvement with the child, this can be a huge gift to the child and help them know, in their bones, the way their family of origin expresses their culture. Adoptive parents may do research about a child's culture and learn recipes or rituals, all of which is good, but pales in comparison to the details available from extended family (e.g., how this particular Hmong family would celebrate

Christmas or how this Mexican family would host a quinceañera for a daughter). In addition, the family of origin can also share what it means to be of that cultural or ethnic group in their day-to-day experience in the dominant society of the United States.

Depending on the extended family's ability to support adoption during the transition, it may be useful to account for the possible complexity of their attitudes and feelings toward the adoption. When they are in favor of the adoption, they can provide an important source of support for the adoption through sending positive messages to the child and adoptive parents or by attending some aspects of the transition. They may have the ability to have post-adoption contact with the child, which is permissible so long as it feels acceptable and safe to adoptive parents. Given that the child's knowledge of their birth parents is very sensitive, the adoptive parents may want to reserve the right to approve decisions about the extended family disclosing further details about them. There is also the question of whether the extended family of the birth parents will accept any restrictions the adoptive parents might place on what they say to the child about the birth parents. A negotiation and agreement process, similar to what might be done between birth and adoptive parents, may need to be considered with other family members. Thoughtfulness about these decisions is recommended. Adoptive parents do not need to make one decision for all the extended family. Keep in mind that these decisions are also an easy place for implicit bias to creep in.

Child's psychotherapist/prescriber

A child's psychotherapist may have an extensive knowledge about the child's emotional and relational functioning and may be implicitly trusted by the child. In some cases, with changes in placements and turnover of caseworkers, the child's therapist may have the longest existing relationship with the child, making them a valuable source of information for the Lifebook. However, with staff turnover in mental health clinics, it is also possible that the child has been with the therapist for only a short period of time, or that the therapist may be new to the counseling field in general, or working with foster/adoptive children and families in particular and not have a close relationship with the child.

One valuable contribution the child's therapist can provide is to translate what this child's surface behavior means about the child's internal emotional world at various points in the adoptive transition. To successfully provide this contribution, the therapist would know the child well and ideally be trained in adoption-competent, adoption sensitive clinical care (e.g., https://adoptionsupport.org/case-training-institute/). Therapists will also have varied skill in translating the meaning of a child's behavior for non-therapists. The level of attention and care they have been able to provide to the child may vary depending on the size of their caseload. It is also useful to note whether the therapist has directly helped to guide transitions or only helped children cope with a transition process that was run without the therapist's collaboration. Whatever the therapist's level of experience with adoptions and this particular child, familiarity with this model is recommended so they can best participate.

If the child is being prescribed psychiatric medications, then the prescriber is essential for the adoptive parents to talk with. Information about the medications, the child's response to them and any side effects will be useful to adoptive parents as visits get longer and stretch overnight and they are administering the medications. It might be noted that some adoptive parents have strong values against psychiatric medications. During the adoptive transition, this is not yet their choice to make and it is important for them to follow the existing medication plan for the child.

CASA/Guardian Ad Litem

These trained volunteers will have provided child-centered advocacy in court proceedings about the child. They may have long-standing relationships with the child and can have useful information for the Lifebook. Their relationship with the child is usually not deep enough for them to be an active participant in the adoptive transition, unless there is a need for child-centered advocacy during it.

Child's attorney

Sometimes a child will have their own attorney appointed for them by the court. This is separate from the attorney representing the state and the child welfare agency. If there are legal challenges interfering with the adoptive transition moving forward, then these attorneys can become involved in the process and advocate for the child's best interests.

Others

Other children and adults in various domains in the child's life can be a resource for the child during and after the transition, depending on the quality and length of their relationship. These domains include:

- School – teachers, classmates, paraeducators, school counselor,

- Birth Family - birth parents and other birth family members,

- Foster home – foster parents and siblings, other hired staff,

- Mental health – psychotherapist, group therapist, skills trainer,

- Special education – tutors, speech-language pathologist, physical therapist, occupational therapist,

- Community activities – coaches, arts personnel, other activity leaders, children in activities (e.g., teammates),

- Church – youth pastor, pastor, other children in religious education,

- Neighborhood – neighbor parents and children

Thus, they could usefully be informed that an adoptive transition is occurring without going into many details. For instance, they may offer support to the child in their day-to-day contacts. They may be invited to a goodbye party at the foster home. Adoptive parents may also want to talk to them as valuable sources of information about the child.

Characteristics of relationships existing pre-transition

We have been reviewing how the qualities of the participants might affect the adoptive transition. In addition, the characteristics of the participants' *relationships with each other* may also have an influence.

One of the most important relationships is between the child and the foster parents. How long has the child been in this home and what is the quality of the relationship that has developed between the child and the foster parents? Do the child and the foster parents know each other very well? Can they predict how the other will respond to various situations in the transition? How much will the child and the foster parents develop feelings of loss as the transition progresses? How good is the communication and trust between the child and the foster parents? These factors are especially important as we are initially asking the child to feel somewhat safe with the adoptive parents based on their trust of the foster parents' recommendation. Conversely, the adults are partly relying on what the child communicates—hopefully openly—about the visits with the adoptive parents to determine the pace of the transition.

Communication, collaborativeness, and *responsiveness* are the most important qualities that define the relationship between caseworker and foster parents for the sake of adoptive transitions. Is the communication clear and mutually understood? Do the caseworker and the foster parent feel like they are on the same team, collaborating towards the goal of doing what is best for the child? When either the caseworker or foster parent have a question or need, do they feel that the other responds in a timely fashion, even if it is not with the answer they want to hear? Having all three of these qualities is a huge asset for the adoptive transition. These same three qualities become relevant for connections between the adoptive parents and caseworker, and between the adoptive parents and the foster parents as these relationships develop (Lanyado, 2008). When communication, collaborativeness and responsiveness are present in all the relationships between the adults then this is a huge asset for the adoptive transition being successful.

In some adoptive transitions, adoptive parents and foster parents have a preexisting relationship (e.g., adoption by kin, a neighbor, the child's teacher, member of the foster parent's extended community). This is often a benefit as they have some sense of each other, even though the relationship will evolve substantially during the adoptive transition. This evolution may feel awkward based on the past relationship and this awkwardness might be openly acknowledged if it arises. If there has been past conflict, then this also needs to be acknowledged but with the goal of supporting the child through the transition. It is often not useful to go back and revisit the past conflict unless an encounter among foster parents and adoptive parents will lead one of the adults to feel such intense feelings that it would interfere with the transition. If that is the case, then it is useful to have a professional therapist help the involved parties to reach some level of resolution to that past conflict, at least to the extent that the collaboration around the transition can move forward.

Pre-transition planning

Legal and administrative policy context

Some states have particular child welfare laws and regulations regarding adoptive transitions. It is important to read these carefully to see how much interpretive flexibility may be allowed by their language.

Within the confines of the statewide rules, child welfare transitions are customarily designed following local practices inherent in the particular branch or region.

Caseworkers would consider:

- Is there a written local policy and, if so, is it being routinely followed?

- If there is a written policy and it is being followed, then what are its details? For instance, is a certain number of visits specified? Or, are there parameters set for contact with foster parents after the child has moved?

- If there is no written policy, is there an oral tradition of how to facilitate adoptive transitions that is often followed?

- Conversely, is there wide variability in how adoptive transitions are done, with each caseworker doing it their own way?

- How much influence have foster parents, adoptive parents, and/or the child had on how adoptive transitions have been conducted previously in this locale?

Sometimes a caseworker may want to use this model but there is no institutional support from higher administration. Given the answers to the above questions, caseworkers may be able to implement some elements of the model that do not go against existing policy. It is possible that exceptions may be granted by administrators, if requested, to try other elements of the model that do contravene existing rules. There may also be times when foster and adoptive parents are implementing the model and the caseworker may choose to not know all the details of what they are doing.

Process and planning

Identify who will be involved in planning the transition. Often, the caseworker leads overall planning. This expectation is assumed in the rest of the outline of this model, because it represents how the vast majority of transitions occur. In rare instances, a consultant specializing in adoptive transitions may lead instead. This consultant may be a specialized child welfare agency staff or a hired outside expert.

It is advisable for planning meetings to occur during significant milestones of the transition, and on a regular basis (Browning, 2015). At minimum, the caseworker, adoptive parents, foster parents, and the child's therapist (if there is one) would attend these meetings, which would be the beginning of any contact between foster parents and adoptive parents. They may be preceded by contact between caseworker and adoptive parents or foster parents.

These meetings would ideally be conducted in-person, if at all possible. Video conferences may be acceptable when necessary, but phone meetings are not because these relationships are just beginning and it's important to build trust and understand each participant's nuances of communication. For best results, share this written model ahead of time, and make explicit the understanding that all parties are putting the child's needs first. Everyone should have access to the same information about the child, participants, process, etc.

When the meetings begin, lay out a potential sequence of steps (see Table 2 for a common sequence) and articulate, clearly, that there is no preset time schedule for taking these steps. A step backwards here or there may be necessary. Come to an agreement about scheduling check-in meetings, and urge everyone to add these meetings to their schedules. Assert that any adult participant can ask for an urgent planning meeting, if they feel the need. Planning meetings would also occur before the overnight visits start and moving day. Additional planning meetings can also be held if any member of the original planning committee wishes. After each planning meeting, the caseworker will send out an email to all attendees summarizing its content and including further scheduled meeting times. All attendees will review these minutes and offer input.

Aside from planning meetings, foster parents and adoptive parents will collaboratively determine when to take next steps in the process. Research supports the foster parent-adoptive parent relationship as key to the success of the transition process (Browning, 2015; Neil, Beek & Schofield, 2020; Reams, 2021), as they have the most invested in the child's welfare.

Table 2

Usual* sequence of steps in this adoptive transition model

- Determine adoptive planning committee and initial planning meetings
- Child(ren) informed of adoption
- First meeting of adoptive parents and child(ren) in foster home
- Subsequent meetings of adoptive parents and child(ren) in foster home
- Short meetings of adoptive parents and child(ren) outside of foster home
- Day-long meetings of adoptive parents and child(ren) outside of foster home
- Planning meeting
- Overnight visits of child with adoptive homes in their residence
- Planning meeting
- Farewell events in foster home
- Moving day
- Reverse visits with former foster parents

*These steps may need to be reordered or repeated depending on events in the transition and the child's emotional state. Planning meetings may be added at any point.

This arrangement empowers the foster parents and adoptive parents. If there is a stalemate, the caseworker can be brought in as a mediator to work towards consensus. The caseworker would also be checking in with both foster parents and adoptive parents individually about how they feel the transition is going and to offer input.

The relationship between foster parents and adoptive parents starts in pretransition

The relationship between adoptive parents and foster parents ideally starts before adoptive parents meet the child. We recommend that they debrief and become acquainted, ideally alone, following the first planning meeting. When foster parents provide information to adoptive parents, this would be provided conversationally over time, and with opportunities for adoptive parents to ask questions (Davis, 2015).

Significant information would also be provided in writing, because both foster and adoptive parents may be overloaded and unable to process and remember all the spoken information without a tangible record. Such useful information is listed in Table 3.

After the foster and adoptive parents have met, foster parents might consider taking videos of some daily routines involving the child, e.g.,

---

Table 3

Information about the child to be transmitted from foster parents to adoptive parents

- child's personality;
- child's daily routines;
- child's like/dislikes including foods, bedtime stories or lullabies, movies, etc.;
- child's behavior and what it signals;
- effective parenting strategies for the child;
- child's history;
- child's health status;
- how the child handled the transition into this foster home; and
- prior work on the child's Lifebook (when available).

---

waking them up in the morning, mealtimes, getting them out the door to school, after school chores, playtime, and/or bedtime. Adoptive parents could watch these videos before meeting the child to get to know the child and develop a feel for the relationship between the foster parents and the child. These videos might also be watched later in the process as preparation for certain steps, e.g. watching the video of bedtime before the overnight visit.

Ideally, foster parents are able and willing to provide emotional support to adoptive parents throughout the transition process, doing some or all of the following:

- voicing their support to the adoptive parents during the stress of the transition process;
- voicing their support for the transition process in general;
- being a support to help the adoptive parents think about the child's behavior and its meaning in the context of the child's history of such behaviors in the foster home;
- making themselves available to adoptive parents for questions during and after transition; or
- being a resource for adoptive parents to share feelings with—without presuming to act as a problem solver or therapist;

Adoptive parents may provide support to foster parents by:

- expressing gratitude to foster parents for their efforts loving and supporting the child currently and in the past;

- inviting foster parents to be involved in the child's life post-move in the capacity of an extended family relationship if foster parents are willing;

- asking for and honoring the foster parents' expertise with this child;

- being a resource for foster parents to share feelings with—without presuming to act as a problem solver; or

- sharing with foster parents photos and short videos of visits that no longer include the foster parents themselves.

In any event, plan for continued daily or near daily contact between foster parents and adoptive parents during the transition.

Informing the child about the adoption.

The first task for the adults to decide in a planning meeting is what will be told to the child about the adoption. Ideally, adults would have some consensus about what is told to the child. Adults would explore together the content, tone, depth, process, etc. of this conversation and how expectable questions might be responded to.

The decision of who tells the child about the adoption is a sensitive one. There are several possibilities and options to consider. The caseworker is the most common option, given that they usually have more experience with these conversations. Many agencies may list this as a policy, even though caseworkers may not have much of a relationship with the child as a result of staff turnover and large caseloads. If the caseworker tells the child, the foster parents would attend, and be prepared to answer the child's questions and provide support.

Foster parents may be a viable option to inform the child, as they often have much more of a relationship with the child than the caseworker, but may need guidance if they are inexperienced (see https://consideringadoption.com/parenting-after-foster-care-adoption/

talking-to-your-foster-children-about-adoption/ for some useful tips). The child's loss issues with the foster parent may come up right away in this conversation—the child may ask the foster parents why they cannot adopt them. It is important for foster parents to have thought through their reasons and responses to this likely question before having the conversation. As mentioned before, listen carefully to the child's question and what the child is asking; "You don't love me, do you?" is different from "Why don't you want me?" Developmental issues are also important in framing the answer– see section 7 below. Regardless of who shares the plan, inform the child's therapist (if they have one) that the child has been told before the next therapy session.

The decision of when to tell the child about adoption is usually best based on the developmental level of the child.

- *Infants and toddlers* are often too young to comprehend, and are consequently not told.

- *Preschoolers* may be told the day before the first visit without being told about the first visit. Because preschoolers do not understand clock-based time, they may be told that the meeting will happen "tomorrow after breakfast." A picture book about adoption may be useful in this process.

- *Early school-age children* (roughly aged 6-9 years) may be told 3 to 4 days before the first visit. These children may also benefit from a book about adoption being read with them as part of this process.
- *Preteens* (10-12 years) may be told a week before the first visit.
- *Teenagers* (13-17 years) may be told two weeks before the first visit.

These time frames are gauged to give the child a developmentally appropriate amount of time to consider the information and ask questions but not so much time that they are burdened with carrying it for any longer than necessary. These suggested time frames might need to be modified depending on specific circumstances of the child and their context.

Informing child of upcoming events (e.g., visits)

Many disclosures to children occur too early or not at all because of an adult's discomfort with some aspect of telling the child or concern about the child's reaction.

- *Infants and toddlers* provide an opportunity for adults to practice language about the adoptive transition. While infants/toddlers live "in the moment" and may not grasp the language shared, describing the transition (and pending goodbye) with verbal language allows the adults to practice the emerging narrative and experience aspects of their emotions that may benefit from support. The infants and toddlers will pick up on the adults' shifts in mood, which will alert them that something different might happen. Maintaining as much daily routine as possible will help these children deal with the changes.

- *Preschoolers* would receive 30-60 minutes of warning of an upcoming visit. Foster parents can help the child through some supportive actions:
  - Help the child with preparations they want to make (e.g., changing clothes, identifying a toy or stuffed animal to take).
  - Talk about who is coming and repeat their role as adoptive parents in whatever language has been decided upon.
  - Answer the child's questions about what is going to happen.
  - Help the child articulate the feelings they are showing directly, or indirectly through behavior, and provide reassurance.
  - If the child asks foster parents repeated questions about when an event is going to happen, reassure them that it will occur and that the adult will let them know when or set a visual timer together.
- *School-age children* would receive 1-2 days of warning, but this can vary with respect to the maturity level of the child.

○ If the child asks foster parents repeatedly about the event's timing, involve the child in developing a visual reminder the child can refer to, such as a paper calendar with each day crossed off leading up to the visit.

○ As with preschoolers, assist the child with preparations, feelings, and questions. For instance, the child might ask, "Do they know about my peanut allergy?" which might be a way of asking if the adoptive parents can keep the child safe. One way of responding might be, "Sure, I've talked with them about it. How about we check with them when they come to be sure they remember?"

- *Teenagers* would know the dates of upcoming events when the foster parents are informed. Upcoming events should be scheduled with their calendars taken into consideration. Teenagers will often claim they need no emotional assistance from the foster parents regarding upcoming visits. Foster parents can still offer the assistance in a way that they have learned that the teenager might accept; perhaps with humor or while doing a joint task (e.g., baking, walking).

Chapter 3

The First Visit

The primary goal for the child of a first visit is to begin to learn about the adoptive parents. It is a very basic goal and easily achievable if the child's boundaries are respected. Even if the child stays hidden the whole visit and the adoptive parents and the foster parents only chat about the child, the child has learned that the adoptive parents were patient and not intrusive, and heard about them from the foster parents and the other children afterwards. For instance, a three year old girl hides under the dining room table peering through the protective first of chair legs at these visiting strangers; listening to the voice tones of her foster mother and the visitors to assess safety and friendliness.

The goal for adoptive parents is to be in the same house, probably the same room, as the child and to be friendly and warm towards the foster parent and the child, if the child is ready for that. Focusing on those emotions rather than the excitement and nervousness is often the challenge. Being warm rather than doing something is the key.

Foster parents have twin goals that are not in conflict but can be a little bit of a juggling act. The first goal is to be present for the child and help them feel safe and protected even though there are strangers present. This may even require gently redirecting the adoptive parents if they are initiating too much towards the child. The second goal is to help the adoptive parents feel comfortable and supported in the foster home so they can be their best selves in the visit. Both are usually achievable but the first goal takes priority. The child's needs take precedence.

Ideally, foster and adoptive parents are clear with each other that foster parents will do all caregiving and comforting of the child during this and other early visits. Even if the adoptive parents know what the foster parents would do to comfort the child and feel ready to provide it, the child is not ready to accept it from them.

The first visit can be anywhere from 10-60 minutes in length. The foster parents and adoptive parents decide together on a prearranged signal that foster parents can use to indicate at any point their sense that the child is nearing capacity and it is time the visit wraps up. The first visit and subsequent initial visits would occur in the foster home with at least one foster parent present. This is essential for the child to feel safe and as open as they can be to starting a new relationship.

Heading into a first visit, it is very expected that adoptive parents will have a lot of feelings. That is fine and adoptive parents might park near the foster home ahead of time to breathe, review plans, cry, exchange hugs, or perform any other emotional regulation that feels right. When the time approaches to start the visit, it is important for adoptive parents to feel relatively pulled together so they can observe and think. It is a paradox: ideally adoptive parents would be authentic as people and sensitive to the other person simultaneously, sort of like a first date. The goal is for the child to feel like the adoptive parents are tuned in and responsive to what the child needs in the moment, not what is going on emotionally for the adoptive parents in the moment.

Children, who are old enough to understand what is going on and that potential adoptive parents are coming over, will likely be activated and may show that in a range of behaviors. Responding to those behaviors as an expression of the child's jumbled feelings is useful. These preschool/school-aged children are old enough to have a direct conversation validating and normalizing their feelings. For example, the foster parent might say, "You've got a lot of feelings going on right now. What are you feeling?" It is also useful for the foster parent to physically reassure the child and tell them that the foster parent cares about them and will be with them through the visit. This is another time when children may start processing their feelings of loss. They may cry, hug tightly, or verbally express that they want to stay with the foster parents forever and not be adopted. Foster parents would accept these feelings and express caring back, without contradicting the child's assertions that they will refuse the adoption.

A child's trauma history may also manifest itself in a first visit. They may flinch at an arm movement of the adoptive parent or scream at the sight of a blond adoptive mother with glasses who resembles a previous abuser. Responding to these reactions is the responsibility of the foster parents. Adoptive parents can most usefully stand still and try not to visibly react.

Foster parents will soothe the child in the ways they have learned previously. Foster parents will decide whether the visit can continue or not. It often can not. A new plan may need to be made for the first visit to take into account the child's trauma reaction. Hopefully, a child with a trauma reaction will be in psychotherapy and so the therapist can provide input into this planning (Zeanah, 2022).

In the time right before a first visit, foster parents may also have their own feelings of sadness and happiness that the child is moving forward but also developing away from them, whether the child is expressing feelings of loss or not. It's a bit like the first day of kindergarten or an adult child getting married. There is not usually the opportunity for foster parents to talk about those feelings in the moment but hopefully those feelings can be shared with one another before the day is out.

Arrival

The physical locations of all parties is a sensitive matter, and requires some planning in order to make the space feel casual and safe for the child. Allow the child to move wherever they want to be in the foster home—including their room. Foster parents would greet adoptive parents and invite them in. This is important to show the child the positive emotion with which the foster parent interacts with the adoptive parent. Ideally, foster and adoptive parents would have agreed ahead of time on how the adoptive parents will be introduced to the child. Especially for the first visit, other foster children should not be in the living room, preferably even not in the home, to provide an uninterrupted space for the adoptive parent and child to meet.

Adoptive parents should not bring a gift—as this puts too much pressure on the child to respond. If the child is in the same room as the adoptive parents, adoptive parents are encouraged to be curious and observant about the child's cues to adjust their level of engagement.

Some general guidelines for adoptive parents:

- Remain silent and observe or talk to the foster parent until the child has at least looked at you, then you might say something to the child.

- A child's actions can be a good guide (e.g., if the child looks at you out of the corner of their eye, then look at them out of the corner of your eye).

- Keep the same distance from the child until they have moved towards you without immediately moving back toward the foster parents.

- When in doubt, choose to go more slowly rather than more quickly.

- Foster parents can help here by sitting on the floor which will lead the child to sit on the floor or the foster parent's lap; then the adoptive parent can join them on the floor which nonthreateningly communicates playfulness without intruding on the child.

During Visit

Ideally, the foster parents and adoptive parents settle in a room with plenty of space to play (living room or family room, perhaps but not a bedroom) and talk about positive aspects of the child (e.g., favorite foods, daily routine, favorite toys).

Some children benefit from a little space to observe adults from afar. Children may listen from another room; adults can keep the conversation focused on each other until the child signals (often with minor movements towards the group) that they might be interested to engage. If, and when, the child chooses to enter, foster parents can use the occasion to invite them to play with them and the adoptive parents.

If the child says yes, the parties all play a simple noncompetitive activity sitting with the child on the floor. After some time, usually after a cue from the foster parent, the adoptive parents move to their knees, and say goodbye and that they will return.

If the child says no, their choice is acknowledged and respected, and the foster parents and adoptive parents continue to talk. After a few minutes, the foster parents invite the child to play while adoptive parents watch.

If the child says no to this second invitation, then foster parents and adoptive parents continue to talk for a while and then end the visit. Remember that this is still a success, albeit a smaller one.

If the child says yes to this second invitation, the foster parents play a simple noncompetitive activity with the child, on the floor, while adoptive parents watch.

After some time, on their knees, adoptive parents say goodbye, and that they will return. It is very normal for adoptive parents to wish for physical contact with the child at the end of the visit. This wish needs to be acknowledged on the inside by adoptive parents but consciously set aside for the welfare of the child. If the child initiates physical contact, adoptive parents can then reciprocate but at the level of the child's affection and be prepared to stop the exchange the second the child disengages. Some examples might be a seven year old boy who raises a hand for a high five and the adoptive parent gently slaps his hand or a two year old hugs the adoptive parent's leg and in response the adoptive parent briefly rubs her back. If the affection goes on longer or is more intense than the adoptive parent is comfortable with, it is fine to gently disengage and remind the child that the adoptive parent will be visiting again.

Departure

At the end of the visit, foster parents show the adoptive parents to the door and warmly say goodbye and indicate verbally that they look forward to the next time they see them. This again illustrates to the child the positive relationships between foster and adoptive parents. It also communicates to the child, directly from a foster parent, that the adoptive parents will be coming again.

Infrequently, the child will show emotional distress upon the adoptive parents announcing that they are leaving. An attachment bond has not formed that quickly, but the feelings are genuine and may be connected to that child's history of losses. The adoptive parents can respond empathically—but briefly—to the feelings, reassuring the child that they will return, and then leave. The foster parents then would take over comforting the child as the adoptive parents are leaving.

Adoptive parents will have feelings upon leaving—this is easily understandable. They may become teary. If it is possible to contain the tears until after leaving the foster home, that is preferable. If the adoptive parents are teary while departing, it is useful for the adoptive parents to acknowledge their feelings of sadness to the child, but add that they are glad they will be seeing them again soon. The foster parents can usefully offer some words of comfort to the adoptive parents also, for the child to witness. It is helpful if adoptive parents can share these feelings and discuss them with each other as soon as possible while they are fresh; perhaps in their car after they have pulled out of sight of the foster home.

Foster parents often also have feelings as they recognize that this meeting marks the beginning of a foundational shift in the relationship that they currently have with the child into a different kind of relationship. This is a real loss. It is very useful for foster parents to talk about those feelings with each other and with friends or other supports they have in their life. It is important that the children in the foster home do not overhear these conversations.

After the first visit

Foster parents would record written notes about the child's behavior and emotional state after the visit. The child may have comments or questions for the foster parents about the visit or the adoptive parents and the foster parents would respond. For instance, the child might say, "They left. They didn't like me." A foster parent might reassure with, "Remember, I like you and they're coming back. Let's watch and see if they smile at you or play with you." If the child says nothing about the visit, the foster parents may make a mildly positive comment about the adoptive parents like "they seemed nice" and see if that stimulates any discussion with the child about the visit. Adoptive parents and foster parents need time later to debrief the visit that same day on a phone or video call. The caseworker would also get updated about how the visit went.

Vignettes

There are a multitude of ways a first visit can go. To give a sense of what each step of a transition will look like, three scenarios will be described to highlight certain characteristics of first visits: the heightened and rapidly shifting emotional states of the child, the questions and uncertainty of the adoptive parents in how best to be with the child, the crucial role of the foster parent in guiding and reassuring both the child and the adoptive parent, and the importance of following the child's lead as opposed to assuming what the child is ready for (which may shift from minute to minute).

A reminder: these are not the stories of actual children, but composite stories that represent true-feeling scenarios.

Diego - 5 years old | the first meeting

The first scenario is about a five-year-old Mexican-American boy, Diego, who has been in Fernanda's foster home for two years. Fernanda is also Mexican-American. Diego was in one prior foster home for two months when he first entered the state's custody. He is meeting his white identified adoptive mother, Sue, a stranger to him, for the first time.

Diego ran from window to window to see every possible view of the street his foster home was on. He knew that the woman who would soon be driving up might be his forever mother. He hoped that she would like him and that he wouldn't do something bad to make her hate him. As he ran, he bumped into a side table and a lamp wobbled but didn't fall.

His foster mother, Fernanda, called to him, "Diego."

"Si, mama." Diego answered.

In a calm voice, she invited Diego to sit with her.

Diego ran over to her side and leaned into her.

She put her arm around his waist and asked, "Are you excited, Diego?"

"Si, mama." he answered while bouncing a little.

"Maybe other feelings, too?"

"I don't know, mama." He started to wiggle more. "Can I go look out the window? Can I?"

"Let's look together. How about that?" Fernanda suggested.

Diego nodded his head.

"Excelente. If we sit on this end of the couch, we can see the whole street at once." directed Fernanda.

Diego and his foster mom moved to the couch and he again leaned into her as he knelt and looked out the window. A car drove up—it is a nice car, thought Diego. Without realizing it, he compared this car to his foster mother's car and the car his birth mother used to drive.

"It's her," Diego exclaimed.

"Si, it is." Fernanda explained, "That's the car she was driving when I met her before."

"Why doesn't she get out?" Diego asked worriedly.

Fernanda reassured Diego, "I'm not sure. Maybe she's getting ready."

Diego's voice got more high-pitched and anxious, "Is she going to drive away?"

Before his foster mother could answer, the car door opened and a woman emerged, looking up at the house. Diego let go of his half of the curtain and hid behind it while still watching the woman, scrutinizing her for clues that she would like him. His foster mother waved to the woman and she waved back as she walked towards the front door. Diego jumped up.

"I've got to go potty." Diego blurted out and ran out of the room to the bathroom. His stomach felt weird, like he might throw up. He heard the front door open and the voices of Fernanda and the other woman float through the house. The other woman's voice sounded sort of like his teacher's voice: different from his foster and birth mother's. He thought "she does not speak Spanish." He went to the archway between the dining room and the living room and peeked in. He thought they didn't know that he was there, so he listened in. He heard the new woman speaking, but could only see the back of her head.

"Please, Fernanda. Just call me Sue," the woman insisted, "only my brother calls me Suzanne."

"Sure, Sue. How's your hotel?" asked Fernanda.

"It's fine," Sue began, "but the food in the restaurant isn't very good. I had some enchiladas last night that were so greasy."

Fernanda nodded. "Chicken enchiladas are Diego's favorite dish, but not too spicy."

"I'd love your recipe if you'd be willing to share it." Sue sounded sincere.

"Of course," replied Fernanda, adding "Diego is such a good eater."

Listening in on this conversation, Diego thought the new lady sounded nice. While wondering if she has other kids, he was startled to hear his own name called.

"Diego!" Fernanda called again.

Diego came out from behind the archway and replied, "Si, mama."

Fernanda explained, "Mrs. Jones would like to know what else are your favorite foods besides chicken enchiladas. Churros?"

Diego nodded his head while staring at Sue, who had turned around to look at him, smiling. He looked down. He saw one of his toy cars on the floor and blurted out, "I like Hot Wheels."

Sue asked gently, "Do you have a lot of Hot Wheels cars?"

Instead of answering, Diego bolted out of the room. Sue looked at Fernanda, who shrugged in response. Diego ran back into the room carrying his Hot Wheels carrying case with dozens of cars inside. He opened the case and dumped them all out in front of his foster mother. A wave of anxiety came over Diego as he remembered that he was not supposed to dump a whole container of toys on the floor at once.

Fernanda smiled and moved to the floor. Diego joined her on the floor. They rolled cars back and forth while Sue watched. After about five minutes, Sue sat on the floor but farther from Diego than Fernanda was. Fernanda smiled at her but Diego looked at Sue with no expression as he scooted a bit closer to his foster mother. Sue leaned back a bit. Fernanda and Diego rolled cars to each other at the same time to see if they would crash. Fernanda then rolled a car to Sue. Sue smiled at Fernanda and then rolled the car to Diego who glanced at Sue and then rolled the car to

Fernanda. Fernanda went to roll the car again to Sue, but Diego interjected, "No."

Fernanda said to Diego, "You want to play cars with me and just have Sue watch?"

Diego nodded in response.

He played cars with Fernanda for a few more minutes before she said, "I think it's time for us to wrap up our visit for today."

Sue agreed. "I think that's a good idea." She stood and said to Diego, "Thank you for showing me your cars."

Diego ran and hid behind his foster mother.

Fernanda reminded Diego, "What do we say when someone thanks us?"

"De nada," answered Diego to Sue.

"Muy bien," complimented Fernanda. "And in English?"

"You're welcome."

Sue remarked to Fernanda, "I had fun being with you both." Sue got her coat and was moving to leave when Diego darted out and hugged her from behind and then ran out of the room.

Sue exclaimed, "Wow. My head is spinning."

"For sure," reassured Fernanda, "let's talk about that when we debrief tonight. Does 8:30 still work for you?"

"You bet. I'm looking forward to it." added Sue as she left.

In their debrief later that evening, Fernanda let Sue know how anxious Diego was and that some of his behavior that seemed inconsistent on the surface (keeping a distance and then hugging Sue at the end) were more about that anxiety. Sue asked how she did and Fernanda reassured her that she did a nice job of giving Diego space while also showing interest. Fernanda also volunteered that she was glad that Diego didn't hide out in the bathroom the whole meeting, which he can do sometimes when he is overwhelmed. His peeking in showed his interest in Sue.

Isabella - 14 years | the first meeting

The second scenario is about a 14-year-old white girl, Isabella, who has been in her current home with her white foster parent Sheila for four months. Isabella has been in five prior foster homes. She is meeting her white adoptive mother and aunt, Julie, for the second time. She met her once when she was five years old, but has no memory of that meeting.

Isabella scrolled on her phone without really seeing anything. She wondered what this new "mom" would be like. She felt her stomach tighten up and switched to fantasizing about a Tiktok video she could create with photos of each prior mom, making fun of them with filters and masks to make each of them look ridiculous.

Sheila interrupted this daydream, announcing, "She's here."

Isabella glanced up and looked at a 40ish woman walking up the sidewalk with clothes that looked terribly lame to her. She quickly looked down at her phone again—letting it be very obvious that she wasn't interested. She assumed her foster mother would insist she interact so she opened her phone's camera. As her Aunt Julie walked in, Isabella took her picture and then shifted to shooting video of her.

"What are you doing?" asked Sheila.

"Just creating a record for history of this life-changing moment," replied Isabella with heavy sarcasm.

"I think of it that way for me for sure," interjected Julie.

Isabella rolled her eyes.

"Do you remember your aunt at all? You met her when you were younger?" Sheila asked Isabella, who shook her head.

Julie offered, "What I remember is you had on this pretty pink dress. You were shy at first, hiding behind your mom. She was so sweet with you. You'd twirl in your dress. Show me some of your -

Isabella interrupted, "Fuck all that ancient history. My therapist brings that crap up, too. I have to tell her, over and over again: I'm not interested."

Julie responded, "Okay, back to the present. What do you think of this adoption idea?"

Isabella angrily stated, "I don't care who I live with — you or Sheila. I'm emancipating when I'm 16, going to fashion school, opening my own design house like Coco Chanel."

Julie tentatively asked, "Tell me about Coco Chanel. Why her and not another designer?"

"She used her own skills, first to make hats and then dresses in her own design house and then all sorts of other stuff like perfumes and purses even though she was in an orphanage after her mother died," replied Isabella.

"She's quite the expert on Coco Chanel," Sheila added.

"I see," replied Julie. "You admire her a lot."

"She was her own boss. Didn't answer to nobody." Isabella was emphatic. After a pause, she asked Julie if she owns any Chanels.

"No, no dresses or accessories or anything like that. I do have a small bottle of Chanel No. 5," Julie answered.

"Me too," said Isabella.

"Really?" asked Sheila.

"Fuck off and die, Sheila. I'll be out of here soon," Isabella blurted before storming out of the room.

"I'm guessing that's the end for today," said Julie.

"Yep. That went better than I thought it would."

"Really? Okay. I'll want to hear more about that later in our phone call."

In their check-in on the phone later that day, Julie expressed concern about Isabella's level of anger. Sheila said that she has seen that often from Isabella and shared that her therapist says it's a strategy for Isabella to keep people at a distance and hide her vulnerability from others and herself. Julie asked how Sheila could feel it went well. Sheila commented that Isabella hadn't refused to meet with her and had even asked her if she owned any Chanels, which, for her, was a vulnerable question to ask. Sheila volunteered that she regretted raising questions about Isabella's Chanel No. 5. She wasn't trying to imply that Isabella was lying, she was just surprised because she had never seen it in her room. Sheila added that Isabella told her later that she hid it so other foster kids in the home wouldn't steal it, and insisted that Sheila text a picture of it to Julie so Julie would know that she wasn't lying. Julie said that she'd text Isabella back a picture of her bottle of Chanel.

Hakim - 18 months | the first meeting

The third scenario is an 18-month-old African-American boy, Hakim, who has been with his white foster mother, Jane, since he was four days old. Jane had wanted to adopt Hakim but had eventually reluctantly decided not to because she was in her 60s. He is meeting his identified adoptive mother and father, LaRonda and Michael, both African-American, for the first time.

Jane let LaRonda and Michael into the house and Hakim toddled to Jane to be picked up, which she did. He buried his head into her shoulder.

Jane welcomed Laronda and Michael warmly, "Please, come in. This is Hakim."

LaRonda responded in a child-friendly voice, "Hi Hakim." Hakim squirmed and buried his face even deeper.

Jane rubbed Hakim's back, gave him a squeeze, and whispered in his ear, "I'm right here, Hakim," before addressing LaRonda and Michael, "Please have a seat. Let's chat." They all sat.

Michael started off with a question for Jane, "You mentioned he might be really shy. Is this what you meant?"

Jane nodded and added, "Yes, he is very nervous around strangers right now. It wasn't always this way but he's at an age where there's a lot of stranger anxiety. He usually warms up after a bit."

LaRonda commented, "We read about that. We're planning on using an attachment parenting approach."

Jane responded, "There's a lot of wisdom in that approach. As you can see, Hakim loves hugs and physical contact—unless he's at a park and then it's all about the swings and the climbing structure and playing bridge monster."

At the same time, Michael and LaRonda asked what a bridge monster is. Hakim looked around at them and then buried his face again.

"Hakim will run across a bridge at the park between two climbing structures while I act the part of a monster making some growling noises. Hakim gets a little scared and very excited. He's a very brave boy; aren't you, Hakim?"

Hakim nodded his head, "Yes," and Jane kissed the side of his head. Jane looked around the floor and asked, "LaRonda, would you please hand me the Black Panther action figure under your chair? That's his favorite."

LaRonda picked up the figure and gave it to Jane.

Jane thanked LaRonda and then said to Hakim, "Look what LaRonda found under her chair," while holding up the action figure. Hakim looked and then grabbed the figure and shifted to sit on Jane's lap but facing away from Michael and LaRonda. He started to fiddle with the figure's arms and legs.

"I wish I could see his face better but I know he's facing away because that feels safer." stated Michael.

"Me too," added LaRonda.

"We'll get there and it'll be worth the wait. Hakim has the biggest, best smiles." Hakim turned and had the action figure start to climb Jane's body.

Jane described the figure's actions, "He's going higher and higher. Not in my face. That's right—he's on the tippity-top of my head." He jumped down to Hakim's head. Jane guided Hakim's hand and the figure—first down to Hakim's hair, then to his stomach, saying, "He's got Hakim's tummy," which made Hakim giggle.

Jane added to LaRonda and Michael, "He's got a tickly tummy."

LaRonda responded with, "I definitely can see that."

Hakim rubbed his eyes and Jane said, "I think it might be time to say goodbye." The adults all stood, with Jane holding Hakim.

Both LaRonda and Michael thanked Jane and Jane acknowledged that it was good to have taken this first step and that they would all talk later that day. She then said to Hakim, "Do you want to wave bye-bye?" Hakim turned and looked full on at LaRonda and Michael for a couple of seconds and then buried his head again.

A few hours later on their phone call to talk about the visit, LaRonda and Michael talked about Hakim not waving good-bye while Jane pointed out that he looked at them without tremendous anxiety, which wasn't true at the beginning of the visit. "That's progress." Jane also praised LaRonda and Michael for restraining themselves despite their strong desire to interact more with Hakim.

These three scenarios all describe a first visit that was a success that can be built on in later visits, even if the actual amount of interaction between child and adoptive parent might be minimal. The child experiences the adoptive parents as respectful and interested in them and observes the foster parent's own positive connection with the adoptive parents. The child-oriented pacing present within each of these first visits is extended over subsequent visits.

Chapter 4

Subsequent Early Visits

Shifting the balance of safety from foster parents to adoptive parents

The goal for the child of these subsequent early visits is to build some basic trust in the safety of the adoptive parents while foster parents are around to guarantee that safety. Be on the lookout for the following signals, which may indicate the child's growing trust in the adoptive parents:

- Easy flow of interaction with adoptive parents.
- Relaxed body posture.
- Infrequent glances at foster parents (if present).

- Absence of stress behaviors (e.g., spitting up for infants, regression in preschoolers, spaciness in school-aged children, unusual defiance or withdrawal in teenagers).

- If there is physical movement during their play with adoptive parents, the child moves short distances away from the foster parent (e.g., in a game of toss with the adoptive parent, if the child misses the catch they feel comfortable moving away from the side of the foster parent to go get the ball).

The goal for the adoptive parents is to enter into a dance with the child where the child is leading and the child knows it. The child comes to trust the adoptive parents to not intrude on the child's sense of safety and, if they do, they back up quickly. Yet the adoptive parents are still also a dance partner that is present in the dance and attentive.

To continue the metaphor, the goal for the foster parents is to be both chaperone to the dance and dance teacher. Thus, like a good teacher, to be active in the beginning, modeling how best to interact with the child, but then also receding more into the background as the adoptive parents progress in their ability. The chaperone function is to make sure the relationship develops at an appropriate pace for the more vulnerable member of the duo.

At the beginning of each of these early visits, adoptive parents would initially visit with

foster parents for at least a few minutes to help the child with the transition of them being present in the home. During this phase of the transition, there is a gradual decrease in the presence of the foster parents over the course of visits as the child starts to develop a sense of security with the adoptive parents. This can be seen in the following sequence:

- Child interacts with foster parents with adoptive parents present.

- Child interacts with both foster parents and adoptive parents.

- Child interacts with adoptive parents, near foster parents who are involved with another child or phone or task.

- Child interacts with adoptive parents, in the same room as the foster parents who are involved in other activities at a distance.

- Child interacts with adoptive parents while foster parents move in and out of the room.

- Child interacts with adoptive parents outside in the foster home's yard—with foster parents in the house.

For each visit, do not begin with the most-engaged level of interaction with the adoptive parents that was achieved in the prior visit. Rather, start with one level *before* that, as a way to begin with a comfortable amount of interpersonal intensity for the child and avoid distressing the child. Try to have at least five minutes of easy, comfortable play at this first level of each visit before moving onto the next level. Play for **at least** 10 minutes at each subsequent level before trying a new level. The most important principle is *"Take it slow"*. Foster parents can give signals to adoptive parents if they feel that the child is ready to try the next level or needs to retreat back to the previous one.

After shifting to a new level, if the child shows any signs of resistance at the foster parent being less available, then stay with prior level for the rest of the visit. Say out loud "Oh, we'll just keep on playing (insert description of level that is being stayed at)." In this scenario, the child has perceived the adult as being somewhat out of attunement, which needs to be recognized aloud and repaired. This is often unforeseen, as the child may have given the adoptive parents every outward sign of being ready to move to the next level of engagement.

If the child shows no signs of resistance but becomes distressed once the shift to the next level of engagement occurs, don't panic. This is an opportunity to demonstrate empathy and attentiveness to the child's feelings, which is crucial information for the child to have. Adoptive parents should stop the play activity and attempt to soothe the child first and, if that is not successful, then the foster parents will take over.

Some tips for soothing by adoptive parents within the first 30 seconds of the child's demonstration of distress:

- Shift your body to mirror the child's body position but don't move any closer

- Let your sympathy for the child's distress show on your face naturally.

- Speak to the child in "parentese", the higher-pitched voice that grown-ups use to talk with babies; use rhythm and tone to communicate concern.

- Body language and voice quality is the most crucial method for communicating empathy, but the content of the communication is also a little important. Despite the possibility that a substantially distressed child will process very little of the content, it is important to use empathic language.

- Label feelings; link the feelings to the shift in the play interaction between you. Tell them that you are there with them. Don't tell the child that everything is or will be okay. That doesn't feel true from their point of view. A stance to consider: your soothing is intended as a gift to the distressed child who could benefit from it rather than an attempt to influence the child to change their feeling state and calm down; which is your agenda, not theirs. An example might be, "Oh, I scared you when I moved closer. I'll back up a little. I'm sorry. I know you're upset right now."

If they begin to calm down within 30 seconds, then continue soothing.

If the child doesn't calm down within 30 seconds, or if they start to move towards the foster parents at any point, then make way for foster parents to start their soothing. As foster parents start soothing, adoptive parents would remain emotionally engaged and interested in how the child is doing. Adoptive parents may have the impulse to disengage and mentally review or wonder what just happened or if they did something wrong. Do that later when the visit is over and instead stay present with the child's mood.

If the adoptive parents' presence seems to be distressing to the child, then adoptive parents say goodbye and exit.

If the child calms either through the efforts of the adoptive parents or the foster parents, then the foster parents would describe what happened (i.e., the child got distressed when the child and adoptive parent shifted between types of playing) and ask the child if that's what happened. If the child agrees, adoptive parents can agree—which becomes a point of joining. If the child disagrees, foster parents would ask them to describe what happened, if they are able.

Ideally, the child would play together with foster parents and adoptive parents for a short period of time before adoptive parents say goodbye and leave to help with repair of the small rupture in the relationship.

In addition to play times, meal times can also be useful for these early visits. Again, foster parents would be in the lead throughout the meal time and the child would sit next to the foster parents and adoptive parents would be far enough away at the dining table that the child does not appear stressed. Because there is less shifting of position when people are seated around a dining table, there can be more opportunity for eye contact but this can be overwhelming for the child too.

Frequency

These early visits are 30-90 minutes in length depending on the child's age and capacity, as well as the foster home schedule. Their frequency may be determined by the child's age:

- *Infants and toddlers*: daily for at least the first week. Following the first week, they can—but don't need to—have a 1-2 day pause between visits.

- *Preschoolers*: most—but not all—days in the first week. This age group needs a break to rest and reconnect with foster parents and familiar routines even though they may miss adoptive parents. After the first week, 3-4 visits per week is good.

- *School-age children*: 3-4 visits per week.

- *Teenagers*: 2-3 visits per week.

As before, the visit may be cut short because the child is inconsolably distressed or the child is showing signs of becoming overwhelmed or dissociated in the view of the foster parents.

Diego - 5 years | hide-and-seek

5-year old Diego found it easy to play with adoptive mother Sue as long as Fernanda, his foster mother, was in view—even if she was otherwise occupied. Any time Fernanda was in another room he would drag Sue and their activity to whatever room Fernanda was in, even if he could hear her from the living room. There were three visits at this level before Fernanda had the brilliant idea of playing "hide-and-seek" with two out of three of them looking for the third person. Diego loved it when both Fernanda and Sue would both be looking for him and he would often give auditory clues so they would find him faster because he enjoyed the three-way hugs upon reunion immensely. As these combinations of seekers rotated, every third time it would be Sue and Diego looking for Fernanda. This was initially somewhat frightening for Diego and he would say "I want to find Fernanda fast." Fernanda made sure to hide in easy spots initially and would exclaim how great a team Sue and Diego made for finding her. Diego and Sue continued this game as a twosome finding each other even when Fernanda began attending to unrelated tasks in different rooms. Diego had made the leap of trusting Sue without Fernanda watching over him.

Isabella - 14 years | Chinese checkers

Isabella, at 14, had the developmental task of not appearing to need Sheila, her foster mother, for safety even though she still did emotionally.

Isabella dragged out her Chinese checkers game that she hadn't played with in two years and solemnly declared that she could whip both Sheila and her adoptive mother Julie at the same time. This activity had the advantage of keeping Sheila close by without appearing dependent. Isabella kept a running score and never managed to lose the piece of paper it was on—this, from a girl who was known for forgetting her homework assignments somewhat regularly. Isabella said they could not stop playing the game until she was in front of both the adults, which somehow she managed to never do. This went on for five visits until Sheila had the idea of suggesting that Isabella show off some of the dresses Isabella had sewn herself before the Chinese checkers game started. Julie engaged Isabella in conversations about her design process and fashion inspirations while Sheila was quiet. Somehow, time ran out in the visit before they could get to Chinese checkers. This became the new pattern. Sheila became able to absent herself to go to the bathroom or cut up some vegetables while Julie and Isabella were deep in conversation. Isabella discovered that interacting with Julie without Sheila around felt good in its own way.

Hakim -18 months | throwing the ball

Hakim gradually moved through each level of shifting safety from his foster parent, Jane, to his adoptive parents, LaRonda and Michael. Besides his Black Panther action figure, he also loved balls. He started out sitting on Jane's lap and rolling or throwing balls to LaRonda and Michael. As he got more comfortable, he enjoyed throwing the ball hard over their heads so that one or the other would have to go chase it while he laughed— though he always stayed securely on Jane's lap. LaRonda moved things along hilariously by throwing the ball over Jane and Hakim's head in a quite exaggerated manner. Hakim laughed at LaRonda's antics and got off of Jane's lap to track down the ball. Initially, he always returned to sitting in Jane's lap before taking his turn flinging the ball as far as he could. Eventually, when LaRonda or Michael comically threw the ball, Hakim would run and get it and then throw it back right away and not need to return to Jane's lap, which allowed her to gradually be involved with her phone or dusting or picking up toys. Eventually, LaRonda and Michael were opposite each other and Hakim would come and sit in each of their laps while throwing the ball far away and then clapping hands with whichever adoptive parent he was sitting in the lap of. He balked initially at taking this play out to the back yard without Jane accompanying, but soon was fine as long as the foster family's dog, Rudy, came along.

As you can see, in each of these scenarios, adoptive and foster parents respected the child's pacing. The foster parent relied on their knowledge of the child and used creativity to find a way to stretch the child's comfort zone without overwhelming the child. Using these approaches, the child can feel the empathy from the adults and their prioritization of the child's comfort.

Chapter 5

Shifting to Visits without Foster Parents

Since the child is comfortable playing with adoptive parents without the foster parents in the immediate vicinity (in the foster home yard while the foster parents are in the house, for example,) then visits may begin with adoptive parents away from the foster parent. The goal of these visits, beyond deepening the relationship between child and adoptive parents, is for the child to begin to view the adoptive parents as their caregivers/protectors. There are important concerns to be mindful of when thinking about initiating visits without foster parents present.

Prior trauma and initiating visits without foster parents present

It is very important for caseworkers to inform adoptive parents of the known details of the major traumas the child has experienced or witnessed in their birth home, foster care, or their community. Foster parents would inform adoptive parents of the child's specific trauma triggers, how the child manifests trauma-based reactions behaviorally and foster parents' responses that have been most helpful. This last aspect is very important because responding to trauma-triggered behavior requires different strategies than if the same behavior occurs outside of a trauma context.

An example of trauma-triggered behavior might be a young child who acts up aggressively and is very resistant to bath time. A child I worked with had had his feet dunked in scalding bath water as a disciplinary method and so the child's resistant behavior was fueled by terror rather than defiance. The foster parent started out with sponge baths and having the child play in the tub without water in it. After baths, the foster parent and the child developed a fun, silly activity out of drying off with a towel that the child looked forward to. The child grew more cooperative with bath time but this was still a work in progress at the time of the adoption. The foster parent explained all this to the adoptive parents who decided to also start out with sponge baths on the overnight visits.

Providing guidance on parenting children with a history of trauma is beyond the scope of this book. Recommended resources include the books of Bryan Post (Post 2009, 2010) and Daniel Hughes (e.g., Hughes et al., 2019) and the resources at the National Child Traumatic Stress Network (www.nctsn.org).

In particular, there are specific situations that may not be trauma triggers but are trauma-relevant for some children and need some advance planning involving adoptive parents, foster parents, the child's therapist (if available,) and possibly the caseworker.

- If there are common triggers for this child in the community (e.g., cars honking, dogs, bearded men), it is useful for the adoptive parents to be aware of those and have a plan for when (not if) they are encountered during outings into the community.
- If the foster home is near the birth home, then driving past certain locations or on certain streets may also produce emotional reactions.

- Create a plan for taking sexually abused children into public or private spaces when they still need adult assistance going to the bathroom.

- A plan may need to be developed around physical touch (e.g., if they need an adult to hold their hands while crossing a street or physical assistance at a park) for adoptive parents and children who are survivors of physical abuse or witnesses of domestic violence.

- Neglected children may gorge food or try to sneak it back to their foster home to eat later; adoptive parents may need a plan when eating out on a visit.

- Children who have witnessed domestic violence may need a plan if they encounter angry yelling or a police siren while with adoptive parents in the community.

Adoptive parents can feel overwhelmed in these discussions about the child's trauma triggers. It is important for foster parents to give a realistic sense of the frequency of these trauma triggers and the intensity of the reactions and how preventive strategies and soothing responses can be very helpful to the child and the parent. It is also useful to remember that these

discussions may activate an adoptive parent's own trauma history to some extent. If that occurs, it is understandable and ideally would be discussed with someone the adoptive parent trusts.

Progression of psychological distance from foster parent

Even though the child is ready to be with the adoptive parent out of the presence of the foster parent, it is still useful to be thoughtful about how to do this little by little. We recommend the following sequence of visit plans to gradually increase the child's sense of distance from the foster parents:

- Child and adoptive parents take a walk in the neighborhood without a foster parent. This can include stopping at a destination within walking distance that is familiar to the child (e.g., school playground, park, small store, coffee shop).

- Child and adoptive parents go for a short drive to a restaurant familiar to the child for a meal without a foster parent. Note that the child getting into a car with the adoptive parents can feel substantially more risky to the child than what has gone on before. Caseworkers may have driven the child away from prior placements never to go back. It's important for both adoptive parents and foster parents to emphasize the destination, the food they like there, and the return plan.

- Child and adoptive parents go for a two-hour visit to an unfamiliar restaurant, a park, a playground, and/or an errand familiar to the child (like buying something at the grocery store or the mall). Avoid high-sugar meals that might dysregulate the child.

Throughout the progression, we recommend the following conditions:

- Visits may be shortened if needed, but not extended. The child needs to feel able to rely on the schedule and the words of the adoptive parents. The end time of the visit would be identified to the child in a developmentally appropriate way ("We'll be taking you back after lunch.")

- If the child is still taking naps, avoid disrupting the nap schedule for the visit.

- Activities during visits should not be especially stimulating child-oriented destinations (e.g., theme park). Ideally, they whould feel like regular life, with the adoptive parents responsible for the child and the child's safety.

- A younger child might fall asleep in the car seat while driving back to the foster home. Waking is a vulnerable time for children unused to new caregivers. If a nap in the car occurs in the middle of a visit, then shift to driving back to the foster home, even if more activities were planned, so hopefully the child wakes back at the foster home.

- If there is going to be a longer than usual time gap between visits, then have another form of contact between the child and the adoptive parents, ideally a video call. (Beek, Neil & Schofield, 2021). If a video call is going to be made with the adoptive parents, then the child would be on the foster parent's lap or next to them for emotional support.

Homesickness and emotional distress

Children missing the foster home or just becoming upset during a visit is perfectly natural and a sign of the attachment between the child and the foster parents. This often is anxiety-provoking for adoptive parents. A sequential strategy for handling this is provided below.

If the child communicates that they miss the foster parents, but is not emotionally distressed during the visit, then the following sequence is recommended.

1. The adoptive parents would validate those feelings and the child's love of the foster parent.

2. Adoptive parents may see if distraction can work with the child by talking about events that are planned for the visit or other items of interest in the immediate environment. This should not be a prolonged attempt to convince the child to continue with the adults' plan.

3. If distraction does not work, adoptive parents can see if the child would like a phone call to check in with the foster parents. Foster parents should be available to take calls during these visits and would reassure the child that they miss them too and will see them after the next event of the visit.

4. Adoptive parents would attempt to do only one more event of the visit after such a phone call even if more than one event remains on the schedule unless the child shifts into a distressed state.

If the child gets emotionally distressed about being away from a foster parent during a visit, then the following sequence is recommended.

1. The adoptive parents inform the child that they have a solution: that the adoptive parents will take the child back to the foster parent starting right away. The child's feelings are validated. The goal is for the child to experience the adoptive parents as helpful, understanding adults.

2. The child and adoptive parents immediately move to the car and drive to the foster home. Adoptive parents narrate the trip as it unfolds so that the child knows the adoptive parents support their goal of reuniting with the foster parents—and are a facilitator of the reunion, not a danger to them or a barrier to the foster parents.

3. When the child is reunited with foster parents, adoptive parents would remain in the foster home. After the child is calm, adoptive parents would act like it's a first visit again where they

interact with the child over time to the extent they can emotionally handle it, while the foster parents are as available as the child needs. This is part of the repair of the attachment disruption the child experienced as a result of realizing they were farther away from the foster parents than felt safe.

4. After the adoptive parents have departed, foster parents debrief with the child about their distress. Ask: Was it caused by fear of adoptive parents? Fear of something or someone other than adoptive parents? Missing foster parents? A distressing memory? Praise the child for voicing distress to adoptive parents and highlight that the adoptive parents listened to them.

5. Later that day, foster parents and adoptive parents debrief what each of them noticed about the child's distress, how each of them responded, and their plans for adapting the next visit. Subsequently, inform the caseworker and child therapist (if there is one) and see if they have any input.

6. Adoptive parents often have some level of concern when a visit is disrupted by the child's desire to reunite with the foster parent.

It is important for them to process these feelings with someone they trust.

7. If the child becomes distressed during two consecutive two-hour visits, go back to shorter visits for a meal or, if necessary, to more visits with foster parents present.

If the child demonstrates an unexpected shift in mood, sudden regression, or spaciness during a visit this may mean a previous trauma has been triggered. The trigger may be something the adoptive parents have inadvertently done, or it may be something that has occurred in the environment. The following shifts are recommended:

- Adoptive parents would increase their own calmness, use a quiet voice, get physically lower than the child if possible (i.e., sit on the floor if the child is sitting on a couch or lay down on the floor if the child is sitting on the floor) and move unhurriedly. This may help them communicate a sense of safety to the child and that they are not a threat. Notice whether this shift in the adoptive parents results in any shift in the child.

- Adoptive parents would stop—or decrease the intensity of—the current activity and see how the child responds.

- Adoptive parents would think about what the child has been doing, saying, seeing, experiencing in the 5-10 minutes before the shift in the child and evaluate if there may have been any obvious triggers. They might prepare to describe the sequence of events to the foster parents in the debrief afterwards.

- Avoid questioning the child, which will not be helpful when they are in this state.

- Adoptive parents would offer to take the child back to the foster parents. It is better to err on the side of caution in order to ensure that the child feels safe and cared for, even if it means shortening the visit.

If the child becomes distressed for another reason, adoptive parents can attempt to soothe them. If this doesn't work in a short period of time then, depending on the age of the child and the intensity of the distress, the adoptive parents would offer the child the option to go back to see the foster parent. Many episodes of child's distress during visits are about being away from foster parents, even if this is not said explicitly or another reason is given. Also, if the distress starts for another reason (e.g., the child falls and skins their knee), the distress may evolve into grief about being away from their familiar soothing person. Follow the sequence of steps pertaining to when the child is visibly distressed about being away from the foster parent, above.

Diego - 5 years | a fright at the zoo

Diego and Sue started with some trips to a neighborhood playground for short visits away from the foster home. After those went well, Sue drove Diego to one of his favorite places: a chain ice cream store. They enjoyed their ice cream, then played catch at a park. This visit went so positively that the adults agreed that Sue and Diego would next do a two-hour visit on a bike ride to a food court that had several food vendors that Diego liked. This visit went without a problem. They planned to visit the local zoo that Diego had been to twice before for the second two-hour visit.

Diego was fine with the car ride. After being at the zoo for a short period of time, a lion roared while Diego was watching it. Diego became scared, started crying, and said he wanted his mom.

Sue squatted down and said, "Yes, let's go to your mom right away."

They turned around and started walking toward the parking lot but then Diego started running ahead faster than Sue. This worried Sue.

Sue called out, "Diego, do you know where the car is?"

Diego stopped and turned and said "No."

Sue caught up to him and reassured him, "I know where it is. Let's hold hands while we run to it. We want to get to your mom fast."

They made it to the car and after they were buckled in, Sue asked Diego, "The plan is going to mom. Right Diego?"

"Right," Diego replied.

A little while into the drive when they were on the freeway on-ramp, Sue said, "We're getting on the freeway, Diego, because the cars can drive fast there and I want to get you to mom as fast as I can."

"Go fast, momma Sue," replied Diego; which brought tears to Sue's eyes because that was the first time Diego had ever used "momma" or any other term for mother to refer to her.

At the red light at the end of the exit ramp, Sue thought to call Fernanda using the hands-free feature. Sue reached Fernanda and told her "We're heading back early from the zoo. I'll let Diego tell you about it."

Diego exclaimed, "Momma, there was a scary lion at the zoo. It roared so loud."

Fernanda replied, "I'm glad you're coming home and that Sue kept you safe. Was the lion big?"

Diego answered, "Muy grande, momma." Diego then added, "Momma, we're passing the gas station where we get gas. It's okay. We're almost home."

"Thanks for letting me know, Diego. And thank you, Sue, for taking such good care of Diego."

"It was my pleasure, Fernanda," responded Sue.

Back at Fernanda's house, Sue hung around while Diego drew two pictures of the lion; one for Fernanda and one for her. In their debrief call *later that day, Sue described the roller coaster of feelings she experienced. Panic, when Diego started crying and also when he started running away from her so fast. But also joy, from being called "momma Sue" and being given Diego's drawing of the lion. Fernanda highlighted how well Sue had handled the situation.*

Isabella - 14 years | Interrogation

Most of the two-hour visits went well for Isabella and Julie. The highlight of the first short visit was the two of them watching a stage play at Isabella's high school, which Isabella had worked on backstage with the costumes. Isabella was very clear though that in no way could Julie let anyone know that she was in any way connected with Isabella. She was proud and enjoyed Julie's admiration when they went out for ice cream afterwards.

During a later short visit, Isabella announced when they were driving away from the foster home that she wanted to change the plan and go see a movie together - an R-rated movie about a pop singer's struggle with substance abuse and eventual death. Julie felt like this plan was sprung on her and the movie was not one she wanted to see, especially when she and Isabella were just starting to get to know each other. She suggested Isabella look and see what other movies might be playing and if there might be another option. Isabella did not directly refuse but said she had already looked at all the other movies and this one was the only one she was interested in.

Isabella asked Julie, "Is it because of the drugs that you don't want to see it?"

"Actually, I just felt the movie would be depressing," replied Julie.

"She did so many drugs - heroin, cocaine, alcohol, pills; probably pot but they don't bother mentioning that" noted Isabella.

"I've heard that," added Julie.

"What drugs have you used? abruptly inquired Isabella.

"Um, you mean ever?" clarified Julie.

Isabella nodded and added, "Let's skip the movie. You didn't want to see it anyway. We can talk about our drug use. Right? I've used alcohol twice but nothing else so far. So back to you?"

Julie now wishes she had agreed to the movie. She feels so unprepared for this conversation and suspects Isabella is enjoying making her squirm. She can't think of anything else to do but answer the question. "I've drunk alcohol a number of times. I used to smoke pot and I have taken mushrooms twice."

"Oooh, mushrooms. What was that like?" asked Isabella excitedly.

Julie had suspected Isabella would focus on the mushrooms. She had been tempted to not mention them but she also didn't want to lie to Isabella. She felt like Isabella might be able to tell when she was holding something back. She told Isabella, "The first time I didn't feel hardly anything. The second time everything got sort of swirly which was interesting but then I got dizzy and threw up."

Isabella launched another question right away, "How old were you when you first used pot?"

"I was 16. Is there pot at your high school?" Julie answered.

"Sure. Lots of kids in the drama club use pot. Alcohol - how old were you?" Isabella replied.

Julie thought for a moment and said, "Sixteen again. Sounds like you could have used pot but haven't."

Isabella paused too, "It looks like they're having fun but they're also sort of out of control. That's not my thing. I'm tired of this. Can we go to that chocolate fondue place?"

Julie heaved a sigh of relief to herself and replied, "Sure. Chocolate fondue it is."

Later, when Julie debriefed with Sheila, the foster mom let her know that Isabella loved to put adults on the spot and that she thought Julie handled it fine.

Hakim - 18 months | the grocery store

Two-hour visits also went well for Hakim, LaRonda, and Michael. They happened in the mornings because he was napping in the afternoons. They would often go to a familiar park with a playground and out for a short meal. LaRonda and Michael parked their sedan and rented a SUV because with the back hatch flipped up there was a nice flat space for diaper changes with lots of talking and face-to-face contact with Hakim (when he wasn't trying to roll around!).

On the third short visit, Michael and LaRonda decided to have a picnic. They had a picnic basket with plates, etc. but had not had time to buy the food. They stopped at the grocery store to pick up some ham, candied sweet potatoes, melon chunks, some sodas and a juice box for Hakim. Hakim would try to reach items on the shelves from the shopping cart; which the foster mother, Jane, had mentioned him doing so they were not surprised. Their plan was that LaRonda would amuse and distract Hakim while Michael was grabbing what they needed. Rounding a corner, Hakim grabbed a bag of cookies. When LaRonda tried to pull the bag away from him, he pulled the bag and her hand to his mouth and bit her. She yelled, "Ow." Hakim started screaming. He allowed Michael to pick him up out of the shopping cart and walk away from LaRonda but stayed in view of her. Michael rubbed Hakim's back and said, "That was scary when Mama Ronda yelled." Over time, Hakim snuggled in closer to Michael. Michael rubbed his back some more. Eventually, Michael turned his body and said to Hakim, "I see Mama Ronda down there by the cart. Do you want to look?" Hakim lifted his head and looked at LaRonda. She waved and Hakim reached out one arm towards her. Michael and LaRonda walked towards each other and Hakim leaned towards LaRonda to be held. After the reunion was accomplished, Michael and LaRonda decided to scrap the picnic idea.

Chapter 6

Day-Long Visits

After the child is able to successfully manage two consecutive two-hour visits with the adoptive parents, it's time to plan for a day-long visit. "Successfully manage" means that the child does not need to return to the foster home early and does not have major emotional upsets during the short visits. It may take a few shorter visits to get up to the two-hour length and also achieve the child's general comfort with them. The goal with day-long visits is to deepen the trust between child and adoptive parents because the psychological distance is greater between the child and the foster parents with the longer time apart.

Scheduling a time for a phone call between child and foster parents for these longer visits is important. Sometimes there are concerns that this added phone contact with the foster parents will lead the child to cut the visit short in order to return to the foster parents. This may happen, but it concretely demonstrates to the child the responsiveness of the adoptive parents and that the adoptive parents prioritize the child's emotional needs over their own. Pleasant interaction between adoptive parents and the child is nice, but what really builds the bond most effectively is the adoptive parents responding to the needs and distress of the child. These instances of the child wanting to return to the foster parents are also part of the child feeling the loss of the foster parents, which—it might be remembered—is one of the two main goals of the transition.

Plan two activities for the day-long visit. The first activity might contain more sensory input like visiting the zoo, science museum, etc. depending on the child's sensory tolerance (Miller, 2014). Avoid high-stimulation destinations like theme parks or indoor play parks that may make some children overly excited. The second might be something interactive, low-key, and unstructured like throwing a ball or Frisbee at a park, or walking in a natural area like a river or lake or ocean. Allow each interaction to proceed at its own pace, set by the child.

If the child is still taking naps, they may need more 2-3 hour visits than older children before they can tolerate napping with strangers. Do not prescribe sleep but do designate periods of mutual quiet time. Have the child lie down on a soft surface with books and/or stuffed animals as you sit in the same room reading a book or lay down also but not in the same bed. Do not refuse communication, but do not offer it. If the child has not fallen asleep in 20-30 minutes, then shift to a regular activity. In one case, the adoptive parent and a two year old first pretended to put the child's stuffed animal, that she brought along on visits, to sleep before the child would lie down next to her "stuffie."

If the child gets distressed about being away from foster parents, follow the same protocol as described in the prior section regarding a two-hour visit.

These visits are a great time to begin talking about and preparing for overnight visits. With the child's input, purchase an item for the bedroom that the child will sleep in during the overnight visits (even if it is a hotel room). This is a visible demonstration that they can have input in their new life situation (e.g., comforter, pillow case, poster for the wall, etc.).

Full day visits may also trigger some trauma reactions that shorter visits do not. Even though children may be told that they will be brought back to the foster home around dinnertime, the longer visit may still create a sense in the child that they have been permanently and traumatically moved yet again. This may create feelings of panic in the child beyond the anxiety displayed before. Reestablishing contact with the foster parent with a video call is important as a first step in reassuring the child and then taking the child back to the foster home right away as described previously is the next step. For sexually abused children younger children, naps may also recreate some of the elements of their prior trauma.

Diego - 5 years | Adding the other adoptive parent

Sue and Diego had a full day visit that went well before the second full day visit which included Sue's wife, Joan, who had flown in. Joan met with Fernanda while Diego was in school. The next day, Joan came to the house and played hide and seek with Fernanda and Sue and Diego.

Diego stayed close to Sue during the full day visit that included a trip to the children's museum, lunch and then throwing a frisbee around in the park. Diego especially enjoyed making Joan run for the frisbee. Diego got quiet and withdrawn when Sue and Joan were holding hands on the walk from the park to the car. Neither Sue or Joan noticed until Joan asked about his favorite cartoon and Diego shrugged and looked down. Sue and Joan had the three of them sit at a picnic table.

Sue asked, "Is something wrong, Diego?" and again he shrugged.

Joan asked, "Is it something about me?" Diego looked down and started sucking his thumb.

Sue sat down beside him and rubbed his back a little. Diego stopped sucking his thumb and put his hand on the table. Without thinking about it, Sue picked up and held Diego's hand and rubbed the back of it with her thumb. Diego looked up at both Sue and Joan and asked, "Can we go to the car now?" His voice tone sounded more upbeat to Sue and Joan so they agreed but remained puzzled about what had just happened.

At the end of the visit, Diego privately told Sue that Joan seemed nice but she smelled of cigarettes. Joan later confessed to Sue that she was so nervous that she had smoked three cigarettes before meeting Diego, something she had not done in five years.

Isabella - 14 years | shopping

Their first all-day visit began at some vintage clothing stores, moved on to lunch, and eventually to see a movie set in the 1950's (Isabella's favorite fashion period). They discussed the movie and its costumes afterwards in a coffee shop. They were getting their coats on to leave when Isabella struggled with one of her sleeves and Julie helped her. Isabella lost her balance a little and leaned into Julie which Julie misinterpreted as a request for a hug. She hugged Isabella who recoiled and pushed her away and stormed out of the coffee shop. Julie was mortified and hurried after her to where Isabella was standing by the car.

Julie apologized, "I'm sorry, Isabella. I didn't mean to—I'm so sorry."

Isabella turned away and replied, "Just drive me home."

In the car on the way to the foster home, Julie asked, "Can we talk?" Isabella responded with a shake of her head and stared out the window.

Julie felt desperate to repair before the end of the car ride and pleaded, "Please. I'm so sorry."

"I don't care how sorry you are." Isabella retorted, "You just want to make me not mad to make yourself feel better. I never want to see you ever again."

Julie was crushed and felt like all the positive energy she had shared with Isabella had been obliterated with one wrong move. When they got to the foster home, Isabella stormed to her room. Julie explained through her tears what happened to the foster mom, Sheila, who reassured her that all was not lost conclusively. She related instances when Isabella had become angry and rejected her—episodes that they had been able to repair over time. Sheila suggested that she would talk with Isabella after she had cooled down a bit and then give Julie a call later that evening. Sheila gave Julie a hug.

Sheila went to Isabella's room later to ask her to share her experience of the visit. By the end of that conversation, Isabella agreed to see Julie again but only as part of one of her therapy sessions with no guarantee that there would be any further visits after that. Isabella met once with her therapist (without Julie) so the therapist could hear from Isabella about what happened and plan together how they wanted to handle the session with Julie. Isabella disclosed that she felt torn—that she was beginning to like Julie but wasn't sure if the two of them could overcome how agitated Isabella now felt about Julie and the hug and the conversation afterwards.

In the therapy session, Isabella started out accusing Julie, "You didn't even know what you were apologizing for. I was just some spilled milk you had to wipe up and make all better."

Julie worked to remain calm and responded, "You're right, Isabella. I panicked. I was apologizing for the hug and for upsetting you but I didn't know why the hug was upsetting."

Isabella replied, "Yeah. It's never going to work out."

"Whatever happens, Isabella, I would like to know about why the hug was upsetting," requested Julie.

Isabella started crying and shook her head no. Her therapist interjected, "It's hard, Isabella, but you said you wanted her to know."

Tearfully, Isabella related, "Whenever I was saying good-bye to my mom or to any of the five foster moms I've had, they always want to hug me goodbye and tell me they're sorry it didn't work out. Fuck that shit. Fuck hugs and fuck you." Isabella stormed out of the session.

Her therapist got her to agree to another session including Julie because Isabella had had her say and it was only fair that Julie have her say. Julie started the session with the statement, "I realize now that hug I gave you was so much more than that hug. I assumed you were upset because I didn't ask first, when it was actually about all those other hugs that were so painful." Isabella nodded yes through her tears. Julie gave her a box of tissues. After Isabella had calmed down some, Julie apologized to Isabella for the hug again, but this time elaborated the apology with recognition of the deep pain that was brought up for Isabella. Julie also apologized for trying to manage Isabella and her feelings after she got upset rather than following Isabella's request to give her some space. Isabella accepted her apology and tentatively resumed full-day visits with Julie but it was three months of further trust-building before she agreed to an overnight visit.

Hakim - 18 months | sleepy time

There were some involved conversations between LaRonda, Michael, and Jane about day-long visits. They recognized that, given

Hakim's age and conception of time and understanding of language, that a day-long visit with a nap might feel as big a step to him as an overnight visit would for an older child. LaRonda and Michael bought a pack and play travel crib for his naps to put in their short-term rental. Jane loaned them some of Hakim's stuffed animals and used baby blankets that had not been laundered so they would have his familiar smells. They spent part of a couple two-hour visits in the apartment Michael and LaRonda had rented short-term, and followed the guide Jane had written to describe Hakim's naptime routine. On the first day-long visit as his usual naptime drew nearer, Hakim started showing signs of tiredness. Michael started a playlist on Hakim's favorite lullabies on his cellphone as Jane did in her home. He also closed the curtains and turned off the lights. LaRonda held Hakim in her arms and danced slowly with him for a few minutes in the room, talking to him about "sleepy time," and then laid him in the crib. LaRonda and Michael laid down in his field of vision but about six feet away. Hakim stood up and cried. LaRonda and Michael knew that this was common at naptime for Hakim. They knew to say they were going "sleepy-time" too. Hakim protested for a few more minutes and then fell asleep. LaRonda and Michael high-fived each other and texted Jane to let them know of their success. This *first nap only lasted 30 minutes—much shorter than his usual naps but subsequent naps were the usual length for Hakim.*

Visits including the second adoptive parent and/or adoptive parents' other child(ren)

For some adoptive families, only one adoptive parent can come for the whole transition. If there is a second adoptive parent, they may come intermittently or only for the latter part of the transition. It is better for both adoptive parents to be present for the whole transition, but doing so is not realistic for some adoptive families. It is better **not** to add the second adoptive parent into the mix during the first visit of a new level, such as the first two-hour visit, all-day visit, or overnight visit. This is because it would combine two different stresses for the child (the new person, a stranger, and the new longer visit) which might overwhelm the child. If the first visit at the new level goes smoothly with the initial adoptive parent, *then* the second adoptive parent can join a subsequent visit at that level.

When a second adoptive parent enters the scene, it is important for them to spend extra time at the beginning of that visit in the foster home so the child can see that the foster parent approves of this new person. To support this, the foster parents would meet and interact with the second adoptive parent in advance. After leaving the foster home, the child will likely recognize the first adoptive parent as their safe person—a possibility that ideally the second adoptive parent will honor. They would interact with the child, but let the first adoptive parent take the lead unless the child initiates with the second foster parent. Some foster children gravitate to strangers or embrace this new attention. This may be out of curiosity but also indiscriminate attachment patterns. Even if the child approaches the new adoptive parent, it is still important to recognize that the child will need the first adoptive parent when they feel emotionally challenged. When adoptive parents already have one or more children, you may follow the same overall pattern as previously described for a day-long visit, but with some additional considerations. Both the foster child and the child(ren) from the adoptive home will likely be monitoring how adoptive parents' attention and other resources are divided. There may be insecurity, jealousy, competition, and other reactions from one or more of the children. These reactions will be partially dependent on the child's developmental age and how/if they were prepared to welcome a new member. Evenly distribute attention rather than engage in one-on-one activities. It may also be productive for the children to interact with each other in an unstructured activity with a parent monitoring but without direct adult involvement. Adults would still be monitoring these interactions given that any of the children may become reactive with intense feelings for a variety of reasons, including the triggering or replaying of past abuse or neglect.

Chapter 7

Overnight Visits

In this model, there is a crucial difference between the overnight visits and the previous visits: the child does not return to the foster parents if they become distressed or want to return. This prepares everyone for the next step: moving the child into the adoptive home. The primary goal is for both the child and the adoptive parents to learn they can survive any distress and homesickness on the part of the child, both of which will likely also occur after the move. It is often useful for the child to experience being away from the foster parents, and perhaps intensely miss them; when they reunite, they discover the relationship continues even though it may have felt like a permanent loss.

Overnight visits can, in some ways, be the most stressful step of the transition for the child. It is very important that the child and adoptive parents develop a strong enough relationship to weather this stress together. Therefore, the transition planners would carefully review the following criteria (taking into account developmental expectations) before determining the child's readiness for overnight visits:

- At least two day-long visits have occurred with tolerable anxiety from the child.

- The child engages playfully and preferentially with adoptive parents a majority of the time when both foster parents and adoptive parents are present.

- The child seeks out emotional comfort from the adoptive parents some of the time.

How foster parents can support child's preparation for overnights

Foster parents' communications with adoptive parents about the child's bedtime routines and particular concerns that tend to arise at bedtime (e.g., resisting toothbrushing, enjoying the same book read three times) are very useful. Foster parents can also be a resource to hear the adoptive parents' worries, validate them, and offer advice about specific scenarios (Lanyado, 2008). In addition, foster parents also have an important role to play in preparing the child for this visit, even though they do not directly participate in it.

- Foster parents involve the child in packing their overnight bag, including their favorite nightlight, books, pajamas, or stuffed animals. It's crucial the child knows, before this conversation, that the "sleepover" will last all night (and just one night initially), that they won't be coming home in the middle of the night, and that adoptive parents will keep them safe. This packing time is a great time to talk about practical matters, like what to pack or when the "sleepover" will end. Once those are settled, move on to more emotional topics. These might include worries the child is having about the "sleepover", excitement that the child is having about the overnight visit, problem-solving about specific concerns that the child has about the overnight (e.g. "Will my adoptive parents know I need to sleep with my bunny?"). This conversation can be a good time to discuss that the foster parent is excited for the child to take this step of the "sleepover" but will also miss them while they are gone for this one night. An example of a social story to help a child understand this is:

Once upon a time a foster child named Aaron/Erin was going to sleep over where their forever family lived. This was the first time they had ever done a sleepover with their forever family. It was just for one night and they would be staying the whole night. While packing his pajamas and favorite stuffed animal, Aaron/Erin told his foster mom about feeling excited but also scared. She told them that they would talk on the phone close to bedtime and that his forever parents would keep him safe and bring him back the next morning. His foster mom gave Aaron/Erin a big hug and said they would miss them while they were gone but would look forward to talking all about the sleepover tomorrow morning.

- If the child has gone on overnights with respite providers or is aware of other children that have done this, bring up these past overnights and remind them that the children returned safe and sound.

- For some children, having a short visit to the adoptive home or where the adoptive parents are staying, accompanied by a foster parent, can help build positive excitement for the overnight visit while also lowering anxiety by making the adoptive residence less of a mystery (Beek et al., 2021).

- Foster parents can productively look for cues that the child needs to talk further about the overnight, even if they don't explicitly ask for it. These cues might be a shift in behavior, questions about the adoptive parents that "come out of left field", or comments about a character's sleep in a book or TV show that the child is enjoying.

- Once the adoptive parents come to pick up the child—and, specifically, while in front of them—the foster parents would remind the child that they will spend the whole night with the adoptive parents and that the adoptive parents will keep them safe. At this time, the adoptive parents also commit to the child and foster parents that they will return the child to the foster home in the morning. The foster parents then acknowledge that agreement.

- Foster parents schedule with the adoptive parents a phone call with the child near bedtime. During that phone call, foster parents can reassure the child and communicate that the foster parents are going to sleep. The foster parents can say again that they miss the child, but also that they are excited for them. Asking about the child's feelings is also useful. Foster parents would include in this conversation that they will look forward to the morning when they will see the child again and talk about the overnight visit.

Adoptive parents handling of the child's bedtime

Although a substantial relationship has developed between adoptive parents and the child by this point, overnight visits represent a new level of vulnerability for the child and require a deeper sense of trust. Many typical children, who have not been in foster care, experience increased fear at bedtime because of their tiredness, vulnerability, and being left alone. The absence of the foster parents, which often has been less noticed by the child because of the activities of the visit, can often grab the child's attention at bedtime. We recommend the following steps to help the child feel somewhat less anxious at this first bedtime in the adoptive home (or wherever adoptive parents are staying).

- Ideally, overnight visits start by lunch time at the latest, and include physical activity.

- To help soothe the child, follow the same bedtime routine employed in the foster home, as much as possible.

- Empathize with the child about the difficulties of falling asleep and reassure them that they will fall asleep eventually. Avoid trying to speed up the process; the child will experience that as pressure and become more likely to shift into negative emotions (including fear, or longing for the foster parent). It is permissible and likely that this process will take 1-2 hours. Adoptive parents need to be emotionally prepared for this.

- It is useful for only one adoptive parent to be in the bedroom at a time with the child to help settle them down. Adoptive parents can call each other in to be the parent in the room based on their own reading of the situation. The adults would be in charge of those changes rather than the child.

- If the child is distressed at the end of the bedtime routine, one adoptive parent may sit in a chair across the room from the bed, visible to the child. The adoptive parent sets the rule that the child needs to stay in bed, and the adoptive parent then focuses their attention on their phone or a book or another self-focused quiet activity rather than the child. This can provide some sense of safety to the child while hopefully not agitating the child.

- It might be noted that adoptive parents may also have more trouble falling asleep than usual because of the emotional intensity of the day.

Disrupted sleep

Have a plan ahead of time for the very likely occurrence that the child calls out in the middle of the night—especially if they are under 12. Children over 12 also wake but may feel too embarrassed to call for a parent like a "little kid". Foster parents may have suggestions for handling middle-of-the-night wakings. It is useful to have an audio baby monitor on (even for children who are older than toddlers) in case the child is crying or otherwise distressed in the middle of the night and does not call out.

In advance, designate which one parent will go in and soothe the child—preferably the one who is most emotionally regulated. This designation may require planning for the other parent to wake them. Soothing can include rubbing the child's back, tucking them back in, rearranging stuffed animal protectors, turning back on bedtime music or any other strategy suggested by the foster parents.

If the child remains distressed after 10-15 minutes of soothing and remains focused on reuniting with foster parents, reassure the child that they will see them in the morning and remind the child that they are staying the whole night with the adoptive parents, as the foster parents wanted. Even though likely exhausted, the most important element is to not get angry or frustrated at the child; they are reasonably scared from their point of view. An adoptive parent stays in the room until the child falls asleep, which may take several hours. Try various strategies. Most will be ineffective and some will only temporarily soothe. This is the nature of supporting a child who is scared in the middle of the night. If the child is unable to be soothed, the parent is encouraged to remain sitting in a chair across the room from the child and continue to calm themselves.

This is the first night, but probably not the last, when the child will be upset because of a nightmare, illness, or nighttime fears. Adoptive parents will develop their own strategies over time based on their parenting beliefs, information from foster parents, advice from their own communities or resources, and their own developing knowledge about the child.

Remember that the child is still developing trust in the adoptive parents. The adoptive parents are developing faith in themselves that they, the child, and their relationship will survive. They are also recognizing their small steps in co-regulation and hopefully will be patient with themselves, the child, and this process. This process of this overnight (and any difficulties experienced) does not reflect the eventual relationship that will be formed within this new family.

Waking

Upon waking and realizing they are in an unfamiliar bed in an unfamiliar room, the child may panic. In their intense anxiety, they may not be able to take in words and first need to be held by an adoptive parent. Their feelings need to be reflected back to them, which may sound like "I know you are scared. I'm right here". Avoid false reassurance like, "Everything is okay." After they have started calming down more, rationality can be used. "Remember you are staying here for the night. You're going home after breakfast." With infants and toddlers, frequent wakings may be the norm. Foster parents can give some good guidance on this.

Breakfast can sometimes be a nice distraction and transition out of the difficult feelings. It's useful to have some of the child's favorite breakfast foods on hand as befitting a special occasion. If the child is still quite upset, breakfast can be skipped to honor the child's feelings and move towards transporting the child back to the foster home. If this happens, talk about it aloud to the child. If the child was distressed in the middle of the night, then praise the child for surviving all those hard feelings. Adoptive parents may also want to praise each other!

Overnight visits are scheduled to end at the prearranged time (e.g., breakfast) even if the child asks for it to be extended. Keeping to the schedule helps to reassure the child.

Trauma and overnight visits

For many typical families, bedtime can be a stressful part of the day. Parents and children are tired and may have little resiliency left. This may have made the bedtime routine a high risk time for physical and/or emotional abuse in the birth family of the child being adopted. In addition, bedtime or the overnight period may also have been a time when sexual abuse may have occurred in the birth family or by foster siblings in a foster home. Thus, anxiety about separation may not be the only source of fear for the child during the overnight visit. The foster parents will be a useful guide for adoptive parents if they have noticed any trauma triggers as part of the bedtime routine. Nightmares may also have a traumatic origin. This is useful for the adoptive parents to keep in mind but not be brought up with the child at the time. If the child has a psychotherapist, then the adoptive parents might check in with them before overnight visits start to see if there are any particular trauma-related issues to keep in mind and receive advice.

Return to the foster home

The drive back to the foster home can be a good time for conversation about the visit. Review memories, especially the fun times shared the previous day, and note the difficult feelings of the night before and acknowledge the ways you made it through them together. Validate their experience of missing their foster parents aloud. This communicates to the child that the adoptive parents support their loving feelings for the foster parents and also understand their feelings of loss. In addition, express pride in the child's capability of spending the night away from the foster home, which supports the child's self-esteem.

The adoptive parents are encouraged to accompany the child back into the foster home and talk with the foster parents about the visit. This is another opportunity to name in front of the child the child's feelings and reinforce positive moments together (Including how well the child expressed those feelings). Recount how the child and the adoptive parents made it through the night together. Foster parents would express admiration for the child's and the adoptive parents' accomplishment.

As with the other visits, after the adoptive parents leave, the foster parents would provide opportunities for the child to describe what they liked about the overnight visit and to express feelings. If the adoptive parents described distress on the part of the child to the foster parents, then the foster parents would raise this with the child. "It sounds like you missed us last night." The foster parents' feelings of missing the child can also be shared. Validating the child's feelings is deeply helpful in affirming and normalizing the element of loss in the transition from foster parents to adoptive parents. This conversation would be invited right away, but the child might not be ready, in which case it can happen hours or days later depending on the child's readiness. As with all other visits, the adoptive parents and foster parent would debrief on the phone afterwards.

Diego - 5 years old | the first overnight

Diego was excited about his "sleepover". He and his adoptive parents, Sue and Joan, had picked out and purchased a pillowcase with Black Panther, his favorite superhero. They had planned out where they would eat dinner—Diego's favorite Mexican restaurant, which had what he considered the best chicken quesadillas in the world with just the right amount of gooey cheese. Diego had requested blueberry pancakes for his breakfast the next morning at the two-bedroom condo that Sue and Joan had rented (since they live about three hours away from his foster mother, Fernanda). Sue and Joan had decorated the condo with pictures they had blown up to 8" by 10" of Diego and Fernanda and also one of Diego, Sue, and Joan when they were at the zoo. Diego had his bag packed with his clothes, toiletries and stuffed animals. He insisted on bringing his rolling suitcase for this important trip, instead of his school backpack.

When Sue and Joan came to pick up Diego, they visited with Fernanda for about thirty minutes. Diego alternated sitting next to Sue and Fernanda. Joan still felt new to him. Diego recounted all the plans for the day and, upon prompting, added that he would be just staying one night with Sue and Joan and that he would come back to see Fernanda the next morning. The adults all confirmed this and Fernanda added that she was looking forward to hearing all about his visit in their phone call tonight and when he was back but that she would miss tucking him in that night. Diego agreed he would miss her at bedtime too and suggested that Fernanda might rewatch one of the movies they had watched dozens of times together. Fernanda and Diego had a big hug and then Diego and Sue and Joan headed out for their big adventure.

They had a fun time again at the zoo—and the chicken quesadilla did not disappoint. They had dropped his bag off at the condo and showed him around before they went to the zoo but when they returned after dinner, Diego seemed subdued. It seemed to become more real to him that he wouldn't be seeing Fernanda that evening.

Sue asked him, "How are you feeling?"

"Sad." Diego replied and he started crying.

"Would you like a hug?" asked Sue. Diego nodded yes. They sat down next to each other on the couch with Sue's arm around his shoulders.

Joan asked, "Is it okay if I sit on your other side? Diego nodded yes again so Joan joined them.

"What are you sad about?" inquired Sue.

Diego replied, "I miss momma Fernanda"

"Of course you do. Fernanda is a great mommy." responded Joan.

Diego asserted, "I want to go back to mommy's house. I want to go home."

"You miss momma Fernanda. You want to see her." stated Sue.

"Yeah." answered Diego and he got up off the couch and put on his coat. "Let's go." he commanded.

Sue and Joan shot a worried glance at each other. Sue had an idea. She offered, "We can't go now. We have the video call with Fernanda coming up." It wasn't scheduled for another 45 minutes but Joan was hurriedly texting Fernanda if they could have it now. Fernanda texted back that she would call in about five minutes after she finished giving another child their bath.

Joan showed the text to Diego and he seemed to relax but kept his coat on.

Sue suggested, "Hey, how about we play tic-tac-toe until the call?" This was a game Diego had enjoyed before. Sue quickly found a pencil and paper and Diego proceeded to somehow win 20 straight games against Sue and Joan. When that got boring, Sue and Joan squared off against each other in tic-tac-toe with Diego coaching each of them about what their next best move would be. Finally, the phone rang.

Diego answered, "I miss you, mommy. I wanna come home." he started crying again.

"O muchacho, I see you are sad." replied Fernanda. Diego nodded yes.

Fernanda asked, "Did you have your quesadilla? Was it good" Diego nodded yes again.

"Tell me about the zoo. What animals did you see?" inquired Fernanda.

"Tigers and seals and elephants and lions and monkeys. The monkey house was stinky. And I ate an elephant ear." relayed Diego.

"Those elephants have very tasty ears. Sometimes the lions are scary. Were they scary today? asked Fernanda.

"A little—one roared really loud." responded Diego.

"Were you brave?" asked Fernanda. Diego nodded yes.

"I thought so, Diego. I'm proud of you. What was our plan for your sleepover?" asked Fernanda.

"That I would stay with momma Sue and momma Joan and then come home in the morning, but I miss you." replied Diego.

"I miss you too. Remember we talked about how Sue and Joan can keep you safe and then you'll come back to my house and tell me all about it in the morning." responded Fernanda.

"Can you come here? I want you and Sue and Joan all together here. I'll sleep on the floor and you can sleep in my bed." pleaded Diego.

"No Diego, I'm sorry. I need to stay with the other kids. We are going to sleep in different houses tonight." answered Fernanda.

Diego started sobbing. Sue whispered, "I"m not sure what to do? He's so sad."

Fernanda told Sue, "He looks like he needs a hug," and asked Diego, "Diego, do you want a hug?"

He nodded yes, so Sue pulled him onto her lap and hugged him and gently rocked him and said, softly, "I know you're so sad. You miss Fernanda so much and you love her so much. She's a great momma." Diego melted into her.

After a while, Fernanda said, "It's time for me to say sweet dreams. Buenos sueños, Diego."

Diego waved weakly to Fernanda and said "Buenos sueños."

Sue thought for a moment and then offered, "How about this, Diego: let's get your pajamas on and then make some popcorn and eat it while we watch your favorite show."

"Okay," responded Diego quietly.

They made popcorn and watched his show. Diego sat on Sue's lap the whole time. Then he brushed his teeth and they read two books that he had brought—Sue read one and Joan read the other. Sue sat in a chair in his room while he fell asleep alongside a framed picture of Fernanda—and his favorite stuffed animal.

Having stayed up late, Diego slept in a little. Once he was awake, he got dressed and toileted in record time. They had planned for blueberry pancakes, but Sue and Joan asked Diego if he wanted to go straight to Fernanda's since he missed her so much. He decided he could wait a little longer to see her and eat the yummy pancakes first.

When they all got to his foster home, Diego ran ahead and gave Fernanda a big hug and cried a little and said how much he missed her. Fernanda cried a little too and said she missed him also. She thanked Sue and Joan for taking such good care of Diego. Sue and Joan both hugged Fernanda. The adults talked about the visit together with Diego piping up to provide details that the adults left out.

That night, Diego was a little tearful as he remembered how sad he was at bedtime the previous night. Fernanda asked him about what helped him make it through the night and he said he liked talking to her on the phone and that Momma Sue gave really good hugs.

Isabella - 14 years | the first overnight

Isabella and Julie both had some worries about an overnight visit. It meant more closeness to both of them, which was complicated for Isabella. Julie had become skittish after Isabella had gotten so upset during a two-hour visit. Isabella's therapist suggested another joint session for the two of them. In the therapy session, Julie asked what would help Isabella and she requested that they plan out the visit. They came up with watching the trilogy of Twilight movies, eating Chinese food, and allowing Isabella to put herself to bed. Isabella's therapist brought up her nightmares and planned what to do if she had one: Isabella did not want Julie to come into her bedroom during the night, so they agreed that Isabella would call Julie on her cell phone if she wanted to talk. This happened in the middle of the second overnight, but it was not because of a nightmare; Isabella had insomnia and was stuck thinking about sexual harassment she was experiencing in her high school. She had already talked with her foster mother Sheila, her therapist, and her school counselor about it. Isabella talked about the incidents and her feelings for over 30 minutes with Julie. Julie felt very tempted to protect Isabella and suggest all sorts of practical solutions.

Instead, Julie asked, "Anything I could do to help you now."

"I don't know. Maybe—if you'd be willing but probably not..." replied Isabella.

"What?"

"When I was littler, one of my foster moms used to tell me bedtime stories sometimes and I really liked that. Would you maybe tell me one?" requested Isabella.

"Oh... sure. Anything in particular?" asked a surprised Julie.

"Whatever," replied Isabella.

After a short pause, Julie started telling a story over the phone about a princess named Isabella who had various adventures, some funny and some scary. After about five minutes, Julie could hear some snoring coming from the phone and so she ended the story with "and Princess Isabella lived happily ever after."

The next morning Isabella was up before Julie. When Julie came out of her bedroom, she discovered Isabella in the kitchen making eggs and toast for the two of them, and coffee for Julie.

Julie was surprised and blurted out, "I was going to make you breakfast."

"Well, I beat you to it," retorted Isabella.

"Well, thank you. I realize I'm still learning about all the skills you have." replied Julie.

Isabella looked down and responded quietly, "Thank you for the story last night. I don't remember it very well."

After breakfast, Julie and Isabella went back to Sheila's where all three talked for over an hour about the overnight and how it was for each of the three of them, including Sheila's wonderings about how Isabella was doing.

Hakim - 18 months | the first overnight

Hakim and his adoptive parents, LaRonda and Michael, had good success with naps during his full-day visits. They planned to use the same routine at bedtime. Hakim usually slept through the night in his foster home but still woke up sometimes and needed soothing. In addition to his familiar baby blanket and stuffed animals that had been used for his naps during day-long visits with LaRonda and Michael, Jane gave them a t-shirt she had worn for a couple of days without laundering that would have her smells on it. Michael, LaRonda, and Jane decided to not do a good night call between Jane and Hakim as that might stir up more confusion at his age than he could put in context.

At bedtime during the first overnight visit, Hakim whimpered a little but went to sleep in about 15 minutes with Michael sitting near him. At about 2 AM, Hakim woke up crying and LaRonda went in and picked him up, walked around with him, and bounced him gently. He stilled in a few minutes, despite the fact there was no rocker in the rental... but the relief that LaRonda felt quickly evaporated when she noticed his diaper was wet. Changing him woke him up even more and, worse, he wanted to play. This was hard because LaRonda loved playing with Hakim and it was hard to not accept his invitation. LaRonda and Michael decided to do the bedtime routine again, which seemed to settle him some. When LaRonda put him down in the portable crib, Hakim started crying and stopped when she picked him up. This happened multiple times. She noticed herself getting frustrated and asked Michael to take over, but the pattern continued. At this point, everyone had been awake for two hours. There was a zippered side door on the crib and LaRonda proposed that she lay down on the floor and have her arm in the crib so Hakim could hold onto it. Michael was against this idea because he thought it would set up a bad precedent. Michael and LaRonda argued for a while until they reached an agreement. They would try LaRonda's strategy for 15 minutes and stick with it for the night if it worked, but agreed not to continue it once they were in their own home. If it didn't work in 15 minutes , then they would go back to what they had been doing. LaRonda's strategy worked; Hakim held onto one of LaRonda's thumbs and fell asleep in five minutes. LaRonda and Michael collapsed back in their bed and were also asleep within five minutes.

Hakim woke up LaRonda and Michael at about 7 AM, a normal time for him to get up in the morning. LaRonda and Michael felt a little groggy but Hakim was perky. After changing his diaper and getting him dressed, Michael fed Hakim a banana and some of his favorite cereal and some milk. After being put down on the floor, Hakim wanted to play with some toys, so he and LaRonda did that while Michael cleaned up. Shortly after that, they all went back to Jane's house. When they arrived, Hakim immediately wanted to be picked up and held by Jane, where he stayed while the adults sat and debriefed the visit. Jane highlighted LaRonda and Michael's creativity under pressure. When LaRonda and Michael said goodbye, Hakim started crying and reached out for them. Because Hakim had initiated this bid for contact, Michael and LaRonda each returned his hugs, telling him that they looked forward to seeing him again soon.

Chapter 8

Highlighting the Transition in the Foster Relationship

The child will eventually signal that they are anticipating the permanent change in the relationships with the foster parents. Often this starts during the longer day visits but might occur earlier, even at the very beginning of the process. Remember that, in this model, the relationship between the child and the foster parents is not ending totally. Rather, the current nature of the relationship as primary caregiver/relationship is transitioning to an extended kin relationship and a new relationship is forming: the new primary caregiving relationship is emerging in the adoptive family. This aspect of the transition can present very differently depending on the child, the nature of the relationship between the child and the foster parents, and the child's and adults' history of losses. It will also start earlier in the process on average the older the child is and the more knowledge they have about the goal of the process.

As adults, foster parents have a history of losses. Their feelings will be activated by the shift in their relationship with this child, if it is—as we hope—emotionally significant to the foster parents. Foster parents' feelings of loss have historically not been attended to (Boswell & Cudmore, 2014; Hebert et al, 2013). This is especially important for the welfare of the foster parents, foster parent retention, and foster parent's open-hearted participation in transitions out of their home. Grief support groups have been offered by some child welfare agencies (Edelstein, Burge & Waterman, 2001; Riggs et al, 2022) and they should be expanded. Examples of ways the loss of the foster child might affect foster parents include:

- interact more matter-of-factly and with less emotion with the child as a way of withdrawing to ease the pain of the loss;

- avoid interactions with the child that might involve more emotional closeness; shift those interactions to the other foster parent or other foster home staff;

- think less about that child than had been previously the case;

- react more intensely than they usually would to the child;

- more frequent/intense crying, even when not interacting with the child;

- greater focus on special time and close physical touch with the child;

- avoidance of planning activities associated with the transition;

- new fault-finding with the adoptive parents (especially notable when that hasn't felt true earlier in the transition);

- heightened need for soothing and less attention paid to other emotional stressors than usual (this may be a good form of self-care—it is just useful to be aware that it is connected to the upcoming transition); or

- feel grouchier with important others in their life.

This is not an exhaustive list - foster parents may know their own unique ways of showing reactions associated with loss. Showing any of these reactions does not mean the foster parent is doing anything bad; the foster parent is going through a normal human grieving process. What these reactions *do* mean is that it would be useful for the foster parent to talk to their emotional support providers (e.g., partner, best friend, therapist, parent, or adult child) about their feelings of loss. These conversations can happen before, during and after the transition. It is also particularly helpful for the foster parent to engage in reliably supportive self-care activities (e.g. massage, walks, journaling, adult play). It might be noted that this process of helping the child shift their attachments may feel especially difficult for foster parents who had wished to adopt this child. They would process those feelings with someone they trust. All of the above is to suggest foster parents put on their oxygen masks first so they can support the coping of the children they are caring for.

We offer the following recommendations to foster parents for managing the child's growing awareness of the loss of the current relationship with the foster parents. They are grouped to match the child's developmental level:

Infant/Toddler

- Use physical gestures and tone of voice to confirm a positive view of adoptive parents when handing the child to adoptive parents.

- Explicitly wave "bye bye" or perform other parting rituals when the child is leaving the foster parents to go with adoptive parents.

- Continue positive touch with the baby but do not get lost in reverie with how special it feels to touch this child.

- Continue to make eye contact with the baby, of course, but do not engage in prolonged gazing at the child while letting loving feelings occupy you.

- When talking with the baby, shift your tone of voice from "best baby ever" to "you're a good baby".

- When the child is leaving for all-day or overnight visits, try to be in touch with your anticipation of the child leaving the foster home permanently and the sad feelings that go with those thoughts. Using that time to journal may be particularly helpful.

Preschool

- Read age-appropriate books about adoption with the child and try to be in touch with the anticipation of the child leaving the foster home and the sad feelings that go with those thoughts. Books for preschoolers include *Zachary's New Home* by Geraldine and Paul Blomquist (1990) and *A Mother for Choco* by Keiko Kasza (1996).

- Look for examples of pretend play that the child is doing that focuses on forming new relationships and/or losing old ones. Tentatively identify feelings that the various characters in the play might be feeling without linking it too directly to the ongoing transition. Young children use pretend play as a format to process this change before facing it in reality.

- When the child is distressed in the foster home, think about the situation before the distress appeared and consider ways it might be connected to the adoptive transition. If you think it is, keep this in mind when responding to the child's distress. At this age, do not suggest or assume that their distress is caused by the adoptive transition.

- Respond to questions at an age-appropriate level about the transition. Remember that the relationship is not ending permanently—rather, it is transforming. In this model there is contact between the child and the former foster parents after the move. The child, based on their past experience, will likely assume that they will never see the foster parents after the move has occurred.

- Preschoolers may regress and want more physical connection and caregiving from foster parents. It is important to provide increased comfort while also labeling those times when they manage emerging emotions and everyday problems/challenges, "Look how you handled that hard time".

- The child may start reacting more intensely to regularly occurring separations from either of the foster parents. These occasions may include leaving for preschool, or when one of the foster parents leaves the foster home to go shopping. The foster parents could usefully devote more time to labeling and validating these feelings of loss than is typical and link these feelings to the emotional connection in the foster parent-child relationship; e.g., "Really gonna miss me, huh?

I'm going to the store and I'll be back. You love me and I love you."

School age - many of these are similar to the process with preschoolers but there are differences.

- Read age-appropriate books (e.g., *Addy's Journey to her Forever Home* by Nicole Schryer or *Elliot* by Julie Pearson) about adoption with the child and try to acknowledge the anticipation of the child leaving the foster home and the sad feelings that go with those thoughts. If the child does not volunteer any questions, overtly give permission for questions without requiring them. "Maybe sometime you might have questions about your new family and moving there and about us. That would be normal. Feel free to ask me anything you want."

- As with preschoolers, look for examples of pretend play that the child is doing that may be relevant to forming new relationships and losing old ones. Tentatively identify feelings that the adult and child characters might be feeling. With this aged child, you can make basic links between the pretend play and the child's experience ("Maybe you and the baby dinosaur are both sad about moving"). If these kinds of statements seem to cause the child to switch their play or to stop playing or move away, then stop making these links..

- When the child is distressed in the foster home, think about the situation before the distress appeared and whether it might be connected to the adoptive transition. If you think it is, keep this in mind when responding to the child's distress. At this age, it may sometimes be helpful to the child to gently suggest that their feelings may also be about something connected with the adoptive transition (e.g. being away from foster parents, a feeling of too many changes, etc.) If the child accepts this suggestion, this may lead to a fruitful discussion. If the child rejects the suggestion, do not push the point.

- Respond to questions at an age-appropriate level. Remember that the relationship is not ending permanently, rather it is transforming. In this model there is contact between the child and the former foster parents after the move. The child, based on their past experience, will likely assume that they will never see the foster parents again once the move has occurred.

- School-age children may regress and want more physical connection and caregiving from foster parents. It is important to give this while also praising them during the times when they are independent and being "big kids". You can also note to these children that they are starting to miss the foster parents even though they haven't moved yet—if that feels relevant—and acknowledge that those feelings are fine and that the foster parents also miss the child.

- Ask (but not require) the child to draw pictures of this family and their "new" family, as a springboard for a conversation about similarities and differences between the two families, without necessarily focusing on the adoptive transition unless the child brings it up.

Teenagers

- Listen for indirect openings from teens for conversations about adoption. For example, "I want to go shopping for clothes" may be a request to repeat a favorite activity with the foster parents before leaving the foster home. Clothes shopping is a future-oriented activity that can lead to a conversation about the future in the new home.

- Current events (e.g., refugee resettlements, community violence) can also spark conversations about families, safety, and differences in thinking.

- Teenagers may act out and be more defiant with the foster parents as a way of distancing themselves and thereby trying to minimize the loss. They may or may not be aware of this motivation consciously. The usual structures and boundaries would be maintained without anger. It's important to talk with the teen after they have calmed down about these feelings and offer the possibility that, in addition to what

they were originally upset about, perhaps they were also having feelings about the adoptive transition.

- Teenagers may want more physical contact from the foster parents, but have difficulty seeking it out. Foster parents would make sure to continue—or even increase—small physical gestures that have been already occurring between foster parent and teen (e.g., a pat on the back, playful touch, request for a hug).

- After several visits, foster parents can ask teenagers for their expert opinion about the adoptive parents and what makes them tick.

- Some teenagers, when calm, have enough imaginative capacity to respond to foster parents' questions about how things will be different with their new family and the positive/negative things they anticipate within this new family.

- Sometimes a teen may be willing to talk about issues if they have and a trusted adult (foster parent, therapist, youth minister) have both read a book about adoption. Examples include *Pieces of Me: Who do I Want to Be* by Robert Ballard (2009) or *Adopted: The Ultimate Teen Guide* by Suzanne Buckingham Slade (2013).

- Teenagers may be more private about vulnerable feelings than younger children. It can be useful for foster parents to initiate conversations with teenagers about the move when those conversations can be held with no one else around. If the foster parent genuinely feels they will miss the teen (even if they have been difficult at times) then that can be volunteered to the teen without expecting it to be reciprocated at the time. This overture may help the teenager be more consciously aware of their own feelings and the fact that they matter to the foster parent. If the foster parent does not have those feelings, then the teenager can be asked about what they think the move will feel like to them and if there is anything or anyone they will miss from the foster home. If the teenager is in psychotherapy, hopefully that may be a place where they can talk about their feelings of loss.

- Although not always true, teenagers and foster parents can have had difficult interactions that have not been fully repaired. The shift to an adoptive home provides a unique opportunity for repair to the relationship. It is useful for the foster parent to consider their contribution to the conflict to model accountability and overt repair for the teen. Any apology does not mean that the foster parent is accepting all of the blame or that the teen is without blame. This can be clear in how they apologize ("We had that big blow-up about the curfew. I just want you to know before you leave that I regret yelling at you and I'm sorry for that.") This may lead to the teen acknowledging the apology but not taking any ownership on their part—or perhaps apologizing themselves for at least some small part of the dispute. Either is a useful step for the relationship before the move. There is, of course, also the possibility that the dispute will resume. It is very important to not respond to the teenager's provocations "I get you are still upset and hurt and angry and I know we still have big differences. I just wanted to apologize for yelling."

- Difficult conversation with teens can sometimes be easier for the teen if direct eye contact is more intermittent; e.g. in the car or on a walk.

- The foster parent may want to give a message to the child but the foster parent believes it is too sensitive for the teen to have a direct conversation about. Such a message can sometimes be successfully communicated through a text or other written communication. The teen does not have to respond right away and can reflect on the contents over time and respond later or never. It is important in written communication to be explicit about your intent and feelings, including mixed feelings, so that the teen does not have to guess. Their guesses about interpersonal communications can be off base given their relationship history. Sometimes, humans default to written communication rather than talking directly with the other person for the conscious reason that it would be too hard for the other person to hear but it may also feel too hard for the original person to deal with the conversation directly themselves. It is useful for foster parents to consider if they are avoiding the direct conversation with the teen because of their own discomfort.

Child's Lifebook

Lifebooks are a wonderful tool for recording both a child's life and the life-changing events of an adoptive transition. It is a collection of materials that documents a child's history, both before and during their involvement with the child welfare system. They include information and documentation about the family of origin, prior foster families, the current caregivers, and the adoptive family, as well as materials representing the child's development, school history, and significant events—including the adoption. These materials can be in the form of narratives dictated by the child or written by relevant adults, photographs, creations of the child (drawings, stories, etc.). This material would be presented in a developmentally appropriate manner, which means some content would be revised or added as the child matures. Children who live with their birth parents and are not in the child welfare system have access to those parents' memories as a resource for their history and identity. Lifebooks function in that important way for foster children.

Lifebooks can also be used therapeutically as a way of helping a child understand and integrate events in their life, and separating their worth from what happened to them (Rose, 2012). When used in this way, they are created and/or reviewed by a therapist with the child. If the child has a therapist, then the adoptive transition can become a valuable time to review their history and create entries about the emotional process of shifting their current relationships with their foster parents and developing their new relationships with their adoptive family.

Not every child in the child welfare system has a Lifebook. Research has reported that only about 50% of children had a Lifebook accompany them into their adoptive home (Reams, 2022). An adoptive transition is a crucial time to update or create the beginnings of a Lifebook so it can go to the adoptive home with the child. The foster parents might take the lead on this in conjunction with the child's caseworker and any others who might hold history about this child (e.g., child's therapist, birth parents and other family of origin members, prior foster parents, lawyer or court-appointed special advocates). The internet contains many resources for this process. (https://www.adoptivefamilies.com/category/talking-about-adoption/adoption-lifebooks-scrapbooks/).

Some tips are listed below for using the Lifebook to process the change in the foster parent-child relationship:

- The work of recording the child's time in this foster home is a great time for conversations about what the child likes the best about this home and what they might miss.
- Update the child's Lifebook with pictures or stories or mementoes about their time in the foster home and about the transition and provide a brief explanation of the why of the transition.
- Include blank pages for adoptive parents to add information, as a tangible reminder that there will be a time with adoptive parents after the time with foster parents is over.

- With the child, review the material about this foster home that is already in, or soon to be included, in the Lifebook. This may prompt feelings in both the child and foster parent. It is useful for the child to see the feelings of the foster parents and be reminded that they are emotionally significant to the foster parent (Lanyado, 2008).

- Consult with the child's therapist before reviewing the entire Lifebook during the transition process. Instead, wait for the therapist's recommendations. There may be material that is not developmentally appropriate yet for the child.

- When foster parents write their own contributions for the Lifebook—whether a memory of the child from an earlier time in the foster home or a description of part of the transition process—it is important to include their own emotional reactions. Children partly learn about their value and significance by the emotional impact they have on others. A Lifebook can also be an opportunity for a foster parent to record how the child is special to them and how they will miss them when they are no longer living with them.

- The beginning of an all-day visit with the child, foster parents and adoptive parents can partly include reviewing the Lifebook and discussing past times. The adoptive parents can comment positively about the relationship between the child and the foster parents and how they might miss each other during visits.

Other children in foster home

Foster parents may not be the only member of the foster family to have feelings about the child being adopted leaving the home. Other children in the foster home, including foster siblings or the birth children of the foster parents, may have reactions to the child's transition process (Younes & Harp, 2007). Foster parents would validate these feelings—whether they include anticipated loss, jealousy, anger or others—and assist the child in putting these feelings into words. These other children may also try to sabotage the process, creating disruptions when adoptive parents arrive or talking negatively to the child who is being adopted about adoption or the adoptive parents. If the foster siblings are in therapy, then their therapists should be informed about the change happening in the foster family and the impact it seems to be having on the foster sibling. The reactions of foster siblings to the upcoming move provide an opportunity for the child who is moving and the foster parents to also talk about their feelings about the upcoming changes. The child who is being adopted may experience guilt about leaving foster siblings behind, or about getting an adoptive home when these other children are still waiting. They may need help processing those feelings from the foster parents or their therapist (if they have one).

Chapter 9

Move from Foster Home to Adoptive Home

Moves between residences for foster children have almost always felt unpredictable and often been traumatic (Unrau, Seita, & Putney, 2008), especially their removal from the birth family (Mitchell, 2016). The primary goal of the move to the adoptive home in this model is to provide a sense for the child of knowing what is coming and having input into the move. This will hopefully reduce anxiety and also identify this move as different from the ones that have gone before. In addition, the emotions of both adoptive and foster parents at this time of transition needs to be expressed, supported and validated by the other adults involved.

The following criteria would be reviewed in a meeting of the transition planners. Criteria are useful for maintaining an appropriately cautious pace, because sometimes adults feel ready to move the process along for a variety of reasons, especially as the end draws near. If the child has little attachment to foster parents because of their limited time in the foster home, then some of the statements below may need to be adjusted given the diminished opportunity for attachment and loss between child and foster parents.

- At least two overnight visits were completed successfully. This does not mean there was no turbulence, rather the child and adoptive parents have survived any turmoil and resumed a positive connection before the end of the overnight visit.
- The child turns to adoptive parents for physical and emotional safety and reassurance in developmentally appropriate ways. For example, the child:
  - seeks assistance from adoptive parents when hurt or in pain, although not necessarily as much as they seek it from foster parents;
  - spends at least half of their time in closer proximity to adoptive parents than foster parents when both are available;
  - comfortable receiving food, affection and hygiene care from the adoptive parents;
  - shows or demonstrates things they are excited about with the adoptive parents, as well as the foster parents;

- greets adoptive parents with positive feelings most of the time.

- The child has started the process of dealing with losing the current form of the relationship with foster parents or other members of the foster home. This is often indicated when the child:

  - shows and/or verbalizes a sense that the relationship with foster parents is changing. Usually they expect a total severance despite verbal reassurance.

  - shows shifts in emotional expression in interactions with foster parents. This includes increases in crying, clinging, anger outbursts, regression, and/or dissociation, especially during separations from foster parents (whether this is before visiting adoptive parents or not). They may resist transitions to adoptive parents when they had been smoother before.

  - demonstrates anger outbursts and aggression with foster siblings.

  - gives their belongings to foster siblings.

- begins to shift language when talking about adoptive parents to talking about "my parents" or other ways of claiming the adoptive parents.

- Adoptive parents and other adoptive family members feel ready for the move to occur.

- Adoptive parents have prepared their home for the child to arrive and live there permanently.

Preparations in the foster home

When foster parents take concrete steps to prepare for the child's move to the adoptive home, everyone witnesses their support for the move, making the transition much more concretely real for the child who is moving, the foster parents, and the other people in the foster home. These preparations are an important step in the shifting relationship between the child and the foster parents, and forces them to deal with the feelings of loss that they may have been avoiding. The guidance presented below will be amended if the adoption is a long-distance one. This will be discussed later in a special section.

- Throw a party to celebrate the child's move, near (but not on) the actual moving day. In addition to all the residents of the foster home and staff that might work there, invite individuals who are important to the child, especially those who may lose contact with the child once they are in an adoptive home (e.g., teacher, coach, neighbors, child care provider, etc.). This party is analogous to a celebration of a child graduating from high school or college; they are graduating from foster care to an adoptive home. The house would be decorated and there would be cake or some other celebratory food.

- Document the lead-up to moving day and send content to the adoptive parents for inclusion in the child's Lifebook. Include:
  - Photos and video of the celebration party.
  - Family photo with the date and names of all individuals present. A framed 8x10 inch copy of this photo would

accompany the child in the move and be displayed in the child's bedroom in the adoptive home.

- A narrative about the preparations for the move as written or dictated by the child, including their feelings, would be added to the Lifebook.

- Foster parents would create a written narrative (or video) about events and emotions pertaining to the move and the child's time in the foster home, including fond memories.

- Foster parents and the child pack the child's belongings together in nice suitcases or boxes. Children should not have their possessions moved in garbage bags.

- Pack one pair of bedsheets or crib sheets that the child has slept in at least once, preferably more, since being laundered.

- Look for opportunities to do one-on-one activities with the child (e.g. going to the grocery store, walking the dog) in which the child and foster parent can reminisce about their time together and share feelings about the upcoming shift. It's a great time for both the adult and child to cry and show how meaningful the relationship has been to them. The foster parent can remind the child that they will still see the child once they are in the adoptive home assuming that is the plan.

- Foster parents can also talk with their support people about their feelings, whether positive or negative, about the upcoming transition.

- Notify adults in other important areas of the child's life (e.g., teacher, coach, therapist, religious youth group leader) of the moving date so that those adults can facilitate a good-bye process for the child with the other children and adults in those venues. Foster parents might help to facilitate a connection between the child's pediatric/psychiatric practitioner(s) and the adoptive parents before the move to make the adoptive parents aware of any ongoing health issues. Ideally, prescriptions will be refilled before the move so that the adoptive parents have an adequate supply and do not need to deal with that right away in addition to the myriad other details in assuming care of the child.

Preparation in adoptive home

When parents welcome a child through birth, they "nest" during the pregnancy. They buy furniture, decorate a nursery, make decisions about cloth versus plastic diapers, inform others of the joyous news, etc. Adoptive parents usually do not have nine months between when they learn they have been selected as adoptive parents and the moving date, but they do also engage in nesting behavior. The recommendations below are nesting behaviors that prepare the home for the child—and the adoptive parents for their new role.

- If the child brings something special from the foster home, it takes priority over replacements. For instance, leave the bed unmade, and dress it with the child's sheets from the foster home. Do not wash these sheets for at least seven nights.

- Childproof the adoptive home in a way that is developmentally appropriate for the child.

- Review foster parents' information about the child's daily routine, likes and dislikes, etc. Consider the constraints of the adoptive parents' life, then plan a daily routine and purchase any needed items. This plan is just a starting point and will need to be revised multiple times as adoptive parents and the child find their own unique daily rhythm together.

- If there are children already in the adoptive home, they will have already encountered the child during overnight visits. Depending on the age of these children, the reality of the new child actually moving in will still often feel like a major upheaval in the family. Invite these other children to assist with preparations to welcome the new child, which can be helpful for them as they adapt to the change. Their adjustment to the new sibling will be a long process in which a significant number of twists and turns can be expected. Adoptive parents need to signal that questions and conversations about all the changes are welcomed.

- It is not helpful for adoptive parents to have lots of new possessions for their adopted child waiting in the home. It will be enough to get used to all the regular objects that will be new to the child; the television remote may work differently, the arrangement of items in the kitchen will feel strange, where outdoor coats are hung up, the list goes on. Even with efforts by adoptive parents to think about the routine in the foster home and what might be imported, there will be so many changes. If the child needs something new (e.g., they are moving to a colder climate), involve them in the purchases after the move has occurred. It can feel very meaningful for adoptive parents (or their families) to prepare for the new child's arrival by buying items in advance, but it can also be an emotionally meaningful bonding experience for the child to select and purchase new items with their adoptive parents.

- As mentioned previously, adoptive parents are entitled to parental leave upon welcoming the child into their home. As the move draws near, it is important to nail down these details. When a moving day is identified, then leave dates can be finalized.

- Sometimes the family and community of the adoptive parents want to throw the equivalent of a baby shower to celebrate the welcoming of the child, even if they are not a baby. This is a wonderful tradition, but preferably it happens before the moving day—it will likely be overwhelming for the child to attend.

- Furnishing the adopted child's bedroom can also be a good time to update the bedroom(s) of any existing children in the adoptive family in some way to reduce the likelihood of jealousy.

- If the adoptive couple has been childless before welcoming the child, it is useful for them to pause and reflect on the upcoming change in their lives as a couple. They are entering a new phase of their relationship as co-parents (South, Lim, Jarnecke, & Foli, 2018). This can include, depending on the age of the child, making decisions about how they want to discipline, reallocating money to a college savings account, or negotiating who will drive in the carpool to school. Parents who acquire a child through birth have time to make these choices gradually over years but adoptive parents have a number of decisions to make in a short period of time.

- Adoptive parents also need to think about the name the new child will have in their family (Milbrand, 2024). By the time the child is a toddler, their name is a part of their identity. It is probably a good idea to keep the child's first name the same. Adoptive families often have the child take their last name as a way to ritualize bringing them into their family. In the case of teenagers who are being adopted, solicit their opinion. Sometimes there may be elements of the child's birth name that may be kept as adoptive middle names. The cultural significance of the child's birth name would also be considered before making any changes.

One other planning item takes a lot of careful thought: how soon after moving day would the extended family be introduced and involved with the child. One line of thinking is that adoptive parents be wary of planning to have their own family visit too quickly while they and the child are still trying to settle in together. Although they are the new adoptive extended family and are eager to bond, adoptive parents' relatives are also strangers to the child, who has just started the process of getting used to these new attachment figures, the adoptive parents. On the other hand, extended family can be a huge emotional support for the adoptive parents. For many cultures, extended family are intimately involved in all major milestones and it would be unthinkable to not welcome the new addition to the family. For some children, this abundance of new loving adults may feel great. Video introductions can be a good alternative first step for introducing relatives to children—it's less stressful and frightening for the child.

Moving day

- The move **must** occur in the morning to avoid keeping the child waiting for most of the day and building up anxiety, but not too early. The child needs to have time for breakfast in the foster home and to finish last-minute packing.

- It is a great occasion for the child to dress nicely, as though they were going to get class photos taken. The photos of this day will follow them throughout their life.

- Preferably, adoptive parents come to pick up the child at the foster home. The second best choice is usually for the foster parents to bring the child to where the adoptive parents are staying. If neither of those locations feels acceptable because of privacy concerns, then a neutral site would be selected. The offices of child welfare should be avoided at all costs because of the negative memories for the child. (Even very young children develop feelings about these offices!) Some other possibilities include a courtroom, the child's classroom on a weekend if the school consents, a friend's home, or a place of worship. It is better to avoid public places like restaurants or parks because of the privacy needed for intense feelings.

- Take pictures and a video of the adoptive parents, foster parents, and child together as a group, to serve as documentation of the handover and the feelings associated with it—even if those are not all positive.

- Unless the handover is occurring in the adoptive family residence, foster parents can walk with the adoptive parents and the child out to the adoptive parents' car. It is fine if foster parents show feelings and voice their love for the child while also sharing the bittersweetness of saying good-bye for now.

They can express happiness that the child has the adoptive parents and that they will see the child again soon. If the handover is happening in the adoptive home, then the goodbye to the foster parents can occur at the front door with all of the adults helping the child respect that boundary.

Some children have a hard time containing the intensity of their feelings. They may scream, sob, jump up and down, yell in anger, or even run away. Validate and give voice to their feelings. Many of those feelings are about the pain of saying good-bye to the foster parents and its resonance with earlier losses. If the child has a meltdown, runs, hides, or becomes aggressive, one foster parent and one adoptive parent can cooperate to help the child. It's often better if the foster parent is leading this team, as the foster parent has the stronger relationship at this point and more experience with soothing strategies with this child, however both caregivers can participate and be emotionally present with the child. Remind them that they will see the foster parents again, even if they won't move back in with them.

The child does not need to reach full calmness for the handover to occur. The child may still exhibit emotions, but become settled enough to listen and express feelings. Thus, the child can express good-byes verbally or nonverbally, but is not required to. The child can still hear goodbyes and "see you later" from the foster family.

Assuming the handover does not occur in the adoptive home, the adoptive parents and the child would proceed to the adoptive home without stopping at other locations if possible. Ensure that the car has sufficient gas and snacks/food for the child and the adoptive family. This may not be possible for some adoptive parents who live a substantial distance from the foster home. The goal is for the child to arrive at their new home as soon as possible. Take photos and perhaps a short video of the child in the car as part of documenting the transition.

Upon arriving at the adoptive home, take a photo of the new enlarged family in front of the adoptive home. Allow the child to move about the home and explore, even though they may have been there before for the overnight visits. That was as a guest, this is as a family member. Adoptive parents might ask the child more than once where and with whom they would like their photo taken. This gives the child some sense of control in this part of the process at a time when their feelings may feel big and somewhat out of control.

It's important to let the child know which activities (e.g., dinner, nap, etc.) will occur throughout the rest of the day, to a level of detail that is developmentally appropriate. If the child is a preschooler or younger, let them know about each activity as it is coming up. The rest of this day then starts to follow the daily routine planned for weekend days.

Unpacking is an important thing for the child and at least one adoptive parent to do together. Placing their belongings on shelves and in drawers is a concrete, yet also symbolic, manifestation of their place in their new home and family.

Another crucial activity is reviewing the wall calendar hung up in the child's room. The current day (moving day) would be labeled and bedazzled with stars and glitter. Another important date would be marked: the date of the first visit with the former foster parents (or, if distance or other circumstances require it, then the first video call). As each day passes, it can be indicated on the calendar in a way the child can recognize as visible progress towards seeing their former caregivers. This calendar strategy can work with children as young as three years of age. This enables the child to have greater faith that this very important prior relationship is not disappearing like other prior relationships may have. Other important dates might also be marked on the calendar (e.g., first day at their new school or next therapist appointment).

Even though the child has already spent the night in the adoptive home, settling down, and falling asleep may be difficult for them to do the first night that this adoptive home is a permanent home. Adoptive parents acknowledging this reality is helpful. Following the usual bedtime routine makes sense to the child, but adoptive parents can expect to sit in the chair in the room for a longer time than usual. Adoptive parents may also have a harder time falling asleep.

Adoptive parents calling the foster parents and debriefing how the rest of the day went helps the foster parents feel involved. It also confirms the adoptive parents' prior statements that they will value the foster parents even after the move.

Whether at bedtime or earlier in this first day with the adoptive family, the child will likely feel sad and miss their foster family. They may demonstrate this clearly with tears and/or words—or they may try to hide it from others and even push it out of their own awareness. It may even come out sideways, through anger directed at the adoptive family. This is not a problem but another opportunity to continue to build the attachment between the child and the adoptive parents through the grown-ups' sensitivity to and acceptance of the child's feelings. The feelings do not have to be fixed or eliminated but rather empathized with, so the child knows they are not alone with them.

Diego - 5 years | moving day

Diego's moving day was somewhat chaotic. He was clear on the plan and had apparently been looking forward to the day. His going-away party went smoothly with many classmates, soccer teammates, and neighbors in attendance, as well as his teacher and soccer coach. Sue and Joan, the adoptive parents, were scheduled to arrive at the foster home at 11 AM on moving day. When Fernanda, the foster mom, went to wake Diego up at 8 AM, his usual time to get out of bed, he was hiding under the covers and declared, "Never leaving my bed."

"What's up, muchacho?" asked Fernanda.

"I want to stay with you forever and ever," asserted Diego.

"I love you, too, Diego and you are not leaving me forever. I will see you next week at our favorite pizza place. Sue and Joan will bring you," reassured Fernanda.

"I know that. But they don't know Spanish and I bet the tamales they make will taste yucky," complained Diego.

"You're going to miss me and the special things we share; I'm going to miss you too." responded Fernanda. Diego started crying and came out from under the covers for a hug and to be held. Fernanda stroked his hair. *"You know what? Momma Sue and Momma Joan are starting to learn Español but they don't know very much. I think you could help teach them."*

"Are they going to school?" asked Diego.

Fernanda laughed. *"No, they are learning it from an app on their phones."*

Diego snickered, *"I could give them homework packets to do."*

"No muy difícil. Don't make it too difficult. They can't spend all their time on homework. They need to take care of you too. How about this? When I come over, part of my visit will be to teach them how to make tamales my way?" suggested Fernanda. Diego nodded his head. *"Right now I need to start cooking bacon. Who wants bacon?"*

"I do, I do." exclaimed Diego while jumping up and down on his bed.

"You know you need to be dressed before breakfast," Fernanda reminded him.

"Si, mama." answered Diego.

Breakfast went smoothly, although Diego was so excited that he needed to be reminded to take his plate out to the kitchen. He was dressed in his church clothes and posed for many pictures with Fernanda and his foster siblings.

When Sue and Joan arrived, Diego hid behind Fernanda. Sue and Joan gave him some space and talked with Fernanda about some of the arrangements at the adoptive home that they had made for Diego. When Fernanda felt Diego clutching to her leg less tightly, she squatted down and asked him about the new desk in his bedroom that Sue and Joan had just mentioned. Diego shrugged his shoulders. At the same time one of Diego's foster brothers hit another sibling in the head with a remote control. Sue and Joan looked over at the conflict and Fernanda moved over to intervene. With the adults distracted, Diego ran out the front door. Sue and Joan noticed the front door open. A child mentioned that Diego had run out. Sue and Joan went to look for Diego in the front yard but couldn't find him. They called for Fernanda and explained that Diego had run out. Joan started crying and Sue hugged her. Fernanda asked her adult daughter to watch the other kids and went out to look for Diego. Sue and Joan conferred and agreed that Joan would wait at the front door in case Diego came back and Sue would follow Fernanda. Fernanda thought he might have run to the neighbor's house where his best friend lived, but he was not there. They both called out for Diego. No answer.

Sue asked, "Has Diego run away before?"

"Never. He was always one to stick close. This is not like him." answered Fernanda.

Sue's voice quavered, "I'm scared."

"We will find him. I'm sure of it." Reassured Fernanda, who added, "Let's look in the backyard."

Sue and Fernanda did not initially see Diego in the backyard but then they heard some crying from behind the compost pile. They squatted down on either side of him and both put a hand on his back.

"What's wrong, Diego?" asked Fernanda.

Diego shrugged his shoulders, "Too many scary feelings inside. I go away. Tummy feels weird too."

"Can I give you a hug?" asked Sue. Diego looked over at Fernanda, who nodded "yes." Sue and Diego hugged and Sue pulled him into her lap. Diego also held onto Fernanda's hand.

"You have had to say a lot of good-byes in your life, Diego. Would you agree?" Diego nodded "yes" again and, as Sue spoke, Fernanda texted Joan one-handed that they'd found him.

"I think you are having feelings about saying good-bye for now to Fernanda but you are also having feelings about all those other good-byes too. What do you think of that?"

Diego nodded his head "yes" a third time and leaned his body and head more fully into Sue. Sue rocked him and said, "I love you, Diego."

"I love you too", said Diego and he added "I love you too momma Fernanda and I love momma Joan."

Fernanda responded, "You are a boy who is loved by a lot of people and loves them back really well." She followed that up with a kiss on the top of his head. The rest of moving day went much smoother.

Isabella - 14 years | moving day

Isabella insisted she didn't need a goodbye party, but Sheila, her foster mother, convinced her that the party was for everybody else that cared about her to say goodbye. Despite her protests, Isabella made a dress to wear especially for it.

In the week leading up to moving day, Isabella and her adoptive mother spent a lot of time on outings picking out a paint color for the walls in her new bedroom and a bedspread to match. This decorating extended all the way down to picking out special knobs for dresser drawers. One hitch was that Isabella and Julie could not find curtains that Isabella thought were right for her new bedroom and she refused to move to Julie's home without them. The caseworker urged Isabella to move and reassured her that she could find the curtains later. Julie worried that Isabella was finding an excuse to sabotage the adoption at the last step. Sheila felt torn; she knew there was another girl waiting to leave residential treatment and enter her home as soon as Isabella left. On the other hand, Sheila also knew from experience that pushing Isabella would likely blow up in the adults' faces.

One day, after looking unsuccessfully at four more stores for curtains, Isabella sighed that her feet hurt.

Julie agreed, "Mine too." Julie slumped, thinking that the move might never happen. After a long pause, Julie asked in desperation, "How about we make them ourselves?"

Isabella looked stunned. "I've never made curtains," Isabella fretted.

Julie reassured her, "You're smart and I'll help."

"You don't know squat about sewing," said Isabella in a playful voice.

"That's right—but I'll be a pair of extra hands." added Julie.

They shopped for fabric, sewed, and finished their curtains late that night. Isabella showed them off at her good-bye party to many oohs and aahs.

Moving day itself went smoothly because the adults respected that Isabella wanted to pack up all her belongings herself and carry them out to Julie's car without any help. She said she had lost too many possessions *when adults helped in past moves. Julie had just pulled away from the curb on the drive to her home, when Isabella said, suddenly, "This is scary."*

"Yeah," responded Julie.

"If I screw this one up…" said Isabella through tears. She started sobbing. Julie pulled over, unbelted and held out her arms. Isabella unbelted and melted into Julie's arms.

"We'll figure this out together," reassured Julie.

"But what if we don't?" Isabella worried.

"It's been about four months since I first met you. Have I given up?" asked Julie.

"No," admitted Isabella.

"You haven't given up either."

"Yeah but I thought about it a lot. Almost pulled the plug a bunch of times." responded Isabella.

Julie gave Isabella an extra squeeze and said, "It's scary, but you did it. We did it… are doing it."

"The fear is different now. I can't back out. It'd be too painful—my mind would explode into a million pieces. So I'm trapped with you—what if it's hell like when I was little?" explained Isabella.

"This will take time, Isabella. You trust me some now and over time, I believe that will grow." reassured Julie.

After a pause, Julie added, "And I love you, so I'm motivated to figure out a way with you to make it work."

"Uh-huh. Okay." replied Isabella as she turned and looked out the window. Julie looked at Isabella for a second, wondering what else to say to reengage her and then decided maybe they had said enough and Isabella needed a break. They put their seat belts back on and drove on to Julie's home in silence.

Hakim - 18 months | moving day

Overnight visits had been going okay for Hakim, LaRonda, and Michael. He would wake up every night and it would often take 30-60 minutes to get him back to sleep. Jane told them that this happened sometimes at her house too. A moving date was set. Jane decided to host a small good-bye party so as to not overwhelm Hakim. A couple of neighbors came by, as did his respite provider. Jane and some of the other adults got a little teary which upset Hakim.

The day before the move, Jane was packing up his belongings, which was very upsetting to Hakim. He tried to take them out of the boxes that Jane was putting them in. He did not understand that he was moving away, but knew he did not like the disruption and change involved in packing up. Jane took him to the playground and then to his favorite ice cream store. His belongings were all packed up by the time he was home. He cried a little and looked for his familiar things. After Jane held him for a while, he settled down.

Jane called LaRonda and Michael the night before moving day, and shared her prediction that Hakim would likely realize that something was different after they didn't bring back to her house the next day—and even more the day after. They scheduled a video call for two days after moving day.

Moving day itself went relatively smoothly. Hakim woke up early that day at 6am and didn't want to go back to sleep. LaRonda and Michael were not scheduled to come until 10am. Jane decided to do one last trip to the park for her and Hakim. They enjoyed the playground equipment and Jane got to play the bridge monster role one last time. Hakim did not notice the tears in Jane's eyes. When they got back to the house, the last of Hakim's belongings were packed. Hakim was distressed and even more clingy to Jane. When LaRonda and Michael arrived, the handover went easily. Hakim, LaRonda and Michael flew back to LaRonda and Michael's home state the next day.

Chapter 10

Post-Move Contact between Child and Foster Parents

Contact between the child and their now former foster parents after the move is part of the plan from the beginning. All along, the child has been told (but probably doubted) that their relationship with the foster parents will continue; that it is changing but not disappearing. This is crucial and now the adults are going to follow through on that commitment. Foster and adoptive parents have known to anticipate and plan for this post-move contact.

In addition to the various forms of contact between the child and the former foster parents that will be discussed in this section, there are other ways adoptive parents can keep the foster parents alive for the child:

- foster parents are an open and ongoing topic of conversation in the adoptive home following moving day,

- prominently displaying a framed photo of the child and foster parents in the child's room,

- acknowledging when a dish is cooked based on a recipe from the foster home,

- adoptive parents mentioning a positive memory of the foster parents to the child,

- daily tracking on the calendar in the child's room the next contact with the foster parents and using that for conversation,

- talking about the foster parents to extended family and friends in front of the child, and

- including the foster parents in the child's prayers (if that is part of the adoptive family's traditions.

Why have any contact between the child and their former foster parents at all?

This model assumes that the child has an attachment to their former foster parents and the visits help the child with processing the loss of the relationship they once had with them. The child is welcome to express their sadness about no longer living with the former foster parents. The comfort they receive from the adoptive parents concretely demonstrates that there is room for these emotions. The visits show the child that their former foster parents still want to see them. This can be important because some children may fantasize that the move occurred because the former foster parents did not want or like them any more. The child may have held similar fantasies about prior caregivers who ceased contact with them. These past relationship disruptions, which started with removal from their birth home, may give the child a sense that relationships don't last and are not worth investing in or counting on—the very things we want them to be able to do with their adoptive parents. The post-move contact provides the child an example of a relationship that continues across time and placement changes.

The adoptive parents' support for this continuity of relationship also demonstrates something to the child about their new parents: that they care about the child's connections, that they are relationship-oriented and their care for the child is not simply contingent on school performance and chore completion. Finally, coordinating the child's contact with the former foster parents helps to keep adoptive and foster parents in contact. This can help the adoptive parents use their child's knowledgeable former caregivers as a resource, if so desired. Contact between the child and former foster parents can come in a variety of forms.

Forms of post-move contact

A mix of post-move methods of contact are often used, including the following:

- *In-person visits* satisfy attachment needs best and allow for the most kinds of contact (including touch). This form works for adopted children of all ages, but requires the most arranging and doesn't work if adoptive and foster homes are far apart.

- *Video calls* allow for emotional contact and show physical spaces (e.g., the child can show off their new home to their former caregivers). These can be scheduled but do not have to be, and can involve more than one person at either end easily. These do not work well for infants and toddlers.

- *Video apps* (e.g., Marco Polo) allow for longer recorded videos to be easily sent and can be rewatched. Thus, this option has some advantages over video calls but loses the spontaneity of an immediate back-and-forth interaction.

- *Phone calls* provide some emotional contact through voice. These ideally occur between two parties off of speaker mode, which presents some loss of privacy. These don't work well for preschoolers or younger and require careful structuring for younger school age children (6-9 years).

- *Written correspondence* (e.g., texts, DMs, emails, letters, drawings) provide limited emotional contact but can happen many times per day without scheduling. These may include photos or short videos as attachments, and work well for children who have their own cell phone. Drawings can be nice for younger children so they can send something tangible to the former foster parent.

- Social media, either their own accounts or access to the adoptive parents' account, is a controversial subject for children and teens. The adoptive parents first need to figure out their values and boundaries about social media. They then get to decide at what age their child may have a social media account, what kind, and whether the child will have the former foster parents as contacts. Communication about social media use between the teen and adoptive parents is crucial. Social media can be a way for a teen to maintain a feeling of connection to their former foster parents while easily regulating how often and to what extent they access information about their former foster parents. It also allows the teen to share information that they select to be shared with their former foster parents. Communication and coordination between adoptive and foster parents is very useful; boundaries about social media that are set by the adoptive parents can be supported by the former foster parents. Adoptive parents should be contacted by former foster parents if the child contacts them or sends a friend request through social media without the former foster parents knowing if the adoptive parents approve, or what the rules are.

Locations for in-person visits

Each potential location presents unique considerations. Documenting in-person visits for the child's Lifebook is recommended at all locations. **Visits should never occur in the former foster home**, regardless of convenience. Doing so is confusing for the child as they may feel they are being returned, no matter how much they are reassured. **Visits should also not occur at a child welfare office.** These have too many traumatic associations. The adoptive home is ideal, as this gives the child the chance to show off their new home to the foster parents and experience the foster parents approving their new home. A neutral location with the opportunity for play and other informal activities, such as a park or playground, can work quite well for all ages of children, especially for visits after the first one. Neutral locations that have more structured expectations for interactions, such as a restaurant or a mall, can work acceptably for preteens or teens. A drawback is that interpersonal distance is not easily shifted in these environments as the child grows more or less comfortable with close contact with any of the adults.

Timing of in-person visits

For a first in-person visit, it's useful to provide the child a few days to settle in, but not so long that the child starts to think they will never see the foster parents again. Remember, that the relationship with foster parents is not ending, but changing to a kind of extended family relationship. Thus, it is useful for the first in-person visit to occur 3-5 days after moving day. As suggested in chapter 8, the child has their own calendar in their room with the date of the next visit highlighted in some way and then adoptive parents and child can cross off each day in a countdown to the next visit.

Initially, in-person visits might occur twice a month before stretching out to once per quarter and perhaps less frequently, depending on the preferences of the adoptive parents and foster parents. As the child grows older, they would also have significant input. The final frequency is up to the adoptive parents but it is recommended that, if the former foster parents are local, they receive invitations to major events in the child's life (e.g., religious rituals, birthdays, graduations, performances). Foster parents are not obligated to accept every invitation, but it is recommended that they communicate with the child when they decline invitations.

Contacts other than in-person visits

Phone calls, texting, and social media contact usually occur between former foster parents and the child at a frequency that they arrange mutually. We recommend that foster parents maintain regular contact with the child within any guidelines set by adoptive parents.

On the other hand, former foster parents do not have to be available 24/7. Boundaries around frequency of contact might be set with warmth and preferably during an in-person visit (or at least on a phone call) since written messages can't communicate emotional tone and are subject to misinterpretation, especially by children with a history of loss and trauma.

During these periods of contact, children may complain to foster parents about their adoptive parents. These complaints partially arise out of real day-to-day concerns but also out of many psychological concerns. Some of these might be the child:

- wanting to reunite with the foster parent;

- wanting to pull the foster parents onto their side against the adoptive parents;

- expecting relationships to fail based on their history and trying to have some control over this by sabotaging the relationship with the adoptive parents;

- being traumatically triggered by some aspect of the adoptive home or the adoptive parents; or

- hiding pain through their anger at the adoptive parents.

Foster parents would validate the difficult feelings but if the child presses them, then redirect the child towards the need to solve the problem with the adoptive parents. Foster parents should not take sides, even though it may be very tempting.

Contact between foster parents and adoptive parents

In-person contact often occurs between adoptive parents and foster parents in situations where children have in-person contact with foster parents. This can be quite important and meaningful, but it is rarely needed under other circumstances. Although not needed, many adoptive and foster parents become friends during transitions and may choose to continue in-person contacts.

Other types of contact, especially phone calls, can allow adoptive parents to use the foster parents as a resource in understanding the meaning and function of the child's behavior and identifying effective methods of response. In addition, foster parents can be updated about the child and ask questions in an easy back-and-forth.

Adoptive parents sharing photos via social media or texting can also be meaningful to foster parents, as it is another way for them to keep up with the child's life. It is useful to keep former foster parents updated about major events in the child's life so that they can be an informed resource and as a way to demonstrate respect for them as individuals who have loved the child.

Cold Feet about Post-Move Contact

The plan for post-move contacts between the child and foster parents is usually finalized before the move. Sometimes foster or adoptive parents want to change that plan last minute because of some change in their lives or a change of heart (Boswell & Cudmore, 2014; Sinclair et al., 2005).

Foster parents may anticipate that it will be too painful for them to see the child again. They may also feel too busy getting a new child settled into their home. They may feel the transition has been a huge burden already and they are ready for it to be done; this feeling may be a stand-in for some other reasons or it may not be. They may have second thoughts about the adoptive parents for whatever reason and not want to continue contact with them. Foster parents may also wonder how to occupy the role of extended family for the child; there are no socially approved ways to make that transition from primary caregiver to a kind of "auntie and uncle." It may also be a combination of these reasons or some other reason.

The hesitance about post-move contact can also originate with the adoptive parents. They may be responding to the child's resistance to contact with the foster parents; children may avoid their prior caregivers as a way to try to avoid the pain of the loss. Adoptive parents may also want to focus on their happier-ever-after future with this child and want to not think about the child's traumatic past and avoid the foster parents as part of that focus on the future. Adoptive parents may have a surge in protectiveness now the child is in their home and may start to view the foster parents as a "threat"; e.g. "It will upset the child too much." or "The foster parents won't want to let go." or "We have to protect our privacy."

Many reasons of foster and adoptive parents to reduce or avoid post-move contact fall in a category of anxious anticipation. It is important to remember that just because we have a thought that some interaction might go poorly does not make that a certain reality. Instead, the anticipated potential complications can be a reason for communication between adoptive and foster parents to work out how to handle them.

Regardless of the adults' concerns, the child needs these post-move contacts to solidify the sense that they are valued by the foster parents even when not living with them and are not forgotten (Neil, Young & Hartley, 2018; Swain, 2016). The post-move contact also gives the child a sense that relationships are not disposable and will continue and so the child will invest in them emotionally. Many times foster and adoptive parents can work out these issues regarding post-move contact on their own. If they are not able to, then it is the caseworker's role to explore the basis both practical and emotional for wanting to make a change and also to mediate and create a plan for the post-move contact to occur.

Diego - 5 years | Fernanda visits

Diego had a brief phone call with Fernanda the evening after the move because he wanted to tell her about having eggs and waffles for dinner. Breakfast for dinner was a revelation to Diego. He was also thrilled that Sue and Joan had his favorite brand of salsa to put on the eggs. As he was saying goodbye, he told Fernanda that he missed her and loved her and Fernanda echoed those sentiments back to him. After the call ended, he cried a little and Joan took him to the calendar in his room so he could count down the days until Fernanda would visit him—only three more. Diego was busy getting to know his new teacher, classmates, and neighbors—so many people in such a short period of time. Both Sue's and Joan's parents wanted to come and visit and meet their new grandson but

Sue and Joan put them off to let Diego settle more. Sue and Joan also started to learn soccer terminology and rules from Diego as they watched Real Madrid soccer games on television. (Fernanda had let them know that Real Madrid is Diego's favorite team in the world.)

The day for Fernanda's visit finally arrived. As the time drew near, Diego ran back and forth between the windows in Sue and Joan's house looking for the blue SUV that he knew so well as Fernanda's. He yelled, "She's here" and ran out the front door to greet her at the curb. Joan and Sue trailed after. All three of them gave Fernanda a welcoming hug. Diego grabbed Fernanda's hand and pulled her toward the house as he exclaimed, "My room—come see my new room." Fernanda dutifully toured with Diego as he pointed out his bed and desk and where he stored his Hot Wheels cars. After the tour was done, they all sat down at the dining room table for cookies (which Diego proudly reminded everyone that he had helped make). Fernanda asked about Diego's school and who his new friends might be. Diego, with the help of Joan and Sue, answered all of Fernanda's questions. Diego also wanted to know how some of the other kids in his old foster home were doing, even though it had only been five days (which felt quite long to

Diego). Towards the end of the visit, Diego asked, "Is anyone sleeping in my bed?"

Fernanda replied, "You are a smart boy, Diego. You remember that when one child leaves, another one comes. Yes—there is a new boy named Oscar in your old bed. He's a nice boy."

"Is he nicer than me?" asked Diego plaintively.

"There may be a new child in the house, Diego but you will always be in my heart." Diego and Fernanda hugged again, longer this time. Fernanda left a little while later.

Diego was quieter than usual for the rest of the day. Sue asked him about his feelings and he shrugged his shoulders. She suggested maybe he could draw something about his feelings. He got a piece of paper and drew a big heart on it and four human stick figures inside. He asked for Sue's help to label them as Diego, Fernanda, Sue, and Joan. He wanted to mail it to Fernanda because he was worried that he had not told her that she was in his heart and the drawing showed that. Sue agreed that they could mail it the next day. Before she put it in an envelope, though, she took a picture of it for Diego's Lifebook.

Isabella - 14 years | Sheila visits

Isabella acted as if contact with her former foster mother, Sheila, was of no great importance and that she might be too busy to be available for it with all the things she had to do to get settled. Isabella had lots of complaints about her new home and life. None of the kids at her school had any fashion sense; Julie wouldn't let her stay up late enough (although she was coming up with ways to sneak around that restriction); Julie didn't "treat her as an equal" often enough. Julie and Sheila worked out a time a week after moving day for an in-person visit. Sheila had sent a couple of texts before then and Isabella had responded curtly to one a day later.

When Sheila arrived, Julie asked Isabella if she wanted to give Sheila a tour of the house. Isabella replied, "Nah, It's just a typical house." Julie and Sheila started walking through the house without Isabella, who eventually rolled her eyes, got up, and trailed along. When they got to Isabella's room, Sheila admired the famous curtains and commented how well they went with the wall color. Isabella piped up then to point out the colors in the bedspread that also complemented the curtains. Sheila agreed and asked about the process of making the curtains and the stitching. Isabella warmed up and became more interactive with Sheila. They shared a lunch of grilled ham and cheese sandwiches on sourdough bread which Isabella pointed out is called a "croque monsieur" in France. Isabella was excited that her new school offered French as a language. Towards the end of the meal, Isabella asked "Who's the new girl in my room?"

"Do you really want to hear about her?" asked Sheila.

Isabella paused and thought for a second, "I guess not." Isabella paused again and said, "My therapist said I don't know what to do with you. Somebody that doesn't disappear."

Julie affirmed this for her. "Lots of people have disappeared."

"Yeah," replied Isabella. After a moment, she walked away without a word. Both Julie and Sheila looked at each other wondering who should go.

"It's your call," said Sheila to Julie.

"Let's give her a couple of minutes." replied Julie and they chatted some about Isabella's new school. Isabella came out a few minutes later and walked over to where Sheila was sitting. Sheila stood.

"Thank you for taking decent care of me and not forgetting me," said Isabella.

"You are unforgettable, Isabella," Sheila said with a smile.

Hakim - 18 months | Jane visits

LaRonda, Michael, and Jane had already set up a private social media group for the three of them before the move happened. Jane had seen pictures of Hakim on the plane and in his new home by the time of the video visit. Hakim cried when he saw Jane on the screen. When she began talking to him, he got even more distressed. The adults agreed to end the video call.

Jane continued to be updated about Hakim online, and over the course of video calls that LaRonda and Michael arranged, two-on-one, with Jane. During the calls, they caught her up and also asked some questions.

When Hakim was four years old, he got more interested in his Lifebook and started looking at it over and over. LaRonda and Michael were sure to highlight Jane when pictures of her came up. On one of their chats, LaRonda and Jane discovered they both had relatives in the Los Angeles area. They made a plan to have an in-person visit there.

Michael and LaRonda had brought Hakim's Lifebook with them on the trip to Los Angeles. They reviewed the pictures of Jane and said Hakim used to live with her. Hakim did not seem that interested in looking at the pictures of Jane. When Jane arrived at LaRonda and Michael's rental, Hakim was shy when he first saw her and hid behind LaRonda's leg. This was unusual for Hakim as he was often outgoing when meeting new people if his parents were present. Jane, LaRonda and Michael hugged and sat down and started chatting. Hakim climbed up on the couch behind Michael and put his arms around Michael's neck and looked right at Jane and said, "You're in my book." Jane agreed and Hakim got down and went and got the Lifebook and started looking at the pictures with all three of the adults. He saw a picture of himself throwing his ball back and forth in one of the visits and said, "That's my ball." He ran and got it out of his suitcase where his parents had packed it. Hakim started playing catch with it with all of the adults but he quickly grew bored with that and so a rather raucous game of soccer evolved with him and Jane against LaRonda and Michael. He gave Jane a big hug goodbye at the end of the visit and video calls resumed when everyone was back home.

Chapter 11

Sibling Groups

Keeping siblings together through the child welfare system is a top priority. These relationships are often the longest lasting in anyone's lifetime. Transitioning sibling groups is one of the most complex of adoptive transition scenarios. It often takes the longest because each child's process of forming an attachment to the adoptive parents and shifting their relationship with the foster parents needs to be respected and honored.

Potential complications of these transitions to be kept in mind

Siblings often occupy different levels of development and understanding of adoption and the transition process. Multiple children being adopted brings extra complexities and needs (see Table 4) to the planning. There will often need to be more planning meetings to deal with

Table 4

Complexities of Adopting a Sibling Group

- More communication is necessary with multiple children, with messages tailored to fit each child's ability to comprehend.
- Each child has a different understanding of what the process is about (i.e., living permanently in a new place with new people, changing caregivers).
- Each child has different thresholds of tolerance for longer visits (all day or overnight) and visits away from foster parents.
- Existing sibling dynamics (see below) may complicate an adoptive transition.
- Some children, but not others, are triggered by aspects of the transition process (i.e., a child who was sexually abused at bedtime becomes reactive on an overnight visit).
- One child may be much slower to attach and trust than another.
- If one child has significant special needs, this might impact the kinds of activities or length of visits that could be done with the sibling group as a whole. This dilemma requires extra planning and creativity to find activities that are inclusive.
- If there are video calls with adoptive parents, sibling groups sharing a screen is not recommended. Jealousy and competition and conflict is much reduced if each child has their own video call.
- Varying attachment, trauma and safety concerns of children in the sibling group may need to be addressed.

these complexities. Different adults on the team may be more concerned about the welfare of differing children. It can be challenging to balance the needs of children at multiple developmental levels, varying trauma/mental health needs, perhaps the children even have different sociocultural identities. There is no perfect solution - in sibling group transitions no child gets as accommodated as they would be if they were the only child being moved.

Mental health services for the sibling group

Even if some or all of the children have individual therapists, it can be extremely useful for the sibling group as a whole to have a therapist (e.g., Kothari, 2017; Linares et al., 2014; Tyndall-Lind, 2010) who helps them process the adoptive transition as a sibling unit and to manage their dynamics. The therapist should have experience with treating children in foster care and not be an already existing individual therapist for any of the children.

This therapeutic support can be art-based (e.g. each child drawing their view of the foster home they are leaving) or play-based (the children dressing up as adults and acting out a meeting they imagine where adults are making decisions about them) or talk-based (the children debriefing their latest visit with the adoptive parents and some jealousy that came up). The process of the adoptive transition can be a roller coaster for the sibling group with various siblings struggling more at different points. The therapist needs to have the ability to improvise what happens in the session based on what has happened since the prior session and which child or children are most in need.

Even before the transition process begins, every sibling group has its own set of dynamics (as mentioned in Table 4). These dynamics will be gone into detail for the benefit of therapists who may be assisting the sibling group; however, other audiences may benefit from having some awareness of them.

When parents are neglectful or abusive, a common adaptation by sibling groups is for one child (often the oldest) to act as a substitute parental figure for the other child or children (e.g., Jurkovic, 2014). This child has often been referred to as a parentified child. This pattern can also happen with an only child who acts as a substitute parent to their own parent(s). With a sibling group, the other children may resent the authority the parentified child attempts to have over them and the parentified child may resent the extra burden they are carrying and the other children's resistance to their efforts. In times of danger, whether real or perceived, the other children will often seek physical closeness and protection from the parentified child, who may also seek out the other children to make sure they are safe. These dynamics may get activated when the group is moving to a new level of visiting that feels, at least stressful, if not dangerous. The parentified child may interfere with the adoptive parents assuming a soothing or protecting role with a distressed child. Sometimes, the sibling group therapist can help to negotiate an arrangement between the parentified child and the adoptive parents to make sure all the children are safe but give a gradually increasing role for the adoptive parents to provide soothing and comforting.

Especially in families with sexually or physically abusive parents, siblings may become violent and/or sexual towards other children in the families (e.g., Linares, 2006; Tidefors et al., 2010). Hopefully, the foster parents have become experts in the level of supervision necessary to ensure all the children's safety and in how to most effectively respond to aggression and sexual activity when it is discovered. If so, they will be excellent guides for adoptive parents. In the sibling group sessions, issues of bodily safety need to be discussed. If children do not feel safe on visits with their siblings, then it will interfere with their forming trusting attachments with adoptive parents. The adoptive parents will be scrutinized by all the children for their ability to ensure safety and that is often a condition for moving to visits away from the foster parents. In the sibling group sessions, the children's sense of safety in the current foster home placement also need to be assessed. Sometimes, but not often, there is aggression or sexual activity going on that the foster parents are not aware of. This may not be directly revealed but the observant therapist may pick up cues. This needs to be addressed immediately, of course.

In sibling groups of three or more children, there may be short- or longer-lived alliances between two or more children that leave at least one other child feeling excluded. When birth parents have been emotionally neglectful and the children have felt a shortage of closeness and caring, then they may seek that from siblings. This can also emerge for children in foster care if they do not feel a sense of closeness with foster parents for whatever reason. These alliances can serve other purposes: to help some children feel special by creating feelings of being devalued or scapegoated in another child, to emphasize the difference between a child with special needs and other children in the family, to isolate one child who is seen as getting too much attention or resources from adults for whatever reason, etc. Sibling alliances can also develop naturally because two or more children are similar in age or gender or temperament or interests. Alliances show up in sibling group therapy sessions by who sits next to who, who sides with who in disputes, who interrupts who, and the like. Structural family therapy interventions (Fishman & Minuchin, 1981), like shifting seating patterns or assigning two children to work together, can be tried to change up the pattern.

Just as with the adoptive parents, the siblings may compete for the therapist's attention, try to be the therapist's favorite, or get another sibling in trouble. This parallel dynamic of the siblings competing for the attention of the adoptive parents and the sibling group therapist provides an opportunity for the therapist to work with the children about their sense of scarcity of love and attention to go around.

The sibling group therapist will also often be a consultant to the planning committee about the transition process, especially when there are hiccups. If any of the children have individual therapists, those therapists can help the planning committee understand at a deep level what is going on with that child. The sibling group therapist will be able to provide insights about the relationships between the children and how they are shifting with each phase of the adoptive transition; e.g., is the parentified child getting more controlling as the sibling group is about to do their first overnight visit? Ideally, the sibling group therapist is a member of the planning committee.

Staggered transition

Moving all the children at the same time is the default option. In one British study, 34 of 37 sibling groups were moved together (Saunders & Selwyn, 2010). There are some circumstances that may lead the planning committee to consider moving one child before the others. Ask yourselves:

- Is one child more fragile and in need of time as the adoptive parents' only child before other children proceed?

- Is one child (usually the oldest) a secondary source of safety and could they, if they went first, provide that for the other children as they transition to the adoptive home?

- Does the child welfare agency policy mandate that all the children move together, or is there discretion in decision-making allowed?

- If children in the sibling group are in different foster homes, the readiness of their respective foster parents to participate in a child-centered adoptive transition process may vary.

- Is one child behaving so disruptively in the foster home that foster parents feel that child has to move first in order to avoid disrupting their foster placement?

- The sibling group is so large that the team believes it will be too unwieldy to expect adoptive parents to integrate such a large group all at once.

Some children may need to be adopted later than their siblings for a variety of practical reasons, including that the children

- are in jail or juvenile detention;

- are in a residential or day treatment program that the team feels they need to complete;

- are in a distant foster home and so will require a different process (see section below on long distance transitions;) or

- the child(ren) temporarily needs medical treatment that requires proximity to a certain medical facility or the skills of a medical foster parent.

Ultimately, this decision is ideally made by the planning committee as a whole rather than just by the caseworker even if that is the caseworker's formally identified role. Every option will have pros and cons and can be second guessed. It is a judgment call that needs to be made on a case-by-case basis. Additional scenarios pertaining to staggered transitions are reviewed in detail later.

Moving a sibling group together

Each new step is taken first by children individually. For instance, each child would have a 2-3 hour visit alone with the adoptive parents before the full sibling group has a 2-3 hour visit. No child takes the next step until all the children have mastered the previous step. Foster parents would continue debriefing each step in the transition process with each child individually, *and* as a full sibling group to help the children develop their shared   reality.

The siblings who feel ready to move on with the transition may try to "reassure" or "push" a child who is unsure about a step in the transition process (e.g., being with adoptive parents without the foster parents present) to move the process forward more quickly. If this occurs, it needs to be addressed with the sibling group by the foster parents and/or the siblings' therapist. The sibling group would be reminded that they are in this together. All of them have felt scared or nervous at times in their lives. If this "pushing" is a reiteration of past bullying, then this needs to be addressed with the child doing the coercing.

During the post-transition phase, reverse visitation with the foster parents does not have to happen as a group even if the rest of the transition has happened as a group. A particular child may have a greater need to see the former foster parents by themselves at least once. Regardless, the full group would reverse-visit at least once so the children can all show the foster parents their new rooms, etc. Reverse visitation by children one by one allows for them each and the foster parent to process the change in their relationship without having to deal with the sibling context for that visit at least.

One child or more in the sibling group may become activated (aggressive, dissociated, panicky, and/or hyperactive) by a step in the transition process. This will often activate other children in the sibling group through behavioral contagion and/or trauma triggering. First, provide emotional safety and containment for the activated child by the foster parent based on methods that have previously worked for this child. Another caregiver in the foster home would contain the other children. If this occurs while children are with adoptive parents, then the adoptive parents need to carefully consider their options.

1. *If the adoptive parents <u>do not</u> feel they know the children well enough to contain the child who was initially activated <u>and</u>* attend to the other children, transport the children back to the foster home ASAP if it is safe to do so, while reassuring the children that they are on the way to the foster home.

2. *If it is an urgent situation and transporting the group of children feels unsafe,* it may be necessary for the adoptive parents to contact the foster parents and have them come to where the adoptive parents and children are. This is a rare situation. While the foster parent is in transit, have them on speakerphone talking with the children to help them calm down. When the foster parent arrives, it may be advisable for some children to ride with foster parents and some with the adoptive parents back to the foster home.

Foster parents would debrief with the child—and with the sibling group—after the child has calmed. Quickly, the planning committee needs to debrief and consider staying on the current step longer, taking a step back in the transition process, or proceeding as planned.

Another issue is if one or more of the children "bonds" very quickly with one or more of the adoptive parents, claims them as their own, and resists sharing them with siblings. This bonding is not a healthy attachment but an emotional grabbing-onto. If there is a therapist for the sibling group, then this would be the focus for some sessions. This may raise some or all of the following dilemmas:

- The child who has bonded with an adoptive parent may jealously—or even aggressively—try to push siblings away from having physical and/or emotional contact with that adoptive parent.

- They may become angry with the adoptive parent and feel betrayed if that parent shows interest or warmth towards another child (a sibling or other child already in the adoptive home).

- Siblings may resent and become jealous of the apparently close connection between the child and the adoptive parent and try to drive a wedge between them or intrusively seek contact with the parent.

- Adoptive parents can feel pressured to take sides by their reactions to the children's adversarial interactions. This is a natural reaction to the emotional pressures of the situation—one that needs to be surfaced and discussed.

Adoptive parents need to communicate a message through words and actions that there is enough love for everybody and that nobody will go without love. It will take long after the transition is over for the children to fully take this in and believe it fully.

Impacts on adoptive parents' state of mind/well-being when moving children together

Adopting more than one child at a time presents challenges and opportunities for adoptive parents and families to keep in mind, and these adoptive parents' issues can also affect the children being adopted. Some of these dynamics can also occur when adopting a single child but are more likely with a sibling group. If there is more than one adoptive parent, there may be comparisons between adoptive parents made by the children, which is natural. A child can find one adoptive parent easier to bond with, understand, manage, follow a routine with, and so on. This can lead to conflict and/or jealousy between adoptive parents. The children will inevitably sense these actual comparisons about them being made by adoptive parents during the transition even without witnessing them.

Children being adopted will also have their own conscious and unconscious fantasies of adoptive parents' views of themselves and of their siblings. These fantasies may include which child is the most loved or which child is going to be ejected out of the family. These fantasies are based on factors including:

- actual differences in how the adoptive parents interact with the varying children;

- differences in how the adoptive parents think and feel about the children regardless of whether they're aware of those reactions or that they may be exhibiting them; or

- differences in the relationship and trauma histories among the children, which leads to the children's fantasies about what thoughts and feelings the adoptive parents are having about them.

Hopefully the children individually, or as a sibling group, have therapists that can help them process their fantasies and not solely act them out. Adoptive parents will inevitably be affected by the children believing and subtly or not so subtly communicating these fantasies.

There are also increased practical burdens on adoptive parents of moving all the children at once that may seem obvious but can be lost in the hubbub of so much going on at once.

- Furnishing all of the children's new bedrooms to a similar state.
- Buying additional furniture and household items as needed (e.g., larger dining room table, seating for the living or family room, dishes, and even larger appliances).
- Ensuring that the adoptive parent's vehicle(s) can comfortably hold all children, including their car seats, at the same time.
- Organizing all of the children's new school registrations, child care placements, pediatric healthcare relationships, sports or arts activities, ongoing therapy appointments, etc.

Impacts on foster parents' state of mind/well-being when moving children together

When a sibling group moves from the same foster home, this can have a pronounced impact on the foster parents, in addition to the usual impacts of a single foster child leaving their care. The combinations of the varied grief responses the foster parents have for each child can exacerbate the impact and make it harder for foster parents to cope and not shut down emotionally. This places a heavy emotional load on foster parents as they support each child to process their grief about all of their changing relationships simultaneously.

Whenever a child leaves a foster home, the remaining foster children can have a variety of emotional and behavioral impacts; this can be exacerbated when multiple children leave together placing even more onto the foster parents' plate also to deal with.

Historically, child welfare agencies have not supported foster parents well with grief and loss issues as has been noted previously. Support options for foster parents include:

- foster parents can seek out their own support through other foster parents they are friends with or their own therapists;

- child welfare agencies or local foster parent associations can offer foster parent support groups or foster parent mentors; and

- child welfare agencies might also include supporting foster parents with grief and loss issues as part of the jobs for foster parent certifiers.

Moving one or more children before other children in a sibling group

Moving one or more children before the rest of a sibling group has an impact on the process for child-centered adoption as described previously. While the child(ren) leaving first are informed of the upcoming adoption, the rest of the children in that biological sibling group need to be simultaneously informed of their siblings' adoption and reassured that they too will also be adopted into the same home with a developmentally appropriate explanation for this process.

To minimize jealousy and acting out, schedule each child's visits with the adoptive parents while the other siblings are not present (perhaps at school) unless the other children are too young to fully understand.

Other steps in the transition process need to be done with sensitivity for the children in the sibling group not yet being adopted. Although they have been told verbally that they will be adopted soon, they have good reasons to mistrust what grown-ups say. There can be a tendency to take more care with the transition of the first child(ren) being moved than the children moving later. This is analogous to the firstborn child being photographed more than their younger siblings. This must be guarded against given how important the adoption transition process is to the lifelong narrative of each child.

The therapy for the sibling group is especially important when one of the children is transitioning before the other children. The separation of the children can stir up jealousies and fears among any of the children about what dangers or treats might be happening with the other children. In the joint therapy sessions, it can be useful for the children to give voice to the imaginings they have had about other children when separated. Younger children might act out these imaginings with family figures in a doll house.

Overnight visits when one or more children are moving first

For the child(ren) moving first, overnight visits involve not just a bigger separation from the foster parents but also from siblings. Although children in foster homes have separate bedrooms, children from sibling groups may sneak into each other's beds in the middle of the night for comfort. This is discouraged because of the potential for abuse, but children are creative in accomplishing this. Thus, all the children—whether they're in the adoptive home or back in the foster home—may feel a loss from this lack of access to co-sleeping with a sibling.

Bedtime routines in the adoptive home may involve the same sequence as they do in the foster home, but the absence of some siblings may make it feel weird. This can be especially true if the children perform affectionate rituals with each other like good night hugs or kisses or prayers.

Moving days when one or more children are moving first

Moving day, and the special rituals and ceremonies around it, make all the separations very real both for the child(ren) moving and the children staying behind. Honoring all of the children's varying feelings and giving them room for expression helps minimize (but not eliminate) the acting out. We recommend the following tangible steps towards that end:

- Make and display a visible photocopy of the current month's calendar in the foster home, with important dates clearly marked (including moving day, first visit between the foster parents and remaining children etc.). Foster homes would have children mark this off in a daily ritual, so they may visually keep track of when these important days are coming. This is an opportunity for foster parents to facilitate discussion about the process.

- Take special photographs of each child leaving with each sibling remaining and display them in each child's bedroom (in the foster home and/or adoptive home).

- Invite the remaining children to draw a picture (if old enough) for the departing child(ren) leaving to take.

- Foster parents can help children discuss some favorite memories of joint fun activities that have occurred while they were all in the foster home. This ideally would occur while the adoptive parents are present, so they can listen and learn. Adoptive parents can also contribute by imagining, with the children, some fun activities for all the children to do together when they are reunited in the adoptive home later on.

- Ideally, each remaining child in the foster home gets a hug from each departing child when they are outside moving toward the adoptive parents' vehicle. For some children, this can bring up feelings more intense than they can handle, causing them to resist or run from the interaction. The hugs should not be forced. The children will see each other soon at the first visit after moving day.

In-person visits with former foster parents when one or more children are moving first

Earlier, I recommended that the first visit after moving day occur in the adoptive home and only include the foster parents. However, this first reverse visit would be different when moving is staggered. The remaining siblings in the foster home would join, to help reassure the whole sibling group that all the children are surviving and that the sibling relationships are being valued. Because the children still in the foster home have not started their process formally, this visit would generally be in a neutral site (e.g., park, playground, etc.) instead of the adoptive home, so that their experience of the adoptive home can occur at the appropriate moment in their own transition process. However, there may be times when, for certain children, these visits can occur in the adoptive home.

While determining when to start the adoptive transition for the remaining children, try to create balance between helping the adoptive parents bond effectively with the child who was moved first and continuing the transition of the remaining children. Use the earlier transition as an opportunity for the planning committee to assess progress and determine when

to start the transitions for the remaining children.

As much as possible, adoptive parents would continue bonding with the first-arriving children *and* support the transition process of remaining children simultaneously. Towards that end, we recommend beginning the transition process for the remaining children *after* the first all-day visit of the child(ren) who have moved first.

If the bonding process between the adoptive parents and the first child(ren) begins going poorly after the move, there are additional considerations. This may be indicated in the following ways:

- the child is actively rejecting the adoptive parents;

- the child is frequently and intensely distressed about missing the foster parents;

- the child is exhibiting major regression in developmental functioning; or

- the child is exhibiting dangerous behaviors toward self or other children in the home or the adoptive parents.

When any of these behaviors are presented, the transition of the other children would be delayed while intensive efforts are made to understand what is happening in the attachment process between the adoptive parents and the child(ren) who are new in their home. Visits among the transitioned child in the adoptive home, the remaining siblings, and foster parents would continue.

Moving one or more children first has impacts on the children, especially confusion. The adults' reasons for making this choice often are complex, nuanced, and difficult to explain to children in developmentally appropriate ways. The words likely won't stick given the emotional stakes involved. Children (both those remaining or leaving the foster home) will imaginatively construct their own scenarios. Some potential ones include:

- The departing child(ren) will be permanently separated from the other children.

- The adoptive parents selected the departing child(ren) first because they are better and are loved more and the remaining children are inferior, bad, or damaged.

- The adoptive parents are reuniting the departing child(ren) with birth parents or other, fantasized parents (royalty, aliens, etc.).

- Adoptive parents are taking the departing child(ren) in order to do bad things to them.

- Foster parents are sending that child(ren) away first as a punishment for a bad deed that may be vague or specifically identified in the children's fantasies. The remaining children are vigilant to not commit the bad deed themselves.

Ideally, these fantasies would get discussed in sibling group therapy. These fantasies may be different for different children and may evolve over the course of the adoptive transition and so need to get revisited in the therapy.

The occasions when adoptive parents arrive to pick up and take the child(ren) for a visit or drop them back off can be very activating for all the children and lead to them acting out, competing for the foster parents' and/or adoptive parents' attention, regression, and chaos; this can spread to other children in the foster home who may not be in the sibling group. If this occurs, the foster parents and adoptive parents will need to consult and create a detailed plan for pickup and/or drop-off.

Once the focus has shifted to the later children, and the adoptive parents are visiting with them, the child(ren) who moved first may feel less prioritized if, for example, they are left with a babysitter while the adoptive parents are out with the other children in the sibling group. This is not recommended; try to schedule these visits while the child that moved first is in school or normally occurring child care.

Impacts on foster parents' state of mind/well-being when one or more children are moving first

The children who are adopted later usually exhibit some level of acting out that foster parents have to deal with. Sometimes there is just more chaos, and sometimes the acting out is directed specifically at the child(ren) being adopted. Possible reasons for this include:

- jealous aggression toward the transitioned child(ren);

- clinging to the transitioned child(ren) out of fear for their safety in the adoptive family;
- sadness/longing at the transitioned child(ren)'s absence; and
- misunderstanding that the separation from that child(ren) is permanent despite adults' assurances to the contrary

The process of staggered adoptive transitions is lengthened for the foster parents and can feel like it is going on for far too long. They may experience it as an endless succession of losses. The foster parents can be challenged if a new child enters the foster home when the first child(ren) leaves. In those scenarios, they are attempting to bond with the new child(ren) while processing the loss of the subsequent children to leave from the sibling group. Ideally, new children do not enter the foster home until all of the sibling group have completed their transition out of the home.

Impacts on adoptive parents state of mind/well-being when one or more children are moving first

This scenario poses its own attachment challenges for the adoptive parents in that they are, of course, attaching intensely to the first child(ren) to move, yet aware that subsequent children are also coming, and under the belief that they need to reserve something for those children (even though love doesn't work that way).

Initial visits with the foster parents and the child(ren) that are moving first would occur without the other children around. During later visits, if the other children in the sibling group act out when the adoptive parents arrive, foster parents would manage this in ways they are familiar with. Instead of acting out, other children in the sibling group may approach the adoptive parents and try to engage. This requires some serious juggling on the adoptive parents' part, in that they are trying to hold all of the following goals:

- communicate a special focus on the first child(ren) to move;

- communicate their interest and warmth to the other children in the sibling group, who may be jostling for and competing for the adoptive parents' attention; and

- keep the process of picking up the child(ren) to a reasonable length of time (15 minutes might be a goal) to avoid difficulty and disruption for the foster home.

If there are two adoptive parents, both would come in for picking up the child(ren) to ease the juggling.

Scenario of sibling group transitioning

This scenario has a family of three children. In the first half of the scenario, the oldest child will transition first with the two younger children staying behind in the foster home. The second half of the scenario will be about the two younger children transitioning together as a group.

Brett, Krissy, and Maggie are, respectively, 7, 4 and 2 years old. They are all white. The two oldest have been in the current foster home for three years and Maggie has been in it since shortly after her birth. Brett and Krissy were removed because of physical abuse and neglect by their substance-abusing mother and father. Maggie was removed because her mother kept returning to the physically abusive father of the two older children. Brett is pleasant and polite with adults but in a superficial manner. He will be physically affectionate if it is requested of him but he rarely initiates that warmth. His foster mother has never seen him have an intense emotion. She has witnessed him be coercive and physically hurtful with his two younger siblings when he thinks he is not being watched, in order to get them to do what he wants. His behavior and performance are fine at school although he has no close friends. Brett has a therapist, Ms. Jenkins, whom he has been seeing for about a year. He has not been on any medication.

Krissy was prenatally exposed to methamphetamine and has symptoms consistent with ADHD although she has not been formally diagnosed and has not been on any medication. She often provokes her brother and resents his controlling behavior. She is jealous of her younger sister and wishes that she could have all of their foster mother's attention. She is affectionate with the foster mother but can also seek out strangers in stores for hugs.

Maggie appears to be securely attached to the foster mother, seeking her out for affection and comfort but also able to play independently for short periods of time. She has stranger anxiety around new people and can be clingy in those situations. Neither Krissy or Maggie have ever been in therapy.

The foster mother, Sharon, has been providing foster care for 23 years and has been through many transitions of children out of her home. She is white. She is a widow and employs two women in their twenties to help her during the day. The adoptive parents are Ryan and Opal and they are also white. They are in their early 30s and have been married for five years. They have no children in their home. Ryan and Opal live in the same city as Sharon. The caseworker is Mr. Gray; he has been a caseworker for 13 years. He has been these children's caseworker for the last four months and is the fourth caseworker they've had in the last three years. Parental rights have been terminated for these children.

Brett's transition begins

The planning committee consisted of Mr. Gray (the caseworker), Sharon (the foster mother), Ryan and Opal (the adoptive parents), and Ms. Jenkins (Brett's therapist). The committee met and, after talking some about the situation, agreed that they felt Brett should move first before his sisters. It was felt that Brett would not attach well to the adoptive parents while focused on his younger siblings and that Krissy would ignore her own process of attachment to interfere with Brett's.

Ms. Jenkins, Brett's therapist, talked with the committee about Brett and how moving him first versus with his sisters might play out given his psychological make-up. Ms. Jenkins described Brett as a boy who did still crave loving contact with adults deep down but he was very guarded against further loss, abuse, and disappointment by adult caregivers. His most significant form of interpersonal contact, in her view, was trying to control his sisters' behavior, which, in his mind, was a way to protect them. He used physically hurtful strategies that he internalized from his parents. Sharon, the foster mother, added that both Krissy and Maggie seemed more relaxed when Brett was off at school. All the adults agreed that both Brett and Krissy might resist the plan to adopt them at different times. The planning committee also decided that Krissy and Maggie would go through each step of the transition together so that Krissy's presence could help Maggie feel safer. Mr. Gray presented this plan and the rationale to his supervisor, who agreed with it.

The next step was talking with the children. Brett's therapist coached Sharon about responding to his potential negative reactions, and advised her to tell him in a one-on-one conversation, which she did, in the backyard the next day. His initial reaction was to declare that he couldn't leave his sisters for visits. Sharon acknowledged that he was worried about his sisters' well-being like a good big brother but that the visits would be in the foster home initially and her assistant, whom he knew well, would be with his sisters the whole time in a different part of the house. Brett begrudgingly agreed (at least consciously) that it couldn't hurt to meet these new adults.

Krissy and Maggie were told, with the help of some dolls, on the morning of the first visit. The message was that there were grown-ups that were going to be meeting them and eventually they and Brett would live with them and that Brett would meet them first. Maggie did not seem to *understand much of this, as was expected. Krissy was upset that Brett got to meet the new people first but was appeased by the idea of getting to play with Sharon's young assistant without Brett around.*

Before the first visit, Sharon went out to lunch with Ryan and Opal. The couple had lots of questions about all three of the children and what they were like. They also planned a little bit of the first visit: what Sharon would tell Brett about them, cues that Sharon would use to let them know to wrap the visit up, etc. Ryan and Opal also talked with Ms. Jenkins on the phone about how he might react to them. She emphasized that, although he might appear to be pleasant and liking them on the outside, inside he was quite likely to feel distrustful or numb about them, and unconsciously quite scared of them. Ryan and Opal felt somewhat overwhelmed, like that they were about to jump in the deep end of the pool, but it helped to talk to each other and their pastor about their fears.

The first visit was planned for a Saturday morning. Sharon had been counting down the days with Brett on a calendar in his room. Brett went into his bedroom to play with Legos just before Ryan and Opal were due to arrive. He left his bedroom door open and sat with his back to the door but with a view of the doorway in his mirror. His sisters were at the playground at a nearby park with Sharon's assistant. Sharon called out that Mr. and Mrs. Anderson had arrived but Brett did not answer. When the grown-ups appeared in the doorway, Brett stood up and held out his hand for a handshake. Ryan and Opal shook his hand.

Ryan commented, "Looks like you are quite the Lego guy."

Brett asked, "Would you like to play with me?"

Sharon suggested, "Let's all play Legos together."

The three adults sat down with Brett around the pile of Legos. Brett quickly took apart the car he had built, added those Legos back to the pile and then pushed a quantity of Legos to each adult. In doing so, he left himself very few Legos.

"You're so good at sharing, Brett. You don't have many left. I'll share some back with you," said Opal as she pushed some Legos back to Brett. Each of the adults shared some Legos back to Brett. Brett looked at Opal out of the corner of his eye but did not say anything to her.

"What should we build, Brett?" asked Sharon.

"Don't know. What would you like to build, Mr. Anderson? We could do that." replied Brett.

Ryan thought for a moment and replied, "Maybe we could build a house together. We could each build a wall and then join them together."

They all agreed. As they all started building their walls, Brett kept an eye on the adults' walls and when a grown-up needed a piece and was looking for it, he would quickly offer the needed piece from his own pile. As a result, Brett's wall was only halfway built by the time the adults finished their walls. Brett realized this and looked embarrassed and quickly finished his wall. They put the four walls onto a Lego base and then Brett giggled.

"What's funny, Brett? asked Opal.

"There's no door." answered Brett. The adults realized Brett was right. They had built four walls and none of them had a door. As the adults laughed, Brett looked at their faces and cracked a small smile.

"What should we do, Brett?" asked Opal. Brett looked at the four walls carefully and quickly spotted which wall had a section where it was easy to take out a few blocks and create an opening for a door.

"Way to go, Brett." exclaimed Ryan.

"Thank you, Mr. Anderson." replied Brett, rather formally.

Sharon remarked, "We haven't done the roof yet but I think it's time for the Andersons to go, Brett."

"Okay." Brett jumped up and held out his hand to shake goodbye. Opal and Ryan shook his hand and said their good-byes.

As they were about to leave, Brett blurted out, "I'll save the house in my closet so my sisters don't ruin it."

"Good idea, Brett." said Sharon.

When Sharon, Ryan, and Opal talked later that night, Ryan and Opal commented how formal Brett seemed and that they couldn't tell if he liked them at all. Sharon reassured them that Brett had agreed to seeing them again and that it was clear to her he'd valued the meeting because he saved the Lego house. Evidently, Brett usually tore apart his Lego creations soon after he finished them before his sisters could get to them. Sharon also reported that Brett had not mentioned their visit at all to his sisters, even after Krissy tried to provoke him with tales of how much fun she and Maggie had at the park with Sharon's aide.

Subsequent visits at the foster home went smoothly, although Brett stayed formal with Ryan and Opal. When he was told that on the next visit, he would go out to lunch with Ryan and Opal at a restaurant two blocks *away, Brett seemed to shut down. When Sharon asked if there was anything wrong or if he had any questions, he just shook his head "no". Sharon warned Ryan and Opal of this reaction before the visit. Ryan and Opal had just entered Sharon's home when Krissy dashed up from the basement where she had been playing with her sister and one of Sharon's aides. She ran to Ryan and wrapped herself around one of his legs and started crying and yelling "Me go too. Me go too." The aide came in the room and apologized; she was holding Maggie who then started crying herself in response to her sister. Brett volunteered, "It's okay with me if she comes." Sharon talked with Krissy and tried to convince her that the fun activities at the house were going to be better than going with Brett but to no avail. Ryan and Opal were wide-eyed, but stayed out of the negotiations. Sharon made the decision and canceled the visit for that day.*

The rescheduled lunch turned into a brunch the next day while Krissy and Maggie were at the grocery store with the aide—a favorite outing. After his sisters left, Brett was told about the visit.

Sharon said, "Do you remember how we had to cancel lunch with Mr. and Mrs. Anderson yesterday?"

"Yeah...?"

"Well, they're coming over soon to take you out to eat." explained Sharon.

"Okay. Are my sisters going to be okay without me?" asked Brett.

"Yes. They'll be back from the store soon and you will see them as soon as you are back home. You will all be back together soon, Brett."

Brett willingly walked two blocks with Ryan and Opal to brunch at a neighborhood restaurant he had been to many times. One of his favorite aspects of this restaurant was that they had big sheets of brown paper as "tablecloths" and he got crayons to draw with. He drew a stove with a pan on the stove with a burner flame underneath the pan. This drawing evolved into the whole stove catching fire and disappearing behind a wall of flame. When Ryan asked what happened in the drawing, Brett shrugged his shoulders. Ryan and Opal tried to engage Brett in conversation but Brett gave such short answers that it felt more like an interrogation. Ryan and Opal switched gears and drew fire engines spraying water on the fire and then Brett drew a flow of water turning into a stream that flowed to the table's edge right in front of Ryan. Ryan exclaimed with mock horror, "Oh no, I've wet my pants!" which made Brett smile. The food arrived to *everyone's relief. A short while later a piece of waffle dripping with syrup dropped off Brett's fork and onto his shirt. Brett looked down at it and burst into tears. Opal and Ryan both tried to reassure Brett, but he was not easily soothed. Eventually, Opal asked if this felt like too much to stay at the restaurant and Brett nodded his head "Yes." They paid the bill and walked back to the foster home. Ryan offered to carry Brett. The boy declined, but he did hold both Ryan's and Opal's hands during the walk back.*

During the debrief on the phone that night, Ryan and Opal were concerned about how their visit with Brett had gone and how the previous day had gone as well. Sharon agreed that Brett was struggling and reported that he had not wanted to talk to her about the visit at the restaurant. She suggested that they all meet with the caseworker, Mr. Gray, and Brett's therapist, Ms. Jenkins, and review how the transition was going.

During a video conference call a few days later, Ms. Jenkins presented her sense that Brett was being typical Brett: self-protective, guarded, trying to please. She felt the scene in the restaurant was a step forward because Brett made a mistake (dropped the food on his shirt) that he was scared the adults would be very mad about. He then was overwhelmed and cried which he did not want to do because it made him feel even more vulnerable and, in his mind, even more of a target for adult anger. Ms. Jenkins went on to explain that Brett's fears were disconfirmed when Ryan and Opal were not angry and instead were empathic and took action to help him get to a safer place, his foster home. The fact that Brett held Ryan and Opal's hands was also a good sign that he had some trust in them as safe people according to Ms. Jenkins. She cautioned them that Brett would still be guarded most of the time but that they might see some more openings over time. Ryan and Opal asked for suggestions about how to proceed. Ms. Jenkins suggested a picnic with finger food in a park, which she thought would be less stressful than a sit-down meal at a restaurant. Sharon suggested that she knew Brett liked grapes, Ritz cracker sandwiches with peanut butter in the middle, and turkey jerky. Ryan and Opal weren't sure they would eat all three of those foods in one sitting but they were fine with that as a menu.

The picnic went well and Brett, Ryan and Opal played frisbee afterwards with all of them dropping it a lot and laughing. Subsequent one-hour and half-day activities went well with Ryan and Opal focusing on activities that Brett would likely do better than they would based on advice from Ms. Jenkins. Their comfort with their own mistakes and losses helped to signal to Brett that they would be comfortable with him when he was less than "perfect".

Full day visits were a step up for Brett that seemed fine for him. Krissy and Maggie showed more concern at the length of time Brett was gone. Maggie would ask for Brett in an anxious voice. Krissy also asked for Brett in a way that seemed less out of her usual jealousy and more out of anxiety. A check-in video call was built into the whole-day visits where Brett would update Krissy about what he was doing and Sharon emphasized that he would be home for dinner. These calls helped Maggie and Krissy be less anxious but did stir up Krissy's jealousy again. Sharon assured Krissy that she would have her own turn with Ryan and Opal, but this didn't seem to make an impact on her.

Krissy was generally acting out more in the foster home and the strategies that Sharon had used in the past were less effective. Sharon herself was feeling more frustrated with Krissy. Sharon talked about this frustration with her best friend who noted that Sharon had often had children in the past who were hard to handle and Sharon had not become this much more frustrated. In this conversation, Sharon realized that she had had fantasies of adopting Maggie even though she knew that was not realistic given Sharon's age and that she did not want to adopt Krissy or Brett. Sharon could let in her sadness that had been building since the beginning of the transition. She felt more clarity about responding to Krissy after recognizing her sadness.

Brett, Krissy, and Maggie all expressed anxiety in their own way at the idea of Brett spending an overnight with Ryan and Opal. This reaction from the three children caused the planning committee to have another meeting—this time in person with Ryan, Opal, Sharon, and Mr. Gray. Ms. Jenkins couldn't make the meeting and it was felt that a good plan could be formed without direct input from her (although she did share some thoughts with Mr. Gray). Recognizing that this anxiety made perfect sense from the children's points of view, the team came up with a plan to help address some of the children's concerns. The first overnight visit for Brett would be delayed for a couple of weeks while Ryan and Opal started the process of visiting with Krissy and Maggie. The goal was to help the girls get to know Ryan and Opal and to show them that they were safe people to take care of Brett for an evening. During this interim period, Brett still had full-day visits with Ryan and Opal. He also had an interesting conversation with Sharon. Based on some advice from Ms. Jenkins, Sharon mentioned that, not only would Krissy and Maggie miss him when he had an overnight visit with Ryan and Opal, but she would miss him too and would think about how he was doing. Brett got tears in his eyes and ran to his room. This was the most sign of an attachment that she had seen to her in the time he was in her home. After a few minutes, she followed him to his room but he refused to talk or look at her.

A plan was also made for dropping Brett off at Ryan and Opal's house, which included Sharon and Krissy accompanying them to see where her brother would be staying. Sharon and Krissy would also see what would be Krissy's eventual bedroom and Sharon would take some photos. Krissy was invited to take one item back to Sharon's house to remember her bedroom. This is way earlier than the model would usually recommend, as Krissy would still be doing visits with Ryan and Opal in the foster home with Sharon present. The rationale was that Krissy would likely become quickly and intensely attached to her future bedroom, which would serve as reminder and affirmation that she and Brett were not being separated. The decision was made to not include Maggie in accompanying Brett to Ryan and Opal's house for his overnight visit because of her younger age and the assumption that including her would be more confusing than beneficial for her.

Krissy and Maggie's first visits

Krissy and Maggie visited Ryan and Opal during the week before Brett's first overnight. The girls had some awareness and even brief contact with Ryan and Opal when they picked up or dropped off Brett. Still, it felt different to everyone when one day, while Brett was at school, Ryan and Opal came to the house and sat down on the living room floor with Krissy, Maggie, and Sharon. Krissy ran and jumped in Ryan's lap, threw her arms around his neck for a big hug, and then squeezed his head between her hands and declared, "You're my new daddy." Ryan and Opal had been told that Krissy would likely be overly affectionate but they hadn't been prepared for the intensity of Krissy's approach.

Sharon approached and said to Krissy, "Krissy, look at my face." Krissy turned and looked at her. "You're really excited to meet Mr. and Mrs. Anderson but I think you forgot something."

Krissy turned immediately and uttered forcefully, "Hello, my name is Krissy. What's yours?"

"Hi, my name is Ryan Anderson." replied Ryan.

"And I'm Opal Anderson, Krissy. It's nice to meet you." added Opal.

Sharon interjected, "Good job, Krissy. There's something else you forgot." Sharon leaned forward and whispered in Krissy's ear.

Krissy said to Ryan, "I should've asked. Can I sit in your lap and give you another hug?"

Ryan responded, "Thanks for asking now, Krissy. Not right now for the lap and the hug. Maybe later when we know each other better."

Krissy said, "Okay," but didn't move.

Sharon directed Krissy, "That means you get down, Krissy."

Krissy got off Ryan's lap and went over to Opal and asked if she could give her a hug next.

"Great job of asking, Krissy." answered Opal and then paused and looked a little torn as there was a part of Opal that really did want to hug this cute four year old girl but said with feeling, "I really look forward to hugging you later when we know each other better."

Meanwhile, Maggie has been watching all of this from the security of Sharon's lap. To draw Ryan and Opal's attention away from Krissy, Sharon said, "Maggie, look at your sister and these new people. Krissy, I bet these folks would like to see your favorite doll—you know, the baby doll that laughs." Krissy ran off at the speed of sound and Sharon quickly advised Ryan and Opal, "Divide and conquer." Ryan and Opal looked at each other and Opal said, 'I'll take Krissy." Ryan gave her a thumbs up as Krissy ran back into the room carrying a baby doll. Opal engaged Krissy in a conversation about her baby doll while Ryan shifted position and scooted towards Sharon and Maggie. Maggie immediately buried her head in Sharon's chest with her back to Ryan. Sharon stroked her back and motioned for Ryan to back up and told him to just watch. Sharon gave Maggie a couple of kisses on her forehead and asked her, "Who's got Sharon's nose?" Maggie quickly grabbed Sharon's nose with her hand and giggled. For the next few moments, Maggie grabbed various parts of

Sharon's face. Sharon also grabbed Maggie's stomach with a little tickle thrown in. Then she asked Ryan to stick out his hand, grabbed his thumb and said "I've got Ryan's thumb." She then held up her thumb for Maggie to grab which she promptly did. In an exaggerated, high-pitched voice, Sharon exclaimed while wiggling her thumb, "Oh, Maggie's got my thumb. I need my thumb. Please Maggie, pretty please can I have my thumb back?" In response to this well-practiced game, Maggie squealed and let Sharon's thumb go. Sharon looked at Ryan and at his thumb in her grasp and wiggled her eyebrows and he got the message and imitated Sharon's previous exclamation. Maggie again squealed. After getting his thumb back, Ryan then foolishly put out both his hands with his thumbs up—one toward Sharon and one toward Maggie. Sharon and Maggie each grabbed a thumb and, of course, Ryan had to beg to get both thumbs released. Sharon indicated that it was a good time to wrap the visit up, which Krissy vehemently protested now that Opal was her new favorite person in the universe.

Brett's overnight visit

The rest of the visits with Sharon present between Krissy and Maggie with Ryan and Opal went smoothly. Ryan and Opal were also preparing to have Brett come for his overnight visit. In talking with Ms. Jenkins in a video call about Brett's overnight, they disclosed feeling emotionally overwhelmed with all of their feelings about the different places they were in building relationships with each of the three children. Ms. Jenkins asked to describe what was going on with each child and their feelings. Ryan and Opal expressed differences in their opinions and feelings. This was hard because they felt it interfered with them supporting each other. Ms. Jenkins let them know these differences were normal and tied how the children were interacting with each of them differently with the differences between them. Ms. Jenkins also asked if they had siblings growing up which both Ryan and Opal replied "yes" to. As she asked this question, they both realized that of course their parents' relationships with them and their siblings were not the same and differed based on age and temperament and needs of the children. This relaxed Ryan and Opal and they each planned to talk with their parents about the juggling act of parenting multiple children. They then talked with Ms. Jenkins more about Brett and his upcoming overnight.

Ryan and Opal had taken Brett shopping for a comforter for his bed at their house. He picked out one with a picture of his favorite superhero. Sharon and Brett packed his bag together: favorite pajamas and books, nightlight, picture of Sharon, change of clothes, extra underwear (just in case of an accident), etc. Krissy and Maggie watched this process and were told, along with Brett, that he would be back home after breakfast tomorrow. Maggie went off to her favorite playground with an aide and then Ryan and Opal arrived. This was a difficult time for Krissy—she wanted to monopolize Ryan and Opal but Brett was in the spotlight, plus she was likely anxious about the idea of him sleeping away. Both Brett and Krissy were given a choice about which car they would like to ride in: Sharon's or Ryan and Opal's. Brett chose Sharon's car and Krissy chose Ryan and Opal's.

At Ryan and Opal's home, there first was a tour and Krissy was fascinated with her future bedroom, as well as what they had in the refrigerator. Brett was interested in showing Sharon his new bedspread and not so subtly suggested he should have one like that at her house too. There was a final review with everyone about the parameters of the overnight visit and the reunion in the morning. Krissy resisted leaving but eventually did. After Sharon and Krissy left, Brett seemed a little lost. Opal and Ryan had bought a Lego kit but Brett did not want to open it. He asked if he could watch television with them and they consented. He sat on the couch and let Opal sit next to him, but when Ryan went to sit next to Opal, Brett asked if he could sit next to him, on the other side from Opal. Ryan readily agreed. They watched a kid's movie—a quiet, passive activity that seemed to help Brett settle down and get more regulated. At the end of the movie, Brett asked which Lego kit they had bought. Opal and Brett worked on it while Ryan got some lunch together.

After lunch, they went to the park and played some frisbee golf, which they had enjoyed before. Ryan and Opal decided a quiet day with familiar activities would be best for the three of them as they dealt with the novel, exciting, and somewhat nerve-wracking prospect of a first sleepover. At bedtime, Ryan and Opal followed Sharon and Brett's routine and Brett seemed to settle down easily. Ryan and Opal had set up a baby monitor in Brett's room so they could hear him in the middle of the night. At about 2 AM, they thought they heard him crying but he had not called out. Ryan went in to check on Brett and he was crying. He begrudgingly admitted that he might be a little bit scared. Ryan sat on the edge of his bed and rubbed his back for a few minutes and then sat in a chair. Brett fell back asleep after about ten minutes and slept through until the morning. After a breakfast of waffles and berries, Ryan and Opal took Brett back to Sharon's where Maggie and Krissy gave him big hugs to welcome him home. Krissy especially wanted to hear about all the food he ate in the adoptive home so she could ask for the same thing for her first overnight.

Even though Krissy asserted she was ready right after Brett, she needed to start with visits with Ryan and Opal away from Sharon before she could stay overnight. Maggie needed these steps away from Sharon to go much slower than Krissy appeared to need. Because they were transitioning to their adoptive home together, Krissy had to wait until Maggie was ready for each step. Sharon, Ryan, and Opal walked together with Krissy and Maggie to the playground at a local park. This was relationally easy for them all. Then Sharon stayed at home and Mary, her aide, went with the other four to the playground. Maggie cried a little while saying goodbye to Sharon, but this was not unusual for her to do when Mary took her places without Sharon. Maggie settled quickly. For Ryan and Opal's first outing by themselves with Krissy and Maggie, they walked the girls around the block with an arranged stop along the way—to see the girls' favorite dog of the neighborhood, a cocker spaniel named Megan. Megan's owners had her out in the yard and Maggie and Krissy exchanged hugs and kisses with her. This outing was successful for Maggie; Krissy was pouty because she could name five other dogs in the area that she wanted to visit but was told "no". Ryan and Opal wanted to do this canine visit two more times before trying something more adventurous. The next level of visit was a walk with the girls to the park. Maggie cried a little again leaving Sharon but was distracted by Opal asking questions about which equipment she wanted to play on at the playground. They made it to the playground successfully and played there for about 20 minutes. At that point, Ryan and Opal did not want to test Maggie's capacity for being away from Sharon and so they announced it was time to leave. Krissy was very upset and had a big tantrum, refusing to leave. Krissy's big feelings quickly upset Maggie and she also started crying. Opal scooped up Maggie who clung to her tightly while Opal assured her they were heading back to Sharon's house. Ryan lifted a squirmy Krissy into his arms after she refused to leave. When

Sharon's house came into view and Opal pointed it out to Maggie, Maggie stopped crying. Krissy was unhappy all the way back to Sharon's house and stomped to her room after they arrived. Ryan, Opal and Sharon talked it over and agreed another trip to the park the next day made sense. The three adults talked to Krissy before leaving for the park. She was told that Ryan and Opal wanted to take both girls to the park but they would only take Maggie on this trip unless Krissy could be a big girl and leave the park when the adults said it was time. Krissy quickly agreed to this condition and followed through.

Visits away from Sharon gradually lengthened all the way up to full day visits and, although Maggie or Krissy would have some upset feelings, they were generally able to be soothed by Ryan and Opal.

Brett's moving day

Brett was ready for his moving day while his sisters were still having their visits with Ryan and Opal. The three children had been having joint sessions with Mr. Anderson, the therapist for the sibling group, once Maggie and Krissy had started their visits. He had two doll houses in his office and lots of family figures as well as other play therapy and art materials. Mr. Anderson talked with Brett and Krissy about their visits with Ryan and Opal. Maggie listened while she played and occasionally interjected a few words. Krissy frequently expressed her jealousy that Brett got to go first rather than her, but that complaint got less passionate as time passed. Brett illustrated his overnight visits with the dolls, and enjoyed being in a position to teach his younger siblings. These sessions increased in importance as Brett's moving day drew nearer. Mr. Anderson asked Brett if he wanted to make something to give to each sister on the day he moved to Ryan and Opal's house, for them to bring along when they moved. Krissy requested that he make her a sparkly necklace and Maggie asked that he make her a hug. Brett seemed somewhat stumped by his sisters' requests until he and Mr. Anderson had a whispered conversation. Brett announced he had a plan. Meanwhile, the sibling sessions continued through Brett's move until his sisters' moving day had also passed.

Lots of planning went into Brett's move. He supervised the process of packing all his belongings. Brett told his classmates about his move, even though Ryan and Opal had committed to transporting him to his current school for the remainder of the school year. Brett and Sharon worked hard creating a guest list and menu for his moving party; this was the part that Krissy most wanted to take over. Brett and Sharon agreed she could put one item on the menu. Sharon designed a schedule for the day of his move with some input from Ms. Jenkins, including how to account for his sisters and their potential reactions. Brett went on a last trip to the ice cream parlor with Sharon to share a banana split. (They took a picture for Brett's Lifebook before they ate it). They shared some favorite memories of each other while they spooned down the ice cream.

The moving party went well; aside from Krissy's short meltdown, which she recovered from fairly quickly after Sharon pointed out that she was missing the party. Brett gave his gifts to his sisters: two drawings. The drawing for Krissy has her in the middle of the picture with Maggie and Brett closest to her, and Ryan, Opal, and Sharon next to them. The finishing touch was some gobs of gold glitter glued around Krissy's neck: the sparkly necklace she'd asked for. Maggie's gift was a drawing of Brett and Maggie hugging inside a big heart. On the bottom of each drawing, he printed "See you soon, Love Brett, your brother". Brett received a big round of applause from his neighbors, soccer teammates and coaches, teacher, classmates, and foster family.

Brett's moving day began with eating breakfast, taking a shower, then getting dressed in his best clothes. A few items had to be packed last minute. Krissy had been promised a trip to the ice cream parlor later in the day if she had no tantrums (tears were okay) and she promised that she would keep the deal. Mary, Sharon's aide, was pressed into duty as photographer and videographer. It had been arranged that Sharon would be waiting outside with the kids when Ryan and Opal pulled up. Sharon held Maggie in her arms and held Krissy by the hand. Brett was standing next to her. When Ryan and Opal approached, Sharon crouched down and had a tearful four-way hug with Brett, Krissy and Maggie. Brett walked over to a three-way hug with Ryan and Opal. Then the three of them waved goodbye, got in the car, and drove away.

At Ryan and Opal's home, they unpacked. Brett made sure to quickly find his photo of himself with Sharon and his sisters. The rest of the day was quiet. Meanwhile, Sharon and the girls had a nice time at the ice cream parlor, despite some sniffles.

Brett's reverse visit

The first time Brett saw Sharon after his move was briefly, two days later, when she brought Krissy and Maggie to the sibling therapy session. Brett, Krissy and Maggie (to a lesser extent) filled Mr. Anderson in about moving day. Brett was curious to hear if a new child had moved in and taken his old bedroom yet. Krissy wanted to make sure that Brett was not going into her future bedroom at the adoptive home. Mr. Anderson prompted them about feelings and the kids all admitted some sadness and excitement. Krissy was especially excited about being the oldest child in her family in the foster home. Maggie missed Brett's hugs and he gave her one during the session. She asked him when he was coming back to Sharon's. Brett answered that he would not be coming back, but reminded her that she would be moving, too. This seemed to confuse her. Mr. Anderson shifted the children's attention to the two doll houses. He demonstrated Brett, Ryan, and Opal in one house and Sharon, Krissy, Maggie, and Mary in the other. He then moved Maggie and Krissy into Ryan and Opal's house and showed them sleeping in beds there. Krissy noted, "There's lots more people in one house than the other house. Mama (Sharon) will be lonely." Maggie reached in and moved her doll back into Sharon's house. Mr. Anderson asked her, "You wish you could stay with Mama?" Maggie nodded tearfully. Mr. Anderson showed Sharon visiting Krissy and Brett in Ryan and Opal's home and then coming back to her house and said, "See Mama visits kids with Papa Ryan and Mama Opal. If you are in this house, then you can be with Brett and Krissy." Maggie went over to Brett and climbed in his lap for him to hold her.

Mr. Anderson met with Ryan, Opal, Sharon, Ms. Jenkins (Brett's therapist), and Mr. Gray (caseworker). He talked about Maggie struggling to understand the transition process and her difficulty letting go of Sharon, the only mother figure she had ever known. It was agreed that Krissy and Maggie's trip to see Brett, Ryan, and Opal in the adoptive home (with Sharon chaperoning) would be moved up before Krissy and Maggie went on any more visits to Ryan and Opal by themselves. It was also decided that Brett be present for at least part of the all-day visits that Ryan and Opal were having with Krissy and Maggie. It was felt that Krissy and, especially, Maggie, needed to see Brett more often. Thus an all-day visit might start a little later and last through dinner time and occur on a school day so that Krissy and Maggie would have some time with Ryan and Opal before Brett was let out of school and joined them. Finally, Ryan asked Sharon to join some of the sibling sessions with Krissy and Maggie to work on the transition in their relationships. The first session with Ryan, Maggie and Sharon focused on Sharon shifting from being a "mama" to being an "auntie". This was played out with the dollhouses. They made sure to emphasize the Auntie Sharon doll continuing to see Maggie when she was in Ryan and Opal's home.

Maggie and Krissy's all-day visits

Ryan and Opal picked up Krissy and Maggie around 10:30 AM. They went to the zoo, saw some animals, and got lunch. They saw some more animals; who had plenty of their own lunch thanks to Maggie's quick popcorn-throwing. Krissy and Maggie asked repeatedly when they would see Brett. Ryan and Opal just told them it would be after their afternoon snack. After the zoo, Ryan drove the SUV on a scenic tour while Opal and Krissy sat in the last row of seats quietly playing with dolls and Maggie napped in the middle row. After Maggie awoke and the kids had their snack:

their usual tradition of bananas and peanut butter, juice… and lots of wiping up.

Ryan pulled up at Brett's school and everyone piled out to warmly greet Brett with hugs all around. The five of them kicked a ball around at the park and there was some squealing at the playground. They all went to Ryan and Opal's house where Krissy ran to her future bedroom and jumped on her bed, chanting repeatedly, "I'm going to sleep here." Maggie gradually got out of Opal's arms and seemed comfortable exploring the house on her own as long as there was an adult close by to help her feel safe. Brett had fun teaching her things about the house—like the little box under the mail slot that would catch the mail. Maggie was very excited when she saw the mail drop into the box. After dinner, either Ryan or Opal took Krissy and Maggie back to Sharon's and the other one would help Brett get started on his homework.

The first full official reverse visit occurred about a week after Brett's moving day. Sharon took Krissy and Maggie to see Brett in his adoptive home. Brett had already shown his new home to his sisters but now he had a chance to show it to Sharon. There was a conflict soon after Sharon, Krissy, and Maggie arrived: Krissy wanted to show Sharon her bedroom first and Brett had been expecting that he would show Sharon his room first. This was a re-creation of the jealousy and competition for Sharon that had been present when Brett and Krissy had lived with her. Maggie did not like her siblings yelling at each other and started crying. She allowed Sharon to hand her to Opal, who distracted her. Krissy, Sharon, Brett, and Ryan all sat on the couch in that order.

Sharon turned to Krissy and said, "Krissy, I'll see your room first when I come here for the first time after you move. Today is Brett's day."

Krissy chanted, "Mine first. Mine first. Mine first. Mine first..."

Brett interjected, "No Krissy. It's my turn. Shut up."

Ryan rubbed Brett's back and whispered in his ear. Brett reluctantly volunteered, "I'm sorry I said shut up but it is my turn."

Sharon turned to Brett and said, "Thank you, Brett." She then turned back to Krissy and said, "I promise you I will see your room first when it's your and Maggie's turn."

Krissy shot back, "You'll go to Maggie's room first."

Sharon replied, "No I won't, because as long as I am carrying her, Maggie doesn't care about who's first like you do."

"Maggie can go first because I'm not moving. I'm staying with you forever." responded Krissy, who started crying, which was very unusual.

Sharon put an arm around Krissy and asked tenderly, "Would you miss me?" Krissy nodded her head and cried harder. Brett looked up at Ryan with his eyes glistening and Ryan gave him a hug. Maggie started crying again which prompted Opal to hold her more tightly and give her a kiss. The grown-ups all had tears in their eyes as well. None of the grown-ups were quite sure what to do next and the therapists weren't there.

Sharon stood and announced, "I'm going with Brett to see his bedroom and then to see Krissy's. Krissy, do you want to come with or wait here on the couch with Ryan?

Krissy responded, "I'll go if Ryan will carry me."

Sharon directed Krissy with "Ask him nicely please?" which Krissy did and Ryan consented. They all trouped back to Brett's room with Brett holding Sharon's hand, Ryan carrying Krissy, and Opal carrying Maggie. They all admired Brett's cool furnishings.

When they moved on to Krissy's future bedroom, which was comparatively quite bare, Krissy complained, "My room needs more stuff! More than Brett's room."

Ryan reassured her, "We will go shopping and you can pick out pretty stuff for your room when you're living here."

The mix continued with all-day visits with Ryan, Opal, Krissy, Maggie, and Brett—interspersed with reverse visits of Sharon, Krissy, and Maggie going over to see Ryan, Opal, and Brett. Ryan's meetings with Brett, Krissy and Maggie continued, as well as Brett's therapy with Ms. Jenkins. The sibling group therapy also continued with Mr. Anderson. It was a busy time.

Krissy and Maggie's overnight visits

Ryan, Opal and Sharon met with the caseworker, Mr. Gray. There was some conversation about doing separate overnights for the two girls because they were so different. Sharon pointed out that Maggie often got up in the middle of the night and climbed into Krissy's bed, which Krissy never complained about. Ryan and Opal wondered about Brett's role in the overnights of his sisters. They created a plan that involved engaging the girls with the tasks of furnishing their rooms, Maggie taking more naps there, and Brett participating in the girls' bedtime routines even though it was early for him. He got a brand new chapter book from his favorite series that he could read in bed until his usual bedtime.

Leading up to the overnight visit, Krissy was excited to sleep in the princess sheets she had helped pick out. Maggie was ambivalent— seemingly scared to be away from Sharon, yet looking forward to sleeping in the same house as Brett again. Maggie also liked that she would be in a "big girl" toddler bed rather than her crib. Both girls struggled a bit at bedtime but liked that Brett gave them hugs and reminded them that it was safe in the house. They accepted the soothing and back rubs and stories from Ryan and Opal and fell asleep after about 30 minutes.

Ryan and Opal had put a motion sensor in the hall outside the bedrooms so they would know if any of the kids got up in the middle of the night, even if it was just to go to the bathroom. At 2 AM, the sensor went off and sent an alert to Ryan and Opal's phones. They found Maggie in the hall crying that she couldn't find Sharon. Krissy came into the hall next, crying that she wanted to go home and that she missed Sharon. Brett even appeared in the hallway, insisting that Maggie needed his help. Ryan and Opal looked at each other with an overwhelmed expression and Opal said, "We'll survive this." Ryan nodded and picked up Maggie, inviting Brett to help tuck her in and give her a kiss goodnight. Brett wanted to stay longer with Maggie but agreed to go back to his room with the assurance from Ryan that he would come get him if he was needed. Ryan rocked Maggie and sang to her. While she was still awake, he put her back in bed and rubbed her back. After a few minutes, he moved to a chair next to her bed and sat there until she fell back asleep. Meanwhile, Opal and Krissy had returned to Krissy's room. Opal invited Krissy to sit on her lap which Krissy did. Opal mirrored back Krissy's feelings of missing Sharon. Of the various things that Opal said to Krissy, the one that seemed to make the most difference was that they would be seeing Sharon in a few hours. They counted together the number of hours left. When they came up with six as the answer, Krissy felt reassured that it wasn't that big of a number. She agreed to get in bed and look at books with Opal while they waited for the time to pass. Krissy fell asleep in a few minutes. Both Krissy and Maggie slept the rest of the night through.

The other overnights went relatively smoothly; at least one of the girls woke up in the middle of each night, but they were soothed relatively easily. Given this success with overnight visits, the adults met and decided *both girls were ready to move to Ryan and Opal's home and a moving date was set for Krissy and Maggie.*

Krissy and Maggie's moving day

Given their ages and sense of time, the grown-ups decided to pack the girls' belongings the day before the move. Sharon did all her preparations with Ryan and Opal's help behind the scenes. The moving party occurred the morning of moving day and was smaller than Brett's because the girls didn't have classmates to invite, and because Maggie would become overwhelmed if the party was too large. Brett, Ryan, and Opal came to the moving party and it was well documented for the Krissy and Maggie's Lifebooks. After the guests left, the girls' belongings were loaded into Sharon's car, which Mary, Sharon's aide, drove while Sharon rode with the kids and Ryan and Opal in their car. The grown-ups felt like it would work better for Krissy and Maggie for the goodbye to happen at the adoptive home. Krissy cried more than Maggie while saying goodbye to Sharon; she seemed to understand the magnitude of the change that was occurring more. Maggie seemed to experience this as another overnight visit, which affected the planning for the first reverse visitation.

The grown-ups met to discuss when the first reverse visit would occur, given Maggie's age and deep attachment to Sharon. One proposal was that it occur the day after the move, but there was concern expressed that this may lead Maggie to believe that Sharon would take her home as if the moving day was an overnight. The other primary option discussed was to wait three or four days to give Maggie more of a sense of the permanent shift that had occurred, but there was concern that Maggie would experience Sharon's "disappearance" as a trauma. To oversimplify, reverse visits have two emotional components: first, the arrival and reconnection, and secondly, the goodbye and loss. Neither option was seen as perfect, but the group decided to go with scheduling the visit for the next day so that Maggie would be reassured of her connection with Sharon. When Sharon left, Maggie would have part two of a goodbye process that had started the day before.

At the end of the first reverse visit, Maggie cried more than she had the day before. Reverse visits were scheduled every 2-3 days to help Maggie understand that she and Sharon still had a relationship, but it was one where they did not live together. This pattern lasted for three weeks and then was lengthened out. A large visual calendar was used with each day crossed off and with pictures of Sharon affixed on days when there were reverse visits.

The incredibly complex nature of multi-sibling transitions is evident in the preceding scenario. Taking into account each child's attachment needs, developmental level, personality and temperament as well as the practical limitations of foster and adoptive parents makes planning these transitions a combination of three-dimensional chess and a 1000-piece jigsaw puzzle, but one well worth doing.

Chapter 12

Birth Parents Still Involved

In some cases, one or both birth parents' parental rights have not been terminated by the court, which may present a legal risk to the adoption. If there are no ongoing visits between the child and a birth parent, then adoptive parents will choose between two major emotional options for themselves after assuming physical custody of the child:

1. Adoptive parents function as pre-adoptive foster parents and the child transitions as if from one foster home to another, even though doing so feels much more emotionally significant for the adults. Much—but not all—of what is contained in this approach will be useful and appropriate for that kind of transition. If and when the birth parents' legal rights are terminated, celebrate the child's shift in status from foster to adoptive child.

2. Adoptive parents function in the role of adoptive parents. This places the child and the adoptive parents at substantial emotional

risk if the birth parents regain physical custody, which would significantly disrupt the carefully constructed adoptive relationship. This option is easier to justify if the termination of the birth parents' rights seems like a certainty.

If there are ongoing visits with the birth parent and the birth parents' rights have not been terminated, then it is important for the adoptive parents to stay in the role of pre-adoptive foster parents. It will be too confusing for the child to try and create an adoptive relationship while they still have contact with their birth parent. If the birth parents' rights are later terminated while the child is living in the home of the hopeful adoptive parents, then they can shift status with the child from pre-adoptive foster parents to formal adoptive parents.

In some cases, the adoptive parents and birth parents plan for ongoing contact between the birth parents and the child post adoption. In this case, modify the overall transition plan by including the birth parents in the planning committee mentioned in Chapter 1. Birth parents, foster parents, and adoptive parents need a solid working relationship with a focus on the best interests of the child going forward, without focusing on birth parents' past behaviors. This may involve a shift in the tone of the relationship between foster and birth parents, depending on the history in their relationship. Although not the focus of this book, there are approaches to connect foster and birth parents (e.g., Biehle & Goodman, 2012; Goble, 2022). It is not the role of the adoptive parent to try and bridge any differences between the foster and birth parents—that is a delicate diplomatic process and the role of the caseworker or other transition facilitator. The inclusion of the birth parents can have some advantages for the adoptive parents. Adoptive parents can learn information about the child that they otherwise would not have had access to. This may include history that is useful for the child's Lifebook.

That all said, even if birth parents are involved in the transition planning, it does not mean they have to be involved in any visits. Before deciding to involve the birth parents in any of the transition visits, an assessment needs to be made to determine if they are ready to handle being present in visits involving the child and the adoptive parents. This is a significant emotional responsibility and challenge for many birth parents. Their task is to communicate to the child that they approve of the adoptive parents and the adoption process—and to withhold any significant reservations. This can be heart-breaking for many birth parents—something they may not be able to do emotionally at that time. The birth parents' readiness can also be measured by their ability to handle questions from the child. Questions like: "Don't you love me? Why aren't I coming to live with you?" "Why did you do drugs?" "I don't like these adoptive parents. Can you stop the adoption?" Birth parents may want advice on handling these difficult questions from their own therapist, parent trainer/coach, the child's therapist, or the caseworker.

Sometimes birth parents may feel able to handle being in these visits, but others on the planning committee (e.g., the caseworker or foster parents) may disagree. This assessment may be based on birth parents' behavior in recent visits they have had with their children, mental health or substance abuse status, emotional ups and downs, readiness of the child at the point in their therapy to have extended contact with their birth parents, etc. These concerns would be openly discussed. Perhaps contingency plans can be made to address at least some of the concerns. It is important that the adoptive parents hear these discussions. The decision to include or exclude birth parents in these visits is first the caseworker's (as the child's guardian,) but also the adoptive parents. Both parties need to agree to go forward.

With all these hurdles, why even consider including birth parents in transition visits at all? It is a great gift to the child if the birth parents can freely give their approval of the adoptive parents and the adoption to the child. This birth parents' approval lessens the loyalty conflicts the child may feel. Although open adoption is explicitly not an ultimate goodbye, the birth parents' collaborative participation in the transition process communicates to the child that they are relinquishing the primary parenting role and transferring it to the adoptive parents. It is a way of starting the open adoption process during the transition in which the adoptive and birth parents work together for the benefit of the child.

If the birth parents are going to participate in the transition, then initial visits between the adoptive parents and the child in the foster home would proceed as outlined before. After two successful 2-3 hour visits between the child and adoptive parents without the foster parent present, birth parents can join for a short meal somewhere out in the community. This allows the child a chance to see the birth parents and adoptive parents interacting cordially in a structured setting. During the afternoon of the second all-day visit, include the birth parent in an activity. Photos of the birth parent involvement would be included in the Lifebook and copies given to the birth parents. There would be a physical calendar that is developmentally appropriate and accessible to the child in the foster home which includes plans for ongoing contact between child and birth parent.

Within a week after moving day, the child would see the birth parents. If the adoptive parents approve, the birth parents would come to the adoptive home. The child would give the birth parents a tour and they would eat a brief meal together. If this contact does not occur in the adoptive home, then the adoptive parents, child, and birth parents would meet in the community, where the child shows the birth parents photos (and perhaps a video) of the adoptive home—especially the child's bedroom. For the child's sake, the birth parent would act admiring and positive in all these interactions.

In some cases, the birth parents' rights have been terminated and there is no plan for post-adoption openness, but contact still occurs between birth parent and child. A goodbye process needs to be planned between the child and birth parent as soon as possible. The structure of such a process is beyond the scope of this document (see Bovingdon & Fabian, 2015) but it should not be a single session and its design would be dependent on the developmental level of the child and the preexisting relationship between the child and the birth parent. If the child has a therapist, involve them in the planning of the goodbye process. After the goodbye process, an interim period is needed before initiating the adoption transition, to give the child time to grieve and come to accept that the relationship with the birth parent has truly ended, even beyond being told so by the grown-ups. The length of the interim period is dependent on the developmental level of the child and the quality of the relationship between the child and the birth parent but almost always at least a month.

Chapter 13

Foster Home is a Short-Term Placement

The attachment between a child and a foster parent whose relationship is only a few weeks or months old is not as deep or as trusted as one built over years. However, the child will likely still see the current foster parents as at least a guarantor of safety. The adoptive parents' initial visits in the foster parent's presence will be the same. Furthermore, even when the child has not been in the foster home for as long as is typical, the foster parents still need to be one of the three voices on the planning committee. Given the shorter duration of the relationship between child and foster parent, it might be expected that the foster parents' grief over losing that relationship as part of the transition would be less. This is especially true for the foster parent who knows that the adoption is in the works when the placement is made. It may also be true that the loss is less acute for the child, but many of these children have had a succession of losses, so a transition where there is room for feelings to be expressed may bring up lots of grieving from the past that is expressed in this foster relationship. It is important to provide room for the child to have a significant loss reaction, even if it doesn't make logical sense given the duration of the relationship.

After moving day, schedule at least one visit for the foster parents to see the child in the adoptive home, even if ongoing contact is likely not needed at the same frequency as described previously. The foster home, even though short-term, still needs to be documented for the child's Lifebook, as any foster home needs to be. Focus documentation of the adoptive transition primarily on the growth of the relationships between adoptive parents and the child rather than including the change in the relationship between child and the foster parents.

A move that is this recent is concerning; the reason why the child was moved so close to being adopted needs to be discussed by the planning committee (foster parents, adoptive parents and caseworker). Here are some possibilities, and any additional consideration that each presents:

If the child moved because the child's behavior was not tolerable in the prior foster home, this needs to be taken into account in the transition planning. Ensure that adoptive parents have been informed of this behavior. The adoptive parents may have questions for the prior foster parent about this behavior and how it was handled. Adoptive parents and foster parents would develop a plan to respond to this behavior if it happens on a visit without the foster parents present. This planning would take into account how the foster parents are responding to the behavior in the foster home when it has occurred in this placement (assuming it has). Adoptive parents would develop a plan for how they will respond to this behavior after the move has occurred, especially if it will impact other children in the adoptive home.

If the child moved because the prior foster parents were not chosen to be adoptive parents, this may present issues. Foster parents who see themselves as prospective adoptive parents form a deeper attachment to the child (Waterman, 2003). The child often senses this and forms a reciprocal deeper bond. If this has occurred in a prior foster home, then the child's attachment to the prior foster parents and its loss needs to be taken into account in order to understand the child's behavior as the transition process unfolds.

If the child was moved to be reunited with a sibling before the adoption started, the relationship with that sibling has likely progressed since the recent reunification, but may not be as developed as other sibling relationships. Identify whether there is anything happening in that relationship that needs to be considered in the transition (e.g., blaming for removal from the birth home, clinging out of a fear of another separation, renewal of a prior parentified relationship between the siblings, etc.).

If the child was moved because of some other conflict in the prior foster home, those concerns need to be thought about carefully. The given reason may inform the child's experience in the context of the prior foster home and they may bring those experiences into this adoptive transition. Dynamics beyond the given reason for the move may also be relevant.

Regardless of the reason for the move, if the child was in that prior foster home for a sizable time, then the recent disruption in the attachment to those foster parents needs to be thought about in the planning. Unless otherwise contraindicated, the prior foster parents would be contacted for multiple reasons:

- Gather the prior foster parents' perspective about the reason for the child's move.

- Review the goodbye process from the prior foster parent to see if it would be useful to supplement it, especially if the move from the prior foster home has been very recent (within the past two weeks). When the move from the prior foster home is less recent, then it is probably not useful to revisit that goodbye process unless there are other considerations (i.e., the child was with prior foster parents for most of their life).

- Involve the prior foster parents to signal to the child their approval of the adoptive parents and of the adoption. It may be helpful to have the prior foster parent attend one of the longer visits for one activity.

- The adoptive parents might gather useful information from that foster parent similar to the information that they have received from the current foster parent.

- There may be information, photographs, or other material that the prior foster parents can provide for inclusion in the child's Lifebook.

- There may be some situations where it makes sense to consider reverse visits for the former foster parents once the child has moved to the adoptive home. This would require the consent of the former foster parents and the adoptive parents, of course. An assessment of whether the former foster parents can be supportive of the adoptive placement also needs to be made by the caseworker. Reverse visits with former foster parents in this kind of situation probably only make sense if the child is older than 6. The benefits for the child can be substantial: they can feel the approval of the adoptive home from trusted attachment figures and they can also continue their working through of the loss of the former foster parents as primary caregivers while getting the bonus of continued contact.

Chapter 14

Foster Parents are Against Using the Model

Understanding the reasons for the foster parents' viewpoint

A first step is to approach the foster parents and seek a dialogue about their concerns. This approach would best be done with curiosity and a nonjudgmental attitude and based on the assumption that the foster parents believe the model will not result in the best transition for the child and involved adults. This dialogue seeks to clarify the foster parents' understanding of the model, their emotions about the plan to use the model with this child, their disagreements with the model, and their assumptions and reasoning underlying why they believe it should not be used. In addition to gathering information about the foster parents' position, another goal is for the foster parents to feel respected and taken seriously. This second goal is crucial if there is to be a true dialogue about how to proceed.

Some of the most common reasons that foster parents have for not agreeing with a part of or the whole model include:

- believing the model is culturally inappropriate for the child, the foster parents and/or the adoptive parents;

- not supporting the adoptive parents as the choice for this child and so wanting to accelerate the transition (to get it over with) or slow it down or block the transition for the child's sake;

- believing the model is too much work given everything else the foster parents have to do with running their household;

- believing that the model will harm the child by drawing out the transition excessively; and

- feeling that the extra work involved in the model is not worth the effort because children are not harmed by the current approach to transitions or are too young to be affected.

Initial response strategies for each of these reasons will now be considered. A common theme running through all these response strategies is deep and respectful listening to the foster parents' concerns. That is always the starting point. What to do if the foster parents continue to be against using the model after dialogue has occurred will be explored later.

General steps for responding to foster parents' concerns are fourfold. A first step is to decide who will try to engage with the foster parents about the transition model. Ideally, this person is someone that believes in the model and knows it well, has a good, substantive relationship with the foster parents without unresolved historical conflicts, can minimize being defensive, and has the authority to negotiate changes in the model or has been delegated that authority. It's rare that one person actually has all these characteristics. The first choice is often the caseworker. Caseworkers, as representatives of the state, sometimes have had to use that power to make and enforce decisions that foster parents do not agree with. Depending on how this was done, this can make for a difficult backdrop to these discussions. The child's therapist can be another possibility. Therapists for foster children often consult with foster parents and so may build a relationship. Depending on the foster parent's perception of the usefulness of those consultations, and of the child's therapy in general, they may be more or less willing to see the child's therapist as a useful resource to be reassured by and negotiate with. Someone else from the child welfare agency whose job it is to help with the implementation of the model or to actually facilitate transitions might also conduct these discussions with the foster parents yet these individuals will generally not have any preexisting relationships with the foster parents.

The second step in this overall process is establishing a dialogue. A first message that needs to be delivered to the foster parents is the genuine desire to hear their viewpoint and that they will not be forced into cooperating with the model. Lessening the perception of a threat by the caseworker or the agency to force them to do something helps to remove the sense of impending coercion.

The third step is to listen humbly to the concerns of the foster parents. The foster parents need to feel fully heard; problem-solving should wait until they have laid out all the issues they have. It's important to not only hear the content of their concerns, but also the emotions associated with that content. To feel fully heard, the foster parent needs to feel that the listener gets, not only what emotions are stirred up, but also at what level of intensity.

The fourth step is to engage the foster parents in efforts to modify the application of the model for this child and these adults. It should not be assumed that whoever is running the transition process will decide the modifications unilaterally. This needs to be a collaborative process between the foster parents and the other adults on the planning team. As has been stated before, this model is intended to be a guide and is not to be applied rigidly.

Initial response strategies to foster parents' concerns

Believing the model is culturally inappropriate for the child, the foster parents and/or the adoptive parents is a very relevant point for a foster parent to raise, especially because the child welfare system has a history of treating members of the global majority poorly (e.g., Cantey et al., 2022; Hanna & Rogers, 2022; Mikell Montgomery, 2022; Roberts, 2001). Thinking together with the foster parents may result in adaptations of the model to lead them to feel it is more culturally sensitive, perhaps, to the extent that they can support it. A cultural consultant can also be used to add further expertise in how the model may be modified to fit the situation. The foster parents, as members of a global majority participating in a dominant white culture child welfare system, may assume that they will not be listened to or that they will be dismissed and devalued. Naturally, they would want to avoid such a painful process. Trust needs to be built through demonstrating that whatever the foster parents have communicated so far in words and actions has been listened to and taken seriously. An invitation for further dialogue is extended on that basis. The foster parents do not have to agree to talk about everything; perhaps, just one new topic could be raised and everyone could see and feel how the discussion goes.

The cultural concerns most often fall into one of two main categories. One is the belief that the model, generally, is in some ways at least not culturally competent and may even be culturally hurtful. Engaging with foster parents about their concerns as experts who may be able to improve the model, rather than individuals with complaints who are to be placated with as many changes as they need, is a necessity.

A second category is a concern that the model is not supporting this particular child's cultural heritage in the transition process or the adoptive placement. If the objection is to the cultural appropriateness of the adoptive family that was chosen, then the concerns need to be listened to. If for some reason, they have not been previously factored into the decision-making then that needs to be done and the foster family needs to see that being done. The issue of transracial placement of children from the global majority is beyond the scope of this book (see Antares, 2023).

Not supporting the adoptive parents as the choice for this child and so wanting to accelerate it (to get it over with) or slow it down or block the transition for the child's sake is a challenging stance to respond to. For foster parents to continue to oppose the adoptive parents after the selection process by the child welfare agency, they will have strong reactions. It is very important to understand the emotional underpinnings to this reaction. If there are two foster parents, it is also relevant if both foster parents share the same feeling or not. The feeling may be sadness or jealousy over not being chosen, a conviction that the adoptive parents are flawed as people, dislike of the adoptive parents based on differences (temperamental, parenting approaches, religious, cultural, etc.), pain from past losses triggered by the adoptive transition, or some other feeling. Sometimes, this emotional reaction is masked by a more logical rationale about the model but with exploration the feelings against the adoptive parents emerge more strongly. These feelings need to be expressed and the foster parents need to feel heard. Hopefully, there is someone that the foster parents have a trusting relationship with; perhaps their certifier, the child's caseworker or therapist, or even their own therapist. It is only after they have felt fully heard that they may be more open to proceeding with the model for the benefit of the child, even though they may still have reservations about the adoptive parents.

Believing the model is too much work given everything else the foster parents have to do with running their household is a very realistic concern shared by many foster parents. The very detailed nature of the model can feel overwhelming to many foster parents. If their sense that the model calls for too much work from them can be heard by the rest of the planning committee, then a negotiation may be able to proceed regarding what aspects of the model feel manageable to the foster parents while retaining as much of the model as possible for the sake of the child. Another approach is to ask the foster parents to only commit to the beginnings of the transition through the adoptive parents visiting with the child in their presence. They can then decide after that phase has been completed if they would agree to any more participation in subsequent phases. In addition to taking the foster parents' concerns seriously about workload, it may also be useful to see if there are other issues that may be contributing to the foster parents' hesitancy to commit to the model.

Believing that the model will harm the child by drawing out the transitions excessively signals that the foster parents care deeply about the child and seek to be protective through the transition. This is an important starting point as the welfare of the child is then a shared value that can organize the discussions. First, draw out the foster parents' concerns about how the model will harm the child and what behaviors from the child would indicate that harm is occurring. Creating an implementation plan for the model that takes into account the foster parents' concerns through setting up an observational plan to look for the signs of harm to the child that the foster parents are worried may occur. An agreement would try to be reached that if signs of harm do occur, then the plan will be modified.

Feeling that the extra work involved in the model is not worth the effort because children are not harmed by the current approach to transitions or are too young to be affected. This stance may originate from a couple of different sources. It may be related to the foster parents struggling with their own emotional reactions to the transition and felt loss of the child[1] and so they minimize the impact of the transition on the child as part of trying to minimize its impact on themselves. If foster parents are able to be engaged in looking at the feelings stirred up for them by the transition, perhaps by someone they trust, then this concern may be quelled. If the foster parents are holding this stance out of a lack of knowledge about attachment and child development, then the first step is to be as genuinely curious as possible about the foster parents' beliefs and to see if there are any aspects of their beliefs that might agree with the model's assumptions. Building on these areas of agreement is much more likely to be successful than confronting directly.

---

[1] See Boswell and Cudmore (2014, 2017) for more on this dynamic.

Next steps if a dialogue with the foster parents is unsuccessful in gaining their cooperation

At this point in the process, it is important to understand if the foster parents are only unwilling to play their role in the transition as laid out in the model or whether they seek to actively oppose the transition. If they actively oppose the transition, which is rare, then this is for the child's caseworker and foster parent certifier and their supervisors to respond to based on agency policy. If foster parents are unwilling to engage in the transition as laid out in the model, either partially or fully, then there are several options that are available to the caseworker and adoptive parent which may be used singly, or in some circumstances, jointly:

- proceed with the foster parents providing as much cooperation in the transition as they are willing;

- use other safe person(s) in the child's life (e.g., child's caseworker, therapist, neighbor, child care provider, teacher or family of origin member) to fulfill some of the roles that the foster parents usually would occupy; and/or

- modify what adoptive parents do in the model to fulfill some of the roles of the foster parents (e.g., hold a party before moving day and invite people that care about the child from their foster home community).

In these kinds of major modifications to the model, it is very important to continue to reflect on the child's experience with these changes and listen to what they are communicating directly or indirectly about the process that is unfolding and how the involved adults can be responsive to the child.

When foster parents are minimally or not involved in the transition process and the child is older, then the child may question why the foster parents are not as available for these new, somewhat scary events as they usually are. It is very important that the adults have thought together and talked about this eventuality. The child will want an answer from the foster parent. When they bring the question up to the foster parent, the foster parent would ideally respond that it is a great question and that the caseworker and them want to talk with the child about it and that will happen in the next day or two. The rationale for having both foster parent and caseworker present is that the child can see the two people that have the disagreement and can see that they are able to talk together with the child about it in a collaborative manner. This will reduce (but not eliminate) anxiety that the child may have about the foster parent not being as involved. An approach that is recommended is for the foster parent and caseworker to lay out that they both care about the child and want what is best for the child but have different ideas about how to help the child shift from living with the foster parents to living with the new adoptive parents. The adoptive parent would not be involved or be present for this conversation. The details of the adults' differences would not be gone into with the child although the child may have other questions that can be answered at this point (e.g., when the next visit with the adoptive parents is, can they call their foster parents during their upcoming overnight visit, etc.).

Chapter 15

Child has Experienced a Prior Disrupted Adoption

Effects of disrupted adoption and subsequent adoptive transitions

Children can often be successfully adopted after an adoption disruption (Fitzgerald, 1979), if approached with much care and forethought. These children have significant mental health effects (Argent & Coleman, 2012) and should be in psychotherapy after the disruption and through any attempt at a second adoption (Bruning, 2007). This is even true for children six months of age and older. (Yes, there is therapy for children that young that occurs with caregivers present and needs to be done by therapists with specific training in infant/toddler mental health. See, for example, Zeanah, 2018.)

Hopefully, after the adoptive disruption, the child was placed back with familiar foster parents with whom they had a positive relationship. The highest priority should be given to this. Contact the child's prior foster parents, even if they have given up fostering, to see if they would resume fostering and take back this child.

How long ago was the disruption? Some second adoptions have been attempted within a month of the disruption because there was a second family that went before the child welfare decision makers. These second adoptions are often disrupted because the child was not ready. This is incredibly painful for the child and those adoptive parents. It is difficult to set a hard and fast rule, but a second adoption should not be considered within six months of the disruption. The child's psychotherapist should have considerable input as to whether the child is ready to attempt a second adoption. The child may look okay on the outside. They may have sealed away the experience, as they have sealed away other traumas. It is very important that the child has done some processing with genuine feeling of the disrupted adoption before a subsequent adoption is attempted.

How long before the disruption was the child in the initial adoptive home? Some children

are only in the adoptive home for a few weeks before disruption, while others are there several months. Adoption dissolution (a disruption that occurs after an adoption has been legally finalized) is rarer but can happen years after the adoption.

Many children who were only in their first adoptive home a few weeks before disruption occurred can be successfully adopted if given time to heal. Children who were in their first adoptive home for months or years before disruption often, but not always, have such strong negative reactions to adoption that it may not be worth the risk of the downside of another disruption to attempt another adoption (even though they may still want it at some level). A long-term placement with a familiar foster parent until the child is 18 may be the best option from an attachment and mental health perspective.

The developmental level of the child affects how the child interprets the adoption and its disruption.

Infants (6 months or younger) will rarely be impacted long-term from an adoption disruption, although it is exceedingly rare for disruptions to occur in this age range.

Young children (7-23 months) can experience severe impacts, but these are often temporary (less than 6 months) so long as they are placed back into a familiar foster home. That said, some impacts will linger, especially when another adoption is attempted.

Toddlers (2-4 years) will often experience enduring impacts, however these do not preclude subsequent adoptive attempts. Children this age have developed some ability to sense the magnitude of what was lost. Thus, they may be able to be distracted from it by caregivers yet they do not have enough cognitive ability to place the disruption into any sort of context.

Children (5-10 years) have some ability to place the disruption into context consciously but they will still internalize many intensely negative messages about themselves, their worth, the reliability of relationships, and the emotional risk of adoption (Argent & Coleman, 2012).

Preteens and teenagers may not want to attempt a second adoption and the risks involved, unless they are part of a sibling group. If a second adoption is attempted because they are part of a sibling group, they may relate to the new placement as another foster home (rather than as an adoptive home) as a way to protect themselves emotionally. This is reasonable on their part and should be accepted and even validated as self-care.

Post-mortem

If it has not already been done, attempt a "post-mortem" regarding the first adoption, to help the team try and understand the disruption and its implications for a second attempt (Argent & Coleman, 2012). There is not one reason for a disruption or one person to blame. The disruption is a relational event.

Your goal for undertaking the "post-mortem" would be to address the following questions:

- What was the child's mental health status at the end of the adoptive placement?

- What relational patterns occurred in the adoptive relationship and how did the back-and-forth of reaction and counter-reaction evolve? The goal here is to look for descriptive information on the relational patterns rather than to assign blame. This would include looking at sibling relationships.

- What guidance might be gleaned from this adoption and its transition process that could be used in an upcoming adoptive transition and placement?

The steps of a "post-mortem" would include the following:

- Review the descriptions of the adoptive transition process.

- Have a mental health professional who is experienced with adoptions interview each of the prior adoptive parents separately (if willing) about the relationship dynamics between them and the child, including how the dynamics changed at each step leading to the disruption.

- Interview the child's therapist (assuming the child had one while in the adoptive home) about the child, the adoptive parents, and the relationship between them.

- Interview the caseworker supervising the adoptive placement.

- Hire a mental health professional experienced with adoptions to interview the child (if they are old enough) to obtain a recounting of the adoptive relationship and events from the child's perspective.

- Interview the prior foster parents for relevant information from the adoptive transition and subsequent contacts with adoptive parents and/or the child.

- Review the information that was shared with the adoptive parents about the child on paper before, during, or after the transition.

All of this information is then integrated, while recognizing that each participant will have their own subjective reality that is separate from what an objective observer might have noted. All of these viewpoints have validity.

Recommended modifications

Depending on the age of the child, some (perhaps many) steps in this adoptive process will inevitably bring back the child's memories from the first adoptive transition, especially if it occurred recently. If the activities from the first adoptive transition are known from notes or foster parents' memories, then repetition of those specific activities would be avoided.

Announcing the adoption

Use great sensitivity when telling the child of the upcoming adoption. Choose whichever adult has the best relationship with the child (usually the foster parents or caseworker). The child would be told as part of a psychotherapy session with the therapist present. Note the child's nonverbal reaction to each piece of information. Pause for questions and gently inquire into the child's reaction if doing so seems helpful. The therapist needs time with the child alone after the child has been informed of the adoptive transition to process the new information with them. Invite a feeling of hope towards the second adoption, without offering hollow or false guarantees. The child may have an initial reaction of resistance to the adoption, which should be accepted, but not taken to mean that the child's reaction will remain negative as time passes.

Pre-transition visits with adoptive parents

Establishing safety in these cases will likely require more initial visits with the foster parents present than are otherwise needed. Adoptive parents need to be ready for the process to be lengthy and include some resistance from the child.

When foster parents debrief with the child about visits, the foster parents would ideally be sensitive to shifts in the child's mood as they reflect. It may be useful to talk about the memories from the first adoptive transition that came up. The child's therapist can also explore that issue.

During visits, sensitivity is very useful on the part of the adoptive parents to unexpected shifts in the child's mood, including sudden regression or spaciness. This may mean the child has been triggered by a memory from the first adoptive transition. As has been mentioned previously, it could also indicate a trigger from a traumatic experience that is not associated with the prior adoptive transition. It is not recommended that adoptive parents try to process trauma with the child at this point in their relationship. If it is suspected that the child has been triggered, then return the child to the foster parent and talk about that reunion plan out loud to the child.

The child may assume that these new adoptive parents will reject and abandon them like the previous ones did from the child's perspective. Waiting for this inevitable rejection may be anxiety-producing for the child. The child may unconsciously seek to relieve the unbearable waiting by provoking the rejection through acting-out behavior. Adoptive parents would usefully keep this possibility in mind when faced with the child acting out for no apparent reason. Explaining the reason behind the child's behavior to the child will not work because it is out of the child's awareness; instead, the adoptive parents would calmly set limits and move on to the next activity or if it feels unmanageable then return to the foster home with the child.

Managing grief

The process of grieving the upcoming change in the relationship with the foster parents is usually altered in this scenario. Dealing with the change in the relationship with the foster parents may be forestalled or lessened since the child often expects they will be returning after this new adoption disrupts yet again to the foster home and this relationship. The grieving of the relationship with the foster parents can't be hurried and will re-emerge later. Often, it will take a sizable period of time in the adoptive home and several visits with the former foster parents before the child recognizes that they will not live with the foster parents again. The grieving process regarding the shift in the relationship with the foster parents can begin in earnest after this recognition occurs.

Not surprisingly, moving day can be very emotionally complex for children who have had a prior adoption disruption. Even more than in a typical adoption moving day, there is hope and there is fighting against hope; there is excitement and fear; there is happiness and sadness; there is gain and loss; there is movement towards connection and there is pushing away; there is hiding feelings and being overwhelmed by the upwelling of feelings. There is rapid movement between these various feelings and states of self, with multiple often present at once. Behaviorally, the child can often find it hard to hold it together.

The child needs several things from the adults on moving day.

- Be present for the child even though the adults may also be experiencing big feelings.

- Celebrate the day in a way that allows lots of scheduling flexibility, and avoids many performance demands on the child, to allow for emotional ups and downs.

- Take pictures and videos when you can; the opportunities to photograph the child in a calm state may be rare and delicate; don't expect any posed shots.

- Minimize attendees on moving day (preferably under 8 adults). No one attends whom the child does not know well, so as not to overwhelm the child with new people.

- Employ an available adult or two (who are known to the other foster children in the foster home) to wrangle other foster children out of the child's presence in the event that they get dysregulated.

Post-transition visits with former foster parents

The first contact would be a video call rather than an in-person visit so that the child feels secure in understanding that the foster parents are not coming to take them back.

The first in-person visit from former foster parents can raise significant anxiety for the child, as they may experience it as an attempt to take them away from the adoptive home (another disruption) no matter how much they are reassured. Children would be informed about the in-person visit approximately five minutes before it happens. The prior disruption would be referenced and the child told explicitly in the clearest terms possible that that is not what is happening. Keep this visit brief (ideally about 10-15 minutes, which will feel like an eternity to the child). Immediately after the visit ends, the adoptive parents would debrief the child and emphasize the point that the child is staying with them but that anxiety is normal. Later in-person visits can lengthen if the child's anxiety stays within tolerable limits for the child and the adoptive parents.

Chapter 16

Conflict among Adoptive Parents

Adoptive parents may struggle with substantial conflict as a couple during the adoptive transition. Adding a child by any means, especially a first one, often puts a strain on a couple's relationship. This is normal; all couples have differences. For many adoptive parents, these differences do not preclude them from communicating well, being supportive of each other, and proceeding with the adoption.

Sometimes adoptive parents have preexisting differences that worsen or new differences emerge during the transition that are substantial enough to threaten the transition process. Some of those threats to the process might be:

- Adoptive parents exhibit enough conflict or coldness in front of the child that the child feels less safe with the adoptive parents.

- Adoptive parents cannot agree with each other on basics, such as the scheduling of visits.

- One or both of the adoptive parents have fairly intense jealousy of the relationship the child has with the other adoptive parent, leading to competition for the child's attention.

- Adoptive parents attempt to enlist foster parents or the caseworker or the child to side with them in disputes with the other adoptive parent.

- Adoptive parents have substantial-enough differences in parenting beliefs and actions that it interferes with the planning and/or execution of activities during visits.

- One or both of the adoptive parents blames the other adoptive parent for conflicts without taking responsibility for any share of the difficulty.

- The differences between a couple can be the result of one or both of the adoptive parents having a strong reaction to the reality of becoming a parent or past struggles reemerging (e.g., infertility, commitment issues).

If these or other threats emerge and are persistent, it is the caseworker's responsibility to confront the adoptive parents with the difficulty they are creating for the child. If this intervention appears successful, then the transition process can continue but would be slowed down to see if the adoptive parents are making genuine progress towards being a unified team or merely papering over the conflicts.

If this intervention is insufficient to shift the couple, then the caseworker—in consultation with her supervisor and/or the child welfare agency's decision makers—decides whether to proceed with the adoption. An intermediate step could be pausing the transition and mandating that the adoptive parents enter couples counseling.

In the very particular situation that the only substantial conflict between the adoptive parents is about the transition model, then the caseworker or whoever is leading the transition could attempt discussions around modifying the model in ways that meet the objections of the parent while still keeping in mind the needs of the child.

Chapter 17

Conflict between Adoptive and Foster Parents

Adoptive parents and foster parents often do not know each other before becoming involved in the adoptive transition. They have not chosen to cooperate with each other, but close bonds (including friendship) have been known to arise between foster and adoptive parents. In a few other transitions, the adoptive parents and foster parents may experience conflict, perhaps from personality differences, philosophical disagreements about the children or parenting, implicit or explicit bias, etc. These differences may be workable, but require serious attention when those differences evolve into conflict.

Caseworkers have an important role in working with these conflicts. They should listen to both adoptive parents and foster parents separately in order to understand each side's perspective of the conflict. Caseworkers need to explicitly identify themselves as neutral as they gather information. The issue could be characterized to the foster and adoptive parents as their struggle to collaborate together rather than the content of the conflict, which tends to lead to blame.

If the child being adopted is older, it is useful to look at whether a triangle of the child, adoptive parents, and foster parents has been set up such that the adults have unwittingly been split into opposing sides. Each set of adults may feel they are the only ones who can keep the child safe or loved or understood.

Sometimes, during planning committee meetings, the caseworker can help the adoptive parents and foster parents negotiate compromises on some topics, avoid others, agree to disagree on still others, etc. If this feels beyond the caseworker's expertise, then the caseworker's supervisor or a mediator might be brought in to assist.

If the conflict is about concrete issues, such as the process of the transition or certain parenting practices, then the caseworker would consider declaring how the issue will be resolved for the sake of the adoptive transition.

If the conflict is that one set of parents has an emotional distaste for the other set of parents, then this is more concerning because there is a less rational basis available that will shift emotionally based judgments. This scenario has some similarity to divorcing parents who struggle to co-parent because of lingering resentments. Sometimes an appeal to the welfare of the child, whose adoption is going forward regardless of this conflict, will help foster parents and/or adoptive parents set aside their aversion for the duration of the transition.

If any of the parents' inability to put to one side their dislike interferes with the adoptive process, or if they try to influence the child's relationships with the other parents, then the caseworker, perhaps in consultation with their supervisor or other expert, will need to amend the process. This would be the last option.

- The hardest aspect of the transition process to adapt are the initial visits when the adoptive parents come to the foster home while the foster parents are present to assist the child in building safety with the adoptive parents. Dislike can undermine this objective. One possible workaround for these visits is sending only the one adoptive parent and the one foster parent who get along most cordially. Another less optimal possibility is to substitute another person the child trusts (e.g., teacher, neighbor, child care provider) for the foster parent.

- If the child has a therapist they are bonded with, then another workaround is for the child to meet the adoptive parents and start the process of getting to know them in psychotherapy sessions.

- Each visit where foster parents and adoptive parents are not needed together would have minimal contact between foster parents and adoptive parents at pickup and drop off. If necessary, pickup and dropoff could occur at a therapist's office, a friend's house, or the child's school without foster parents and adoptive parents seeing each other.

- Foster parents and adoptive parents debrief each adoptive home visit with the caseworker rather than each other.

- When the foster parents debrief the child about each contact with the adoptive parents, they would listen and validate the child's feelings only. If they have any concerns about what they hear from the child about the adoptive parents, they communicate them to the caseworker only and do not discuss them with the child.

- Moving day rituals at the foster home with foster parents still occur. The caseworker picks up the child from the foster home and takes them to the adoptive parents who wait nearby. The caseworker documents both the pickup and drop-off for the child's Lifebook.

Conflict between foster parents and adoptive parents has implications for the contact between the child and foster parents after moving day.

- The child would have video visits with former foster parents for the first month after placement. Adoptive parents can monitor those video calls.
- Unfortunately, no in-person visits would occur at any point.
- As the new parents, adoptive parents would decide if any contact between the child and the former foster parents

would continue after the first month. It's usually better for the child if that contact can continue in some form, as long as the former foster parents are not undermining the placement.

Chapter 18

Long-Distance Adoption

Long-distance adoptions create many practical hurdles for the adoptive parents. The child welfare system may not prepare potential adoptive parents that they will be making sacrifices during the adoptive transition process. Many adoptive parents know that pursuing an international adoption may have requirements set by countries to stay within their borders for substantial lengths of time as a prerequisite for adoption. The same expectation would be communicated to parents seeking to adopt from the child welfare system and that they will reap many benefits in the long-term for the child and for their relationship.

It is recommended that at least one adoptive parent stay near the foster home for at least 30 days and book accommodations that have two bedrooms and kitchen facilities to allow for overnight visits. The words "at least" in the prior sentence worry some adoptive parents because of its uncertainty. This situation is like an adult child going to help an older parent who has had a stroke. It is not entirely clear how long you will be needed.

Adoptive parents will be more dependent on the foster parents and the caseworker for recommendations of activities to engage in with the child during visits and child-friendly places to eat, etc. This condition would be made clear to adoptive parents after they indicate an interest in a particular child who lives at a distance—even before they are selected as the adoptive family. The child's caseworker would explore with the adoptive parents how they might meet this condition creatively (e.g., one adoptive parent works remotely for the month they are living near the foster parents, adoptive parents and any children plan a vacation near the foster parents that includes sight-seeing and other fun activities as part of the transition). FMLA leave can also be used before an adoptive placement, even though it is usually available only from the date of the placement[2]. In addition to the usual training provided to prospective adoptive parents, an additional unit on long-distance adoption should be developed and disseminated that provides information on the special circumstances of long-distance

---

[2] See the fact sheet from the U.S. Department of Labor (undated) listed in the references for more details.

adoption and how it can impact the attachment between child and adoptive parents and the need for bonding while the child feels safe with their foster parents.

There would be a prerecorded video tour of the adoptive parents' home city that would include their home, neighborhood (including nearest park,) and the school the child will attend as part of one of the half-day visits. This would be followed by a video call with any other adoptive parents or other members of the adoptive family that did not travel.

If there is a second adoptive parent, they would join for at least one all-day visit, all overnight visits, and moving day. These would not be crammed together in the schedule. The child needs time to process each step.

Moving day involves the child saying goodbye to the foster parents and traveling to the adoptive home by car or plane. If possible, avoid breaking this into two steps (in which the child and the adoptive parents stay a night or two in the local rented residence). If flying, and if the child has enough possessions, then some of the possessions may get shipped ahead of time to the adoptive home.

Some foster and adoptive parents arrange for a foster parent to travel with the adoptive parents and the child on the airplane at the adoptive parents' expense. If this is the case, then schedule both moving day, which is the day of the airplane flight, and goodbye day, which is the day the foster parents say goodbye and fly back home. This option is the best possible but is beyond the practical reach of many foster and adoptive parents. It gives the child a sense that the big leap to the adoptive home is with a long-term trusted adult as well as the new adults that they are still developing trust in.

Long distance adoptions also ask more faith from the child in a system and individuals who, from the child's point of view, have not earned it. Separation anxiety and/or dissociation may be more intense, especially as moving day draws near. Consider the following:

- The change in the relationship with the foster parents is greater, as there won't be in-person visits after moving day—only video calls and other contacts. This can intensify the loss.
- The overnight visit will likely be in a hotel suite, with its anonymity. Children who are adopted across shorter distances

get an important sense of the adoptive parents from their home when they visit it, which will be missing in this scenario.

- Sibling groups must, for practical reasons, move together to the adoptive home.

- If the child will be transported to the adoptive home via airplane, then it is useful to consider that some children may be very frightened by their first plane trip. For these children, visiting the airport as an activity of one of the visits (although not the first visit without the foster parents) or having airplane /airport toys for the child to play with on visits, in the foster home, or in the therapy office can be quite useful. Older children may benefit from a nonfiction book about air travel.

Long distance adoptions also exacerbate the sense of loss for the foster parents as they may never see the child again in person. Video visits between the child and the foster parents after moving day would be regular and scheduled. Adoptive parents might consider returning for an in-person visit with the former foster parents in a year or two. This has some similarities to the families of international adoptees taking the child back to the child's country of origin.

Chapter 19

Older Child Resists the Adoptive Transition

A child who is nearly of adult age—and even younger teens who have needed to behave independently as a result of living on the streets and/or without adult supervision—may have a sense of near-adulthood, like Isabella in the earlier scenarios. As a result, they may be less willing to trust or depend on anyone, and wind up rejecting the chance to attach to a new parental figure. They may resist certain aspects of the transition, or even the whole process. Listen to their concerns—they may fear the loss of the relationship with the current foster parent, loss of friends from their school or neighborhood, or a feeling of powerlessness in the decision-making process.

Even though a traditional attachment bond may not form, an emotional connection can still happen between a teenager and an adoptive parent. This can occur in a similar way that a teen may form a bond with a stepparent who marries into the family when the child is older. It is important to not rush this process, and to let the youth decide for themselves over time what level of trust and emotional connection to invest in with this new adult. In addition, it is important to not consider that the teen has only until they turn 18 to form an attachment to their adoptive parents - attachments can continue to develop during young adulthood as there may still be elements of dependency continuing.

It can be useful for these teens to separate out the two aspects of the transition from each other: the loss of the current placement and caregiver, and the excitement about the emotional relationship with the new caregiver. Teens may be surprised that they will continue to have contact with their current foster parents after the move. Adoptive parents who live relatively near to the foster home may be able to continue the teens' involvement on sports teams or other activities that they value. It is also important to emphasize that the teens have power in constructing what the relationship looks like with the new caregivers. No one gets to tell them what they have to feel about their adoptive parents. It can emerge over time. Teens may even benefit from having a copy of this model so they can see what the adults are up to with a degree of transparency. Giving this to them can build trust, because it shows the teen that the adults do have the child's best interests at heart.

Chapter 20

Recommendations for Child Welfare Agencies

Hopefully child welfare agencies will make changes to support the success of adoptive transitions as outlined in this model. For example, they may:

- Provide separate, group-specific trainings on their model used for adoptive transitions (possibly this one) for caseworkers, foster parents, adoptive parents, interested child psychotherapists treating children in foster care, and relevant court personnel (family court judges, Guardian Ad Litems also sometimes called Court-appointed Special Advocates, Assistant DAs, and interested attorneys that represent children or adults in family court matters).

- Hire Adoptive Transition Specialists who will guide adoptive transitions rather than caseworkers. These specialists should have training and experience in attachment theory, child welfare casework, and children's mental health. Providing those specialists with adequate training and supervision to prevent burnout and/or inappropriate reactions to the intense emotions generated among participants in the adoptive transition process will be important.

- Hold regular professionally-led support groups for foster parents to process their grief over the departure of foster children through adoption, return to family of origin, or emancipation.

- Contract with child mental health agencies to provide professionally-led psychoeducational support groups for children going through adoptive transitions.

- Require all sibling groups undergoing adoptive transitions to attend psychotherapy as a group with a child therapist.

- Inform all prospective adoptive parents who live at substantial distance from the foster home that at least one adoptive parent has to stay nearby the adoptive home for at least 30 days as part of the adoptive transition.

- Conduct research on the satisfaction of participants with this model compared to existing practices and track adoption disruptions before and after this model is introduced.

- Even if the agency does not choose to use the model, they should develop their own clear, specific model for how adoptive transitions would be done and train their staff on it and disseminate it to foster and adoptive parents. They can still borrow aspects of this model that they see as valuable.

References

Argent, H., & Coleman, J. (2012). *Dealing with Disruption in Fostering and Adoption Placements.* London: British Association for Adoption and Fostering.

Antares, K. (2023). *Transracial Adoption, Identity, and Racism in the United States: Between Two Worlds.* Lanham, MD: Lexington Books.

Ballard, R. (2009). *Pieces of me: Who do I Want to Be.* Warren, NJ: EMK Press.

Beek, M., Neil, E., & Schofield, G. (2021). *Moving to Adoption: Using the UEA Model to Help Children Move from Foster Care to Adoption.* London: CoramBAAF.

Bekman, S., & Bellas, V. (2022). Holding multiple perspectives: A toddler's journey with traumatic grief in the child welfare system. *Zero to Three, 43(2), 5-11.*

Biehle, K., & Goodman, D. (2012). *Icebreaker Meetings: A Tool for Building Relationships Between Birth and Foster Parents.* Baltimore: Annie E. Casey Foundation. Available at aecf.org.

Blomquist, G., & Blomquist, P. (1990). *Zachary's New Home.* Washington, DC: Magination Press.

Boswell, S., & Cudmore, L. (2014). 'The children were fine': Acknowledging complex feelings in the move from foster care into adoption. *Adoption and Fostering, 38*(1), 5-21. DOI.org/10.1177/0308575914522558

Boswell, S., & Cudmore, L. (2017). Understanding the 'blind spot' when children move from foster care to adoption. *Journal of Child Psychotherapy, 43*(2), 243-257. DOI.org/10.1080.0075417X.2017.1323946

Bovingdon, T., & Fabian, K. (2015). Relinquishment visits: Saying goodbye is an unnatural process. In *Applications of Family and Group Theraplay* ed. by E. Munns. Lanham, MD: Rowman & Littlefield.

Browning, A. (2015). Undertaking planned transitions for children in out-of-home care. *Adoption & Fostering, 39*(1), 51-61. doi.org/10.1177/0308575914565072

Bruning, P. (2007). The crisis of adoption disruption and dissolution. In *Play Therapy with Children in Crisis: Individual, Group and Family Treatment* ed. by N. Boyd Webb. NY: Guilford.

Buckingham Slade, S. (2013). *Adopted: The Ultimate Teen Guide*. Lanham, MD: Scarecrow Press.

Cantey, N., Smith, L., Frazier Sorrells, S., Kelly, D., Jones, C. & Burrus, D. (2022). Navigating racism in the child welfare system: The impact on black children, families, and practitioners. *Child Welfare, 100*(2), 163-184.

Davis, J. (2015). *Preparing for Adoption: Everything Adopting Parents Need to Know about Preparations, Introductions and the First Few Weeks.* Philadelphia: Jessica Kingsley Publishers.

Dozier, M. & Bick, J. (2007). Changing caregivers: Coping with early adversity. *Psychiatric Annals, 37*(6), 411-415.

Dozier, M., Stoval, K., Albus, K., & Bates, B. (2001). Attachment for infants in foster care: The role of caregiver state of mind. *Child Development, 72*(5), 1467-1477. doi.org/10.1111/1467-8624.00360

Ebensperger, L. (1998). Strategies and counterstrategies to infanticide in mammals. *Biological Review, 73*(3), 321-346.

Edelstein, S., Burge, D., & Waterman, J. (2001). Helping foster parents cope with separation, loss, and grief. *Child Welfare, 80*(1), 5-25.

Fishman, H., & Minuchin, S. (1981). *Family Therapy Techniques.* Cambridge: Harvard University Press.

Fitzgerald, J. (1979). After disruption. *Adoption and Fostering, 3*(4), 11-16.

Fonagy, P., & Campbell, C. (2016). Attachment theory and mentalization. In A. Elliott & J. Prager (Eds.), *The Routledge handbook of psychoanalysis in the social sciences and humanities* (pp. 115–131). Routledge/Taylor & Francis.

Goble, J. (2022). *A Love-Stretched Life.* Carol Stream, IL: Tyndale Momentum.

Goldberg, A. (2019). *Open Adoption and Diverse Families: Complex Relationships in the Digital Age.* NY: Oxford University Press.

Gray, C. (2015). *The New Social Story Book, Revised and Expanded 15th Anniversary Edition.* Arlington, TX: Future Horizons.

Gray, D. (2012). *Nurturing Adoptions: Creating Resilience After Neglect and Trauma.* Philadelphia: Jessica Kingsley Publishers.

Hanna, M., & Rogers, S. (2022). Real or imagined: Racial bias in family assessments. *Child Welfare, 100*(2), 137-162.

Hebert, C., Kulkin, H., & McLean, M. (2013). Grief and foster parents: How do foster parents feel when a foster child leaves their home? *Adoption and Fostering, 37*(3), 253-267. doi.org/10.1177/0308575913501615

Heineman, T. (2001). Hunger pangs: Transference and countertransference in the treatment of foster children. *Journal of Applied Psychoanalytic Studies, 3*(1), 5-16.

Heineman, T. (2007). Weaving without a loom: Creating a self in foster care. *Fort Da, 13*(1), 55-68.

Hughes, D., Golding, K., & Hudson, J. (2019). *Healing Relational Trauma with Attachment-Focused Interventions: Dyadic Developmental Psychotherapy with Children and Families.* NY: Norton.

Jacobsen, H., Ivarsson, T., Wentzel-Larsen, T., Smith, L., & Moe, V. (2014). Attachment security in young foster children: continuity from 2 to 3 years of age. *Attachment and Human Development, 16*(1), 42-57.

Jurkovic, G. (2014). *Lost childhoods: The Plight of the Parentified Child.* London: Routledge.

Kasza, K. (1996). *A Mother for Choco.* NY: Puffin Books.

Kim, A., & Del Prado, A. (2019). *It's Time to Talk (and Listen): How to Have Constructive Conversations about Race, Class, Sexuality, Ability and Gender in a Polarized World.* Oakland, CA: New Harbinger.

Kothari, B., McBeath, B., Sorenson, P., Bank, L., Waid, J., Jade Webb, S., & Steele, J. (2017). An intervention to improve sibling relationship quality among youth in foster care: Results of a randomized clinical trial. *Child Abuse and Neglect, 63*(1), 19-29. doi.org/10.1016/j.chiabu.2016.11.010

Lanyado, M. (2003). The emotional tasks of moving from fostering to adoption: Transitions, Attachment, Separation and Loss. *Clinical Child Psychology and Psychiatry, 8*(3), 337-349.

Lanyado, M. (2008). Playing out, not acting out: The development of the capacity to play in the therapy of children who are 'in transition' from fostering to adoption (pp. 155-167). In *The Emotional Experience of Adoption: A Psychoanalytic Experience* ed. by D. Hindle & G. Shulman. NY: Routledge.

Lee, R., & Whiting, J. (2007). Foster children's expressions of ambiguous loss. *American Journal of Family Therapy, 35*(5), 417-428. doi.org/10.1080/01926180601057499

Linares, O. (2006). An understudied form of intra-family violence: Sibling-to-sibling aggression among foster children. *Aggression and Violent Behavior, 11*(1), 95-109. doi.org/10.1016/j.avb.2005.07.001

Linares, O, Jimenez, J., Nesci, C., Pearson, A., Beller, S., Edwards, N., & Levin-Rector, A. (2014). Reducing sibling conflict in maltreated children placed in foster homes. *Prevention Science, 16*(2), 211-221. doi.org/10.1007/s11121-014-0476-0

Lynes, D., & Sitcoe, A. (2019). Disenfranchised grief: The emotional impact experienced by foster carers on the cessation of a placement.

Adoption and Fostering, 43(1), 22-34. doi.org/10.1177/0308575918823433

Mikell Montgomery, D. (2022). 'They don't understand us and are afraid of us': Black social workers' perspectives on the role of anti-Blackness within foster care service provision to Black children. *Child Welfare, 100*(1), 141-164.

Milbrand, T. (2024). What's in a name? For an adopted child, a lot! Available at: https://www.adoptivefamilies.com/adoption-process/naming-adopted-child-culture/

Miller, L. (2014). *Sensational Kids: Hope and Help for Children with Sensory Processing Disorder, Revised Edition.* NY: Perigee.

Miller Wrobel, G., Helder, E., & Marr, E. (Eds.) (2020). *Routledge Handbook of Adoption.* NY: Routledge.

Mitchell, C. (2007). *Welcome Home, Forever Child.* Bloomington, IN: AuthorHouse.

Mitchell, M. (2016). *The neglected transition: Building a relational home for children entering foster care.* NY: Oxford University Press.

Neil, E., Beek, M., & Schofield, G. (2020). *The UEA Moving to Adoption model: A guide for adoption social workers, fostering social workers, and children's social workers*. Norwich, UK: University of East Anglia, Centre for Research on Children and Families. Available at: https://www.movingtoadoption.co.uk/resources/

Neil, E., Young, J., & Hartley, L. (2018). The joys and challenges of adoptive family life: A survey of parents in the Yorkshire and Humberside region. Centre for Research on Children and Families. www.researchgate.net/profile/Louise_Hartley2/publication/337171 004_THE_JOYS_AND_CHALLENGES_OF_ADOPTIVE_FAMI LY_LIFE_A_SURVEY_OF_ADOPTIVE_PARENTS_IN_THE_ YORKSHIRE_AND_HUMBERSIDE_REGION/links/5dc9a9599 2851c818046aeae/

NICHD Early Child Care Research Network (Ed.)(2005). *Child Care and Child Development—Results from the NICHD Study of Early Child Care and Youth Development*. NY: Guilford.

Pearson, J. (2016). *Elliot.* Toronto: Pajama Press

Post, B. (2009). *The Great Behavior Breakdown*. Palmyra, VA: Post Publications.

Post, B. (2010). *From Fear to Love: Parenting Difficult Adopted Children.* Palmyra, VA: Post Publications.

Reams, R. (2021). Transitioning Children in Foster Care to Adoptive Homes. *Child Welfare, 98*(5), 27-51.

Reams, R. (2022). Lifebooks in child welfare: Why isn't a great idea used more often? *Adoption Quarterly, 25*(1), 70-79. doi.org/10.1080/10926755.2021.1978024

Reams, R. (2023). Reverse visitation between former foster parents and adopted children. *Journal of Public Child Welfare, 17*(1), 167-189.

Riggs, D., Allain, T., Browne, L., Endacott, F & Quince, A. (2022). "There's no disenfranchisement when you're sitting in that room": Evaluating a South Australian loss and grief support group for foster and kinship carers. Children and Youth Services Review, 138, 106501 doi.org/10.1016/j.childyouth.2022.106501

Roberts, D. (2001). *Shattered Bonds: The Color of Child Welfare.* NY: Basic Books.

Rose, R. (2012). *Life Story Therapy with Traumatized Children: A Model for Practice.* Philadelphia: Jessica Kingsley Publishers.

Rustin, M. (2008). Multiple families in mind (pp. 77-89). In *The Emotional Experience of Adoption: A Psychoanalytic Experience* ed. by D. Hindle & G. Shulman. NY: Routledge.

Saunders, H., & Selwyn, J. (2010). *Adopting Large Sibling Groups: Experiences of Agencies and Adopters in Placing Sibling Groups for Adoption from Care. Bristol, UK: Hadley Centre for Foster Care Studies.* Available at: https://research-information.bris.ac.uk/ws/portalfiles/portal/189523706/Report.pdf

Schryer, N. (2021). *Addy's Journey to her Forever Home*. Chesterland, OH: Compassion Enriched, LLC.

Selwyn, J., Meakings, S. & Wijedasa, D. (2015). *Beyond the Adoption Order*. London: BAAF.

Sinclair, I., Baker, C., Wilson, K., & Gibbs, I. (2005). *Foster Children: Where They Go and How they get on.* Jessica Kingsley Publishers.

South, S., Lim, E., Jarnecke, A., & Foli, K. (2018). Relationship quality from pre- to post-placement in adoptive couples. *Journal of Family Psychology, 33*(1), 64-76. doi.org/10.1037/fam0000456

Steele, M., Hodges, J., Kaniuk, J., & Steele, H. (2009). Mental Representation and Change: Developing Attachment Relationships in an Adoption Context. *Psychoanalytic Inquiry, 30*(1), 25-40. doi.org/10.1080/07351690903200135

Stock Kranowitz, C. (2022). *The Out-of-Sync Child: Recognizing and Coping with Sensory Processing Differences, 3rd edition.* NY: TarcherPerigee

Swain, V. (2016). Keeping connected: Maintaining relationships when moving on. The Fostering Network. https://www.thefosteringnetwork.org.uk/sites/default/files/2021-03/keep_connected_4_feb_v2_0.pdf

Tidefors, I., Arvidsson, H., Ingevaldson, S., & Larsson, M. (2010). Sibling incest: A literature review and a clinical study. *Journal of Sexual Aggression, 16*(3), 347-360. doi.org/10.1080/13552600903511667

Trozzi, M. (1999). *Talking with Children about Loss: Words, Strategies, and Wisdom to Help Children Cope.* NY: TarcherPerigee.

Tyndall-Lind, A. (2010). Intensive sibling group play therapy with child witnesses of domestic violence. In J. Baggerly, D. Ray & S. Bratton

(Eds.) *Child-Centered Play Therapy Research: The Evidence Base for Effective Practice.* (pp.69-83) Hoboken, NJ: Wiley.

U.S. Department of Health and Human Services (2024). AFCARS Report #30 - Preliminary FY 2022 Estimates as of May 9, 2023. Available from https://www.acf.hhs.gov/sites/default/files/documents/cb/afcars-report-30.pdf

U.S. Department of Labor (undated). Fact Sheet #28Q: Taking Leave from Work for Birth, Placement, and Bonding with a Child under the FMLA. Available at: https://www.dol.gov/agencies/whd/fact-sheets/28q-taking-leave-for-birth-placement-child

Unrau, Y., Seita, J. & Putney, K. (2008). Former foster youth remember multiple placement moves: A journey of loss and hope. *Children and Youth Services Review, 30*(11), 1256-166. doi.org/10.1016/j.childyouth.2008.03.010

Van der Kolk, B. (2015). *The Body Keeps the Score: Brain, Mind, and Body in the Healing of Trauma.* NY: Penguin Books.

Waterman, B. (2003). *The Birth of an Adoptive, Foster or Stepmother: Beyond Biological Mothering Attachments.* Philadelphia: Jessica Kingsley Publishers.

White, E., Baden, A., Ferguson, A., & Smith, L. (2022). The intersection of race and adoption: Experiences of transracial and international adoptees with microaggressions. *Journal of Family Psychology, 36*(8), 1318-1328. https://doi.org/10.1037/fam0000922

Wise, J. (2007). *Flying Solo.* London: BAAF.

Younes, M., & Harp, M. (2007). Addressing the impact of foster care on biological children and their families. *Child Welfare, 86*(4), 21-40.

Zeanah, C. (Ed.) (2018). *Handbook of Infant Mental Health, 4th Ed.* NY: Guilford.

Zeanah, C. (2022). Advocating for planful transitions for young children in foster care. {Webinar]. Early Trauma Treatment Network. https:youtu.be/OwqgrMXAB78

Index

Figures are indicated by an f. Tables are indicated by a t.
Page numbers referring to vignettes appear in *italics*.

A
adoption, types of
  disrupted, 380–387
  kinship placement, 68–70, 93 (*See also* Isabella)
  long-distance, 248, 403–408, 413
  open, 41–42, 83, 354–357
adoptive children. *See* children, foster to adoptive
adoptive parents
  birth parent involvement and, 353–358
  building attachment with child, 25–27, 244–245, 251, 306–307, 311–
    312, 404–405
  characteristics and experiences of, 66–71, 74–79
  conflict involving, 93, 296–297, 394–396, 397–402
  discrimination by child welfare system, 77–79
  emotional regulation, 111, 117–118, 162–163, 194, 353–354
  goals for visits, 109–110, 139, 152, 173, 186, 311–312
  grief and loss experienced by, 76–77
  guidelines for visits, 110–111, 114–118, 139–145, 159–165, 183–185,
    191–193
  home preparation for move, 52, 240–245
  kinship placements, 68–70, 93
  parental leave, 72–74, 242, 404–405
  selection of, 66, 240, 373–374, 403–405
  sibling group considerations, 296–298, 303–309, 311–312
  supporting the child, 34–35, 142–145, 154–156, 159–165, 194–197,
    389–390
Adoptive Transition Model
  child's needs prioritized, 28–32, 30t
  developmental considerations, 32–35
  goals of, 24–28
  modifications to, 377–379, 387–393, 396, 399–402
  overview and steps, 18–24, 21f, 98t
  participants in, 23–24, 91–93, 95–96
  responding to resistance to, 367–376, 396, 409–411

anxiety. *See also* mental health support
  child's experiences with, 42–43, 50, 186–187, 389–390
  strategies to reduce child's, 161–162, 192–193, 196, 233, 245, 378–379, 392–393, 406–407
attachment. *See also* mental health support
  between child and adoptive parents, 25–27, 244–245, 251, 306–307, 311–312, 404–405, 409–411
  between child and foster parents, 27–28, 55–58, 91–92, 159–163, 215, 233, 263–266, 360–366
  disrupted adoption and, 380–382
  mental health needs of child related to, 19, 48–52, 118–119, 184, 293–296, 380–382
  model's focus on, 19, 24–28, 31, 412–413
  secure, 25–27, 29, 55–58
  sibling group considerations, 282, 283t, 286–287, 293–296, 306–307, 311–312
attunement, 20–22, 25, 68–70, 110–111, 141–142

B
behavior concerns
  due to emotions and trauma, 32–33, 111–113, 153–154, 222–223, 293–294, 306–307, 389–390
  impacting foster placement, 56, 361–362
birth parents
  characteristics of, 82–84
  emotional regulation, 38–41, 82–84, 354–357
  goodbye visit, 36–41, 84, 358–359
  grief and loss experienced by, 39–40, 82–84
  level of involvement with child, 36–42, 353–359
Brett, 12, *313*
  pre-move visits, *315–328, 332–337*
  moving day, *337–340*
  post-move reverse visit, *341–343*
burnout, 82

C
caseworker

characteristics of, 79–82
discrimination by child welfare system, 59, 77–79
information sharing by, 153, 386
legal and policy considerations for, 94–95, 103, 290, 377
qualities of relationships with participants, 92, 369
responding to conflict among participants, 395–396, 397–401
role in Lifebooks, 38–39, 228–229
role in planning transition, 95–99, 275, 289–292, 355–357, 365, 369–371, 377–379, 404–405
child welfare system
  child's feelings about, 246, 268
  current U.S. statistics, 7
  discrimination by, 58–66, 77–79, 371–372
  opportunity to support foster parents, 213, 299–300, 413
  recommendations for, 412–414
  role in facilitating transitions, 369–370
  trauma by, 22
child's needs prioritized
  during visits, 110, 113–118, 138–141, 151, 173–174
  foster parents as extended family, 27–28, 262–265, 269, 273–275
  goodbye meeting, 40–41
  long-distance adoption, 403–406
  model's focus on, 20–23, 25–27, 28–32, 79–82, 96, 374–375
  moving to adoptive home, 240–245
  parental leave, 72–73
  readiness for next step, 33–34, 47, 48–52, 69–70, 141–142, 186–187, 233–236
  safety levels, 30t
  sequence of steps, 21f, 97, 98t, 140–141, 156–157
  sibling group considerations, 282–284, 292, 305–307
children, foster to adoptive
  attachment (*See* attachment)
  degree of contact with birth parents, 36–42, 353–359
  disrupted adoption history, 380–387
  goals for visits, 109, 138–139, 152, 173, 186

grief and loss experienced by, 27–28, 46–48, 103–104, 118–119, 359, 360–366, 390–392

kinship placement, 68–70, 93

mental health needs, 48–52

ongoing relationships with others, 31–32, 47–48, 90–91

responding to emotions of, 25–27, 50, 111–113, 142–145, 159–165, 194–197, 247–248

trauma history, 42–45, 112–113, 153–156, 197–198, 271, 380–382, 388–390

communication

among adoptive parents, 77, 119, 394–396

between adoptive parents and foster parents, 100t, 109–111, 113–118, 187–188, 198–199, 251, 267, 271–275

between birth parents and child, 355–356, 358

between foster parents and child, 31–35, 37, 91–92, 103–104, 191, 263–267

during pre-transition planning, 23–24, 95–102, 98t

information sharing about child's history, 87, 89, 99–102, 100t, 153–156, 187–188, 197–198, 361–365, 386–387

sibling group considerations, 283t, 293–296, 300–301, 311–312

steps to resolve hurts, 60–66, 76, 78–79

strategies to soothe child's distress, 142–145, 159–165, 194–197, 215–227

to child about adoption and visits, 103–108, 300–301

visual forms of, 51, 107–108, 249–250, 262–263, 269, 303, 358

with other important adults in child's life, 31–32, 47–48, 85–91, 237–239

conflict

among adoptive parents, 296–297, 394–396

between adoptive and foster parents, 93, 397–402

between foster parent and child, 225–226

steps to resolve hurts, 60–66, 76, 78–79

within sibling groups, 283t

coping strategies, 43, 47–48, 75–76, 214–215

Court Appointed Special Advocate (CASA), 89

cultural considerations, 22, 85–87, 368, 371–374. *See also* Diego; Hakim

D
developmental factors
   disrupted adoption impacts, 383–384
   distress signals, 32–35, 139
   in sibling group transitions, 282–284, 300–301
   informing child of adoption and visits, 104–108
   moving day, 249–250
   resistance to adoptive transition, 409–411
   transition support and, 69, 212, 215–228
   visits and, 111–112, 146–147, 194–196, 265–267
Diego, 12, 122
   pre-move visits, *122–128, 147–148, 165–168, 176–177, 200–206*
   moving day, *251–255*
   post-move reverse visit, *275–277*

discrimination
   by child welfare system, 58–60, 77–79, 371–372
   extended family of origin experiences with, 85–87
   steps to resolve hurts, 60–66, 78–79
disrupted adoption, 380–387
distress
   developmental stage and signs of, 32–35, 139
   tips for soothing child's, 142–145, 159–165, 194–197, 217, 220

E
emotional regulation
   attachment and, 25–27, 48–52
   of adoptive parents, 111, 117–118, 162–163, 194, 353–354
   of birth parents, 38–41, 82–84, 354–357
   of foster parents, 119–120, 213–215, 299–300
   tips for soothing child, 142–145, 159–165, 194–197, 247–251, 293–294,
      390–392

F
Family Medical Leave Act (FMLA), 74, 404
family of origin, extended, 85–87, 244–245

feedback
  after hurt has been caused, 58–66
  on a goodbye letter, 38–39
fertility challenges, 53, 66, 76, 395
foster children. *See* children, foster to adoptive
foster parents
  as extended family, 27–28, 102, 212, 262–265, 269, 273–275
  attachment to child, 27–28, 55–58, 91–92, 215, 263–266, 360–366
  characteristics of, 52–54
  conflict involving, 93, 225–226, 397–402
  discrimination by child welfare system, 58–66, 371–372
  emotions of, 119–120, 213–215, 273, 299–300, 309–310, 370, 373–376
  goals for visits, 110, 139–140
  grief and loss experienced by, 53–56, 119–120, 213–215, 299–300, 373–
      376, 406–408, 413
  guidelines for visits, 111–121, 139–142, 144–145, 173–174, 176, 184,
      187–191, 388–390
  informing other participants about child's history, 99–102, 100t, 153–
      156, 187–188, 197–198, 361–365, 386
  move support by, 237–239, 245–247
  other children in foster home, 231–232, 299
  post-move contact, 249–250, 265–267, 293, 360–366, 392–393, 401–
      402, 406–408, 409–411
  processing transition with child, 31–35, 37, 103–108, 120, 198–199,
      215–227, 228–231, 378–379
  resistance to supporting transition, 57, 367–371, 377–379
  sibling group transitions, 292–294, 299–300, 303–310
  soothing child, 50, 111–113, 144–145

G
goodbye visit, 36–41, 358–359, 364
grief and loss. *See also* mental health support
  adoptive parents experience with, 76–77
  avoid triggering, 22
  birth parent experience with, 39–40, 82–84
  child experience with, 27–28, 46–48, 103–104, 118–119, 359, 360–366,
      390–392

during visits, 118–119
foster parent experience with, 53–56, 119–120, 213–215, 299–300, 373–376, 406–408, 413
model's focus on, 22, 27–28, 263–264
processing of, 103–104, 112, 198–199, 215–227, 235–236, 263–264, 413
Guardian Ad Litem (GAL), 89

H
Hakim, 12, 133
pre-move visits, *133–136, 150–151, 171–172, 181–183, 209–211*
moving day, *259–261*
post-move reverse visit, *280–281*
home preparation, 52, 240–245
hurt, steps to address, 60–66, 76, 78–79

I
infant/toddler
disrupted adoption impacts, 380, 383
disrupted sleep, 194–196
distress manifestations, 33
informing of adoption and visits, 104, 106
post-move contact, 265–266
transition support for, 215–216
vignette (*See* Hakim; Maggie)
visit frequency, 147
informing child of adoption and visits, 103–108
Isabella, 12, 128–129
pre-move visits, *129–132, 148–149, 168–171, 178–181, 206–209*
moving day, *256–259*
post-move reverse visit, *278–280*

J
jealousy
among sibling groups, 184–185, 243, 283t, 295–296, 301–302, 309–310
between adoptive parents, 296–297, 395

foster parent emotions, 373–374

K

kinship placement, 68–70, 93. *See also* Isabella
Krissy, 12, *313–314*
  pre-move visits, *328–331, 343–350*
  moving day, *350–351*
  post-move reverse visit, *351–352*

L

legal factors, 84, 89–90, 94–95, 353–354, 382
Lifebooks
  artifacts and information to include in, 38–39, 45, 84–89, 237–238, 268,
    358, 361, 365, 401
  purpose of, 37–39, 227–231
  tips and resources for, 229–231
long-distance adoption, 248, 403–408, 413
loss. *See* grief and loss

M

Maggie, 12, *313–314*
  pre-move visits, *328–331, 343–350*
  moving day, *350–351*
  post-move reverse visit, *351–352*
mental health support. *See also* anxiety; attachment; grief and loss; trauma
  communicating transitions to therapist, 104, 231–232
  consultation by therapist, 87–89, 198, 369–371
  following disrupted adoption, 380–382, 385–388
  for sibling groups, 284–289, 301–302, 306–308, 413
  psychiatric medication, 50, 88–89
  recommendations for child welfare agencies, 412–414
  therapist role in transition, 31, 37–41, 87–89, 93, 224, 228, 230, 369–
    371, 400
moving to adoptive home
  considerations for sibling groups, 283t, 289–293, 303–304
  criteria to determine readiness for, 233–236
  foster parent preparations, 237–239, 304

goals for move, 233
moving day, 22, 84, 245–251, 303–304, 390–392, 401, 405–406

N
neglect, 45, 155, 285–286, 287
neurodivergence, 51–52

O
open adoption, 41–42, 83, 354–357

P
pace, child-oriented. *See* child's needs prioritized
parentified child, 285–286, 289
physical contact, 117–118, 155, 215, 218, 221, 223, 265
post-move contact
    forms of, 262–263, 265–267, 270–272
    hesitancy about, 273–275
    long-distance adoption, 406–408
pre-transition planning
    child's needs prioritized, 20–23, 28–32, 30t, 98t
    collaboration of participants, 23–24, 90–93, 95–99, 233–236, 354–357
    considerations for sibling groups, 282–284, 288–292
    information sharing about child's history, 87, 89, 99–102, 100t, 153–156, 361–365
    informing child about adoption and visits, 103–108
    legal and policy context, 83–84, 94–95, 353–354
    long-distance adoption, 403–405
    preparing for visits, 95–99, 98t, 100–101, 110–111, 153–156, 187–191, 194
preschoolers
    disrupted sleep, 194–196
    distress manifestations, 33
    informing of adoption and visits, 104–105, 107
    post-move contact, 265–267
    transition support for, 216–219
    vignette (*See* Krissy)

visit frequency, 147
Provence, Sally, 20
psychiatric medication, 50, 88–89
psychotherapy. *See* mental health support

Q
questions, responding to child's, 34–35, 103–108, 120, 217–221, 356,
    378–379

R
relationships. *See also* communication; conflict
    between foster and adoptive parents, 93, 99–102, 100t, 397–402
    birth parent involvement, 36–42, 83–85, 353–359
    caseworker's approach to, 79–82
    foster parent shift to extended family, 27–28, 102, 212, 262–265, 269,
        273–275
    kinship placements, 68–70, 93
    Lifebook to help reflect on, 37–39, 227–231
    model's focus on, 7–8, 23–24, 27–28, 90–93, 96
    other important adults in child's life, 18, 31–32, 47–48, 85–91, 237–239
resistance to using Adoptive Transition Model, 367–376, 396, 409–411
resources
    adoption books, 216–217, 219, 223–224
    Lifebook online resource, 229
    parenting a child with a trauma history, 154
reverse visits. *See* visits, reverse

S
safety
    child's sense of, 42–45, 68–70, 110, 138–139, 156–165, 193, 388, 404–
        405
    levels of, 30t
    model's focus on, 22, 24–27, 29–31
    sibling groups and, 283t, 285–287, 293–294
school age children
    disrupted adoption impacts, 384
    disrupted sleep, 194–196

distress manifestations, 33
informing of adoption and visits, 105, 107–108
post-move contact, 265–267
transition support for, 219–221
vignette (*See* Brett; Diego)
visit frequency, 147
secure attachment, 25–27, 29, 55–58
sensory processing considerations, 52, 174
sibling groups
  attachment considerations for, 282, 283t, 286–287, 293–296, 306–307, 311–312
  honoring children's feelings, 303–304
  jealousy, 283t, 295–296, 301–302, 309–310
  mental health support for, 284–289, 301–302, 306–308
  moving day, 303–304, 407
  parentification, 285–286, 289, 363
  staggered transitions, 289–293, 300–312
  transitioning together, 292–300, 407
  vignette (*See* Brett; Krissy; Maggie)
social media, 266–267, 270–272
social stories, 51, 189
strengths. *See* coping strategies
stress. *See* distress

T
teenagers
  disrupted adoption impacts on, 384
  distress manifestations, 33
  informing of adoption and visits, 105, 108
  post-move contact, 266–267
  resistance to adoptive transition, 409–411
  transition support for, 222–227
  vignette (*See* Isabella)
  visit frequency, 147
touch. *See* physical contact
trauma. *See also* mental health support

adoptive parent history of, 71, 74
child's history of, 42–45, 112–113, 153–156, 197–198, 271, 380–382, 388–390
model's consideration of, 19, 22
sibling groups and, 283–284, 283t, 285–287, 293–294
triggers, 43–44, 153–156, 163–164, 175–176, 197–198, 293–294, 388–390
trust
   between child and adoptive parents, 25–27, 47–48, 91–92, 138–139, 173, 195, 406–407, 409–411
   between participants, 96, 371–372
   model's focus on, 23
   sibling group considerations, 283t, 286–287

V
visit, goodbye, 36–41, 358–359, 364
visits, pre-move
   birth parent involvement in, 354–358
   child-oriented pacing of, 33–34, 137, 142–145, 151, 186–187
   emotional regulation during, 111–113, 142–145, 159–165, 173–176, 191–196
   ending early, 113, 117, 158, 161, 164–165, 389–390
   frequency and length of, 110–111, 146–147
   goals of, 109–110, 138–140, 152, 173, 186
   guidelines for, 113–118, 140–146, 156–159, 173–176, 183–185, 191–193, 196–199, 388–390
   informing child about, 106–108
   long-distance adoption, 403–407
   modifications based on child's needs, 50–52, 388–390
   modifications due to conflict, 399–401
   preparing for, 95–99, 98t, 100–101, 110–111, 153–156, 187–191, 194
   progression of, 19–20, 21f, 98t
   sibling group considerations for, 286–287, 292, 300–301, 302, 311–312
visits, reverse
   as final step in Adoptive Transition Model, 19–20, 21f, 98t, 263–265
   calendar to track upcoming, 249–250, 263
   guidelines for, 268–269, 271–272, 361, 365–366, 392–393

hesitancy about, 273–275
importance of, 263–266
long-distance adoption, 406–408
sibling group considerations, 293, 305–309
vulnerability, 20, 64–65, 191–192, 224